HANDBOOK OF DISCOURSE ANALYSIS

VOLUME 4
Discourse Analysis in Society

HANDBOOK of DISCOURSE ANALYSIS

VOLUME 1: Disciplines of Discourse
VOLUME 2: Dimensions of Discourse
VOLUME 3: Discourse and Dialogue
VOLUME 4: Discourse Analysis in Society

HANDBOOK of DISCOURSE ANALYSIS

VOLUME 4
Discourse Analysis in Society

Edited by
TEUN A. VAN DIJK
Department of General Literary Studies
Section of Discourse Studies
University of Amsterdam
Amsterdam, The Netherlands

1985

ACADEMIC PRESS
(Harcourt Brace Jovanovich, Publishers)
London   Orlando   San Diego   New York
Toronto   Montreal   Sydney   Tokyo

COPYRIGHT © 1985, BY ACADEMIC PRESS, INC. (LONDON) LTD.
ALL RIGHTS RESERVED.
NO PART OF THIS PUBLICATION MAY BE REPRODUCED OR
TRANSMITTED IN ANY FORM OR BY ANY MEANS, ELECTRONIC
OR MECHANICAL, INCLUDING PHOTOCOPY, RECORDING, OR
ANY INFORMATION STORAGE AND RETRIEVAL SYSTEM, WITHOUT
PERMISSION IN WRITING FROM THE PUBLISHER.

ACADEMIC PRESS INC. (LONDON) LTD.
24-28 Oval Road
LONDON NW1 7DX

United States Edition published by
ACADEMIC PRESS, INC.
Orlando, Florida 32887

LIBRARY OF CONGRESS CATALOGING IN PUBLICATION DATA
Main entry under title:

Handbook of discourse analysis.

Includes indexes.
Contents: v. 1. Disciplines of discourse — v. 2.
Dimensions of discourse — v. 3. Discourse and dialogue —
[etc.]
1. Discourse analysis.   I. Dijk, Teun Adrianus van,
Date   II. Title.
P302.H343   1985   001.51   84-6482
ISBN 0-12-712004-1 (v. 4 : alk. paper)

PRINTED IN THE UNITED STATES OF AMERICA

85 86 87 88   9 8 7 6 5 4 3 2 1

Contents

Contributors	ix
Preface to the Four Volumes	xi
Preface to Volume 4	xiii
Contents of Volumes, 1, 2, and 3	xv

1
Introduction: The Role of Discourse Analysis in Society
Teun A. van Dijk

The Uses of Discourse Analysis in Society	1
The Problem of Application and Social Relevance	3
The Relevance of Discourse Analysis	4
Critical Discourse Analysis	6

2
Interpersonal Conflict
Janet Beavin Bavelas, L. Edna Rogers, and Frank E. Millar

Introduction	9
Studies of Interpersonal Conflict	10
Summary and Suggestions	22
References	24

3
Ideological Structures in Discourse
Gunther Kress

Text and Discourse	27
Language and Ideology	29
Exemplifications	32
Bibliography	42

4
Political Discourse Analysis
Gill Seidel

Approaches to Political Discourse Analysis	43
Discourse Analysis with Particular Reference to Paraphrase and Synonymy	46
Discourse Analysis with Particular Reference to Syntax	48
Discourse Analysis Focusing on Enunciation	53
Bibliography	55

5
Power
Roger Fowler

Language as Social Practice	61
The Pronouns of Power and Solidarity	63
Directive and Constitutive Linguistic Practices	64
Ideology in Sociolinguistic Varieties	65
Linguistic Checklist	68
A Brief Example	75
References	81

6
Discrimination in Discourse
Mary Sykes

Introduction	83
The Question of What Constitutes Unfavorable Treatment	87
Example: Syntactic Analysis	88
Example: Semantic Analysis	94
Conclusion	99
References	100

7
Gender, Language, and Discourse
Candace West and Don H. Zimmerman

Introduction	103
Language and Speech of Women and Men	104
Gender and Discourse in Context	108
Conclusions	119
Appendix: Transcription Conventions	119
Bibliography	120

8
On the Discourse of Immigrant Workers: Interethnic Communication and Communication Strategies
Norbert Dittmar and Christiane von Stutterheim

Interethnic Communication: Problem Space	125
Aspects of Verbal Interaction between Natives and Immigrants	128
Discourse Organization	137
Consequences for Social Relations	148
References	149

9
The Problem of Justice in the Courts Approached by the Analysis of Plea Bargaining Discourse
Douglas W. Maynard

Introduction	153
Theory and Research	154
Sentencing Decisions	156
Methodological Problems	164
Gestalt Approach to Defendant Attributes	168
Conclusion	176
References	176

10
The Interaction between Judge and Defendant
Ruth Wodak

Introduction: The Aims and Goals of Sociolinguistics	181
Review of the Literature: The Impact of Institutional and Cultural Norms on Language Behavior	182
The Language of Defendants in Austrian Courts	184
Class-Specific Justice: The Goals of Interdisciplinary Research	190
References	190

11
Doctor–Patient Discourse
Aaron V. Cicourel

Aspects of Doctor–Patient Communication	193
Contradictory Beliefs about Illness: An Example of Miscommunication	197

| | Concluding Remarks | 201 |
| | References | 201 |

12
Cross-Cultural Communication
Deborah Tannen

Introduction: The Importance of Cross-Cultural Communication	203
Paralinguistic Signals in Communication	203
Examples of Cross-Cultural Differences	206
Effects of Cross-Cultural Differences	209
Appendix: Transcription Conventions	212
Bibliography	213

Biographical Notes   *217*
Index   *223*

Contributors

Numbers in parentheses indicate the pages on which the authors' contributions begin.

JANET BEAVIN BAVELAS (9), Department of Psychology, University of Victoria, Victoria, British Columbia, V8W 2Y2, Canada

AARON V. CICOUREL (193), Department of Sociology, University of California at San Diego, La Jolla, California 92093

NORBERT DITTMAR (125), Fachbereich Germanistik, Freie Universität Berlin, 1000 Berlin 33, Germany

ROGER FOWLER (61), School of English and American Studies, University of East Anglia, Norwich NR4 7TJ, England

GUNTHER KRESS (27), Faculty of Social Sciences and Humanities, New South Wales Institute of Technology, Broadway, N.S.W., Australia, 2007

DOUGLAS W. MAYNARD (153), Department of Sociology, University of Wisconsin, Madison, Wisconsin 53706

FRANK E. MILLAR (9), Department of Communication, Cleveland State University, Cleveland, Ohio 44115

L. EDNA ROGERS (9), Department of Communication, Cleveland State University, Cleveland, Ohio 44115

GILL SEIDEL (43), The Modern Languages Centre, University of Bradford, Bradford, West Yorkshire BD7 1DP, and URL3 Lexicologie et Textes Politiques (CNRS and INALF), École Normale Supérieure de Saint-Cloud, 92211 Saint-Cloud, France

MARY SYKES (83), School of Economic and Social Studies, University of East Anglia, Norwich NR4 7TJ, England

DEBORAH TANNEN (203), Department of Linguistics, Georgetown University, Washington, D. C. 20057

TEUN A. VAN DIJK (1), Department of General Literary Studies, Section of Discourse Studies, University of Amsterdam, 1012 VT Amsterdam, The Netherlands

CHRISTIANE VON STUTTERHEIM (125), Max-Planck-Institut für Psycholinguistik, 6522 BC Nijmegen, The Netherlands

CANDACE WEST (103), Board of Studies in Sociology, Stevenson College, University of California at Santa Cruz, Santa Cruz, California 95064

RUTH WODAK (181), Institut für Allgemeine Sprachwissenschaft, Universität Wien, A-1090 Wien, Austria

DON H. ZIMMERMAN (103), Department of Sociology, University of California, Santa Barbara, Santa Barbara, California 93106

Preface to the Four Volumes

One of the most conspicuous and interesting developments in the humanities and the social sciences in the past decade has undoubtedly been the widespread, multidisciplinary attention paid to the study of discourse. This development began to take shape in the early 1970s, after some scattered attempts to the late 1960s, in such disciplines as anthropology, linguistics, semiotics, poetics, psychology, sociology, and mass communication research. This shared interest for various phenomena of language use, texts, conversational interaction, or communicative events soon became more integrated, under the common label of discourse analysis (or, e.g., *Textwissenschaft* in German).

The variety of theoretical and descriptive approaches to this new interdisciplinary field is impressive; for example, the study of narrative in nearly all disciplines mentioned above, the attention paid to natural forms of language use in the social context in sociolinguistics, the experimental or computer-simulated study of text processing in psychology and artificial intelligence, the construction of text grammars in linguistics, the ethnography of speaking in anthropology, as well as the continued attention to the analysis of style, rhetoric, argumentation, and persuasive communication in several branches of the humanities and the social sciences.

To document the development and the current state of this new field of discourse analysis, it became imperative to unite these various directions of research in one multidisciplinary publication. The present *Handbook of Discourse Analysis*, in four volumes, is the result of this enterprise. This *Handbook* provides surveys of and introductions to the respective approaches in discourse analysis. In concrete sample analyses, its chapters show how discourse analysis actually works at several levels of description. It summarizes our insights into the structures and functions of various discourse types of genres. And it demonstrates for a number of important social domains and problems how discourse analysis can be usefully and critically applied. The four volumes deal, respectively, with these major aims: presentation of the various disciplines of discourse analysis, introduction to descriptive methods, study of important genres of (dialogical) discourse, and application in critical social analysis.

For each topic we have invited leading scholars to contribute essays in their area of specialization. Most of these scholars were widely known, in and beyond their own fields. Young researchers have also been invited to write about the topic in which they have become specialists. To make the *Handbook* not only interdisciplinary but also international, care has been taken to include scholars from several countries.

The *Handbook* has been set up according to a few basic leading principles. First, as an introductory state of the art, its chapters satisfy a number of didactic criteria so that it is accessible at least to advanced and interested students in all disciplines of the humanities and the social sciences, and not only to specialists in some area of research. Second, the *Handbook* has a descriptive and analytic bias, to allow more direct application in concrete discourse research. Detailed attention to theoretical issues, as well as excessive formalization, have been avoided. Third, in line with the important interest in spontaneous uses of language, illustrations are given predominantly of natural discourse forms. Fourth, within the constraints of the thematic setup of the *Handbook*, authors are free to present their own perspectives and to summarize their own research findings. The variety of approaches, however, guarantees that the major directions, theories, or methods of research are represented.

Despite its multidisciplinary and wide-ranging scope, even a four-volume handbook must have self-imposed limitations. There are, of course, more disciplines involved in discourse analysis than could be represented here. Thus, space limitations forced us to exclude, for example, the study of mass communication and literary scholarship. Similarly, of the hundreds of discourse genres, only some of the most important could be treated here. The same holds for various details of discourse structures. And, finally, not all directions of research or schools of thought could be covered (such as discourse analysis in France). Yet the selection we made should result in a coherent, representative, and up-to-date state of the (new) art of discourse analysis.

The preparation and editing of this *Handbook* have been a considerable task that would have been impossible to perform without the help, the advice, and the assistance of many people—too many to mention here. I hereby thank them all for their cooperation.

University of Amsterdam TEUN A. VAN DIJK
Autumn, 1984

Preface to Volume 4: Discourse Analysis in Society

In this fourth volume of the *Handbook of Discourse Analysis*, attention is paid to the role of discourse analysis in society. After one or two decades of increasingly sophisticated analytic and theoretical approaches to the many dimensions of text, talk, and their cognitive, social, and cultural contexts, the time has come to reflect on the implications of the new discipline and the tools it has provided. This means that application in various social domains, as well as formulation of relevant social problems or conflicts in terms of the role of discourse, becomes imperative. Also, the old question of the discipline's potential for social criticism needs to be answered here.

The chapters in this volume provide relevant suggestions and directions for this important development of discourse analysis: The discourse dimension of first- and second-language learning receives attention, as do pathologies and interpersonal conflicts in communication; the special problems of intercultural communication are also studied; the central political and ideological nature of discourse in the account, for example, of discrimination, sexism, racism, or exploitation as expressed or enacted by discourse is investigated; and specific social contexts, such as trials in court, are examined for the social implications of discourse.

Obviously, many other problems, conflicts, or social contexts could and should be evaluated from a point of view of social discourse analysis—for example, education, the media, politics, and public health services. The chapters in this volume can do only part of this job, but they show that it can be done and contain suggestions of how it can be done. Applied and critical discourse analysis should be a central, not marginal, task of our research in the future.

Contents of Volumes 1, 2, and 3

Volume 1: Disciplines of Discourse

1. Introduction: Discourse Analysis as a New Cross-Discipline
   T. A. van Dijk
2. Linguistics as a Tool for Discourse Analysis
   C. Fillmore
3. Text Linguistics in Discourse Studies
   R. de Beaugrande
4. Cognitive Psychology and Text Processing
   G. Bower and R. Cirilo
5. Social Psychology and Discourse
   W. P. Robinson
6. Artificial Intelligence: Modeling Memory for Language Understanding
   R. Schank and M. Burstein
7. Sociological Approaches to Discourse Analysis
   W. A. Corsaro
8. Sociocultural Dimensions of Discourse
   A. Duranti
9. Philosophy and Discourse Analysis
   A. Kasher
10. Historical Discourse
    N. S. Struever
11. Legal Discourse
    B. Danet

Volume 2: Dimensions of Discourse
1. Introduction: Levels and Dimensions of Discourse Analysis
   T. A. van Dijk
2. On the Integration of Linguistic Description
   J. M. Sinclair
3. Dimensions of Discourse Analysis: Grammar
   M. A. K. Halliday
4. Phonology: Intonation in Discourse
   D. Brazil
5. Morphology
   W. U. Dressler
6. Lexicon
   J. S. Petöfi
7. Semantic Discourse Analysis
   T. A. van Dijk
8. Pragmatics
   A. Ferrara
9. An Analysis of Argumentation
   J. Kopperschmidt
10. Narrative Analysis
    E. Gülich and U. Quasthoff
11. Analysis of Nonverbal Behavior
    K. Scherer and H. G. Wallbott
12. Text Processing: A Psychological Model
    W. Kintsch
13. Extracting the Proof from the Pudding: Coding and Analyzing Experimental Protocols
    N. Johnson
14. Protocol Analysis
    K. Ericsson and H. A. Simon

Volume 3: Discourse and Dialogue
1. Introduction: Dialogue as Discourse and Interaction
   T. A. van Dijk
2. The Inference-Making Machine: Notes on Observability
   H. Sacks
3. An Exercise in the Transcription and Analysis of Laughter
   G. Jefferson
4. Everyday Argument: The Organization of Diversity in Talk
   D. Schiffrin
5. Children's Conversations
   J. Dore
6. Parent–Child Discourse
   S. Ervin-Tripp and A. Strage
7. The Discourse Symptoms of Developmental Disorders
   J. R. Johnston
8. Analyzing News Interviews: Aspects of the Production of Talk for an Overhearing Audience
   J. Heritage
9. The Structure of Classroom Discourse
   H. Mehan
10. Analyzing the Use of Language in Courtroom Interaction
    P. Drew
11. Meetings
    E. C. Cuff and W. W. Sharrock
12. Refusing Invited Applause: Preliminary Observations from a Case Study of Charismatic Oratory
    J. M. Atkinson
13. Conversational Storytelling
    L. Polanyi
14. Verbal Dueling
    J. H. McDowell
15. Puns and Jokes
    J. Sherzer
16. Rumors and Gossiping
    G. A. Fine

CHAPTER 1

Introduction: The Role of Discourse Analysis in Society

Teun A. van Dijk

THE USES OF DISCOURSE ANALYSIS IN SOCIETY

In the three previous volumes of this *Handbook* the many facets of the emerging discipline of discourse analysis have been highlighted. Against the background of developments in several disciplines in the humanities and the social sciences, it was shown how discourse in general, and specific discourse genres in particular, can be analyzed at several levels of description. One of the prevailing features of this new discipline of discourse analysis appears to be the explicit account of the fact that discourse structures, at several levels, may have multiple links with the context of communication and interaction. Discourse analysis, thus, is essentially a contribution to the study of language "in use." Besides—or even instead—of an explication of the abstract structures of texts or conversations, we witness a concerted interest for the cognitive and especially the social processes, strategies, and contextualization of discourse taken as a mode of interaction in highly complex sociocultural situations.

One important dimension is still lacking in this account, however. Having obtained some insights into the social functions of discourse, we also might ask what the social role of discourse analysis as a discipline is. That is, what are the "external" goals of this new approach to language and communication? Or, to put it even more bluntly: What are the uses of discourse analysis? Especially for linguists, such questions may appear irrelevant. If the "internal" or academic goals, such as those of observational, descriptive, or explanatory adequacy, or maybe empirical validity, in the account of language and language use are reached, who cares about the possible usefulness of our insights? Possible applications, for example, for practical purposes in several social domains, are seen as by-products of linguistic inquiry, and applied research does not seem to have the same status as theoretical and descriptive work. And the same holds for possible external constraints upon the selection of our research objects, problems, or goals: What discourses, by what participants, and in what contexts do we study? Pressing social issues or problems thus, have little bearing upon the research goals of the linguist. And applications have been limited mostly to the field of first- and second-language learning, or are left to the discretion of psycho- and sociolinguists. Traditionally, social scientists paid more attention to this problematic issue. Their insights into the nature of social interaction and institutions may also be evaluated as to their possible contribution to the understanding, or even the solution, of important social problems. To be sure, many social scientists may ignore such external expectations or demands, either because they just are not interested or because they deem their knowledge to be too fragile to be relevantly applied. Any effective use that might be made of their work is considered premature or superficial, if not an abuse of theoretical subtleties and complexities. Obviously, however, whatever good reasons both linguists and social scientists might have for avoiding this kind of involvement, there is also much ideology at stake; that is, justification patterns for professional interests. Although it would be interesting to analyze such an ideology in detail and to try to explain the reasons for the lack of interesting contributions of linguistics and discourse analysis to the insight of relevant social problems, I here mainly sketch some of the conditions and the modes of the role of discourse analysis as social analysis. The various papers in this volume of the *Handbook* then spell out, more concretely, how relevant social issues can be addressed in terms of our understanding of the role of discourse in society and culture.

The attention paid to this issue in a full separate volume of the *Handbook* is not merely based on the personal, social, or political responsibility of a number of linguists or social scientists (myself included). It has been stressed in the general introduction to this *Handbook* that it should serve both academic and practical goals: It should be shown what we can do with discourse analysis. Obviously, I here mean more than to provide adequate descriptions of text and context. That is, we expect more from discourse analysis as the study of real language use, by real speakers in real situations, than we expect from the study of abstract syntax or formal semantics. Together with psycho- and sociolinguistics, discourse analysis has definitely brought linguistics to the realm of the social sciences.

So we now may expect some rather concrete requests for help by other social scientists in the account of social problems. As long as we dealt with abstract grammars, sophisticated formalisms, or idealistic speech act theories, our preoccupations were possibly respected or admired, but further ignored, in the majority of the social sciences. Now that we claim to have better insights into the nature of actual language use, and into the intricate relations between discourses and social situations and institutions, we may have to deliver more than just another sophisticated theory or fancy description.

THE PROBLEM OF APPLICATION AND SOCIAL RELEVANCE

When we address the problem of possible applications and social relevance for the study of discourse, we enter a confused discussion. This discussion is far from new and has flared up periodically since the work of the scholars of the Frankfurter school, for example, and since the reformulation of their ideas during the student movements at the end of the 1960s. I cannot even try to review the main tenets of this debate here. What is at stake is the sociopolitical function of the scientific and academic work we do, and hence interests and ideologies. One party in this debate claims that the choice of our research goals, our methods of inquiry, our theories, and the objects of analysis cannot be independent of our own sociopolitical positions—and interests—and of the wider social context of research. That claim can be backed with many examples from the development of the social sciences. Maybe the more prominent contemporary example is the widespread and rapid development of feminist research in a number of disciplines. Others include the emerging ethnic studies and research programs in several countries. Male chauvinism, ethnocentrism, racism, middle-class interests, Western dominance, and so on have become familiar types of criticism and reasons for action, both in our society at large and within our academic domains. Another party in this debate might go along a little bit with these arguments or criticisms, but it will firmly refuse to mix science with "politics": Maybe we should indeed adapt the goals of our research, extend the domain or object of analysis, and revise the overall perspective a bit, but on the whole, academic scholarship should remain autonomous, and not be put under the constraints of external social or political developments, decisions, or policies. Of course, intermediary positions are possible too.

Although we feel an affiliation with the first position mentioned above, this does not mean that we have a clear picture in mind, let alone an explicit methodology, about what it means exactly to do socially relevant research, especially in the field of discourse analysis. On the one hand, we may have directly effective applications in language-learning programs or therapies, which would fall under the scope of what could be called "practical relevance." On the other hand, it will often be claimed (though seldom proved by a thorough analysis of the history of science) that even the most abstract and apparently irrelevant theoretical endeavors may later turn out to be of utmost practical relevance. The usual examples in this case generally come from physics, chemistry, or biology and their possible applications in new technologies or as medical treatments. Against this background, therefore, we must indicate some of the difficulties and possibilities for the adequate application of discourse analysis in socially relevant research.

THE RELEVANCE OF DISCOURSE ANALYSIS

An obvious first claim that could be made about the possible social relevance of discourse analysis is that the very choice or extension of the object or field of linguistic research—actual language use in its social context—already satisfies a condition of social relevance—it provides insight into the forms and mechanisms of human communication and verbal interaction. Clearly, such insight is necessary for relevant applications, but this is hardly a sufficient condition. It only places the study of language where it belongs in the first place: namely, among the social sciences. It still has few implications for the methods of inquiry, for the structure of theories, for the choice of specific discourse types or discourse properties, or for the analysis of specific social contexts. The development of discourse analysis in the 1970s has also shown, on the one hand, that structural analysis of texts or conversations may be as abstract and as far removed from actual language use as the earlier sentence grammars, and, on the other hand, that studies of language in the social context may pay attention to rather trivial or hardly critical examples of language use and communication. And similar remarks may be made for the development of models of discourse processing in psychology and artificial intelligence. We now know much more about the rules, the moves, and the strategies of everyday talk. We know about coherence and cohesion, and we have some insight into the structures and the conversational occasioning of stories or into the cognitive processes involved in the understanding and representation of stories. However we also begin to grasp some of the constraints of the various features of the social context, such as gender, status, power, ethnicity, roles, or institutional settings, upon the style, the thematic structure, or the cognitive interpretation of text and talk. Clearly, these latter contributions to the study of discourse in its social context provide a next step on the difficult route toward relevant applications, and some of the studies in this volume explicitly try to give answers to these important issues in the sociology of discourse.

Yet, although we draw closer to the issue at hand, one aspect is still lacking. It is certainly important to know how women's and men's speech may differ, how young urban American black men may be experts in the art of verbal dueling, how judges and lawyers address the defendant in court, or what style of talk a policeman adopts when giving us a speeding ticket. The same holds for the interesting observations in studies of newspaper discourse, parliamentary debates, laws, advertising, or TV programs. We have selected important and even relevant objects, phenomena, or locations of inquiry. But this does not yet guarantee that we pose relevant questions. We simply do not yet know whether a study of pauses, hesitation phenomena, local coherence, paraverbal gestures, or style in a job interview, a court trial, or a TV program will provide socially interesting answers about what is really going on in such communicative events.

We only tell a tiny fragment of the story if we do not specify how such discourse details serve a function in the creation, the maintenance, or the change of such contextual constraints as the dominance, the power, the status, or the ethnocentrism of one of the participants. Analysis of the discourses in the classroom, the office, or the social welfare agency can hardly be called complete if we do not thereby show how a teacher, a boss, or a social worker enacts social roles, shows power, and exerts control. An explication of the complex structures of everyday talk becomes even more interesting if we can relate them to the social parameters mentioned above and if we can show what kind of personal problems people may have in the adequate participation in such talk, what kind of individual pathologies may surface by such discourse, or what conflicts can be at stake in such interactions. If we study (as in a project being carried out at the University of Amsterdam) what people tell us or each other about the ethnic minorities in their town or neighborhood, we may, just for fun, study sociocultural variations in style, storytelling, and argumentation, or the strategies of talk and interviews. Yet, such analyses show that at these levels of description people will, sometimes indirectly, express contradictory ethnic attitudes. And the analyses become really interesting when they expose the cognitive and social strategies used by people both to express their negative experiences and opinions and to present themselves as kind, tolerant, nonracist citizens. Arriving at such insights, we learn more about the formation, the change, and the spread of ethnic prejudice through everyday interaction, and thus about some of the underlying mechanisms of social attitudes and discrimination practices.

Several of the chapters in this volume not only take socially interesting objects for analysis but also try to answer some of the questions mentioned above about the social problems, conflicts, or predicaments related to such discourse and context types. It hardly needs to be stated in these cases that, in order to try to answer such specifically selected questions, we need the theoretical instruments and the more general analytic data and descriptions that constitute the wider framework. If we want to know how judges in court may display bias, prejudice, or power in interrogations or the justification of a verdict, we must of course first know about the general discursive structures of court trials, about the procedures of questioning or the structures of verdicts. And the same holds for the other examples we have mentioned. Yet these obvious preconditions for the solution of specific puzzles should be handled with care in our research strategies. More often than not they are used as avoidance arguments, as part of a strategy employed to mask lack of interest or to justify one's own hobbies. Clearly, we need not wait until the full general picture has been filled in, or the preliminary theories completely worked out. We started to study discourse without a complete theory of the sentence. In fact, we also started to do discourse analysis because we hoped to say more about sentence structures (a hope that turned out to be realistic). Similarly, if we try to answer specific relevant questions, we may well obtain insight into the more interesting and critical dimensions of what discourse and social interaction are all about. We are here back to the arguments of the more critical developments in the social sciences, such as feminist research, that would claim that the choice of relevant and sociopolitically motivated goals and objects of research will also affect, and maybe ameliorate, our very methods of inquiry and hence our theories and analytical instruments.

CRITICAL DISCOURSE ANALYSIS

There is another possible extension to relevant discourse analysis: the formulation of criticism and alternatives. Although we here leave the confines of academic control and enter clearly sociopolitical realms, this does not mean that we are powerless. There are many domains about which discourse analysis is able to provide relevant insights: the use of sexist discourse, racist reporting in the news media, the enactment of power in and by the discourses of authorities, the inequities confirmed

1 Introduction: The Role of Discourse Analysis in Society

by the prevalence of white middle-class discourse styles in multi-ethnic schools, and so on. But even the choice of such specific research domains and problems, and even the formulation of relevant questions, does not yet provide solutions to problems or strategies to fight inequality. These will among other things depend on who will benefit from our insights, and what perspective is given to our results. Without a thoroughly founded criticism of those authorities or institutions who are responsible for the inequalities, we are no more than "free-floating intellectuals," paper tigers. It follows that a next step in the research program will be to make decisions about priority, about who to "sell" our work to, about the adaptation of our specific research goals and methods to those who are most in need of them. The groups of people and the areas of social problems concerned hardly need to be spelled out here. There are few but yet crucial studies, within or close to the purview of discourse analysis, that have shown that such critical discourse analysis is necessary, useful, and realistic. Work on the portrayal of industrial disputes in TV news, on the misrepresentation of political demonstrations as "violent riots," or on the bias in favor of the police or the authorities in the media coverage of "race riots" has shown that detailed discourse analysis can be brought to bear in the wider context of the challenge of authority and power and as a basis of political action. That such work is not necessarily linked to a socialist or Marxist tradition, or to predominantly European ways of doing research, may be illustrated by many other examples: as in the United States, where participation in such traditions is limited, but where the democratic and liberal ideals of a social context in which our universities not only have concrete professional tasks but also wider ranging responsibilities is taken seriously. Academic freedom also means the freedom to criticize. Discourse analysis provides us with rather powerful, while subtle and precise, insights to pinpoint the everyday manifestations and displays of social problems in communication and interaction. It is here that we witness the realization of the macrosociological patterns that characterize our societies. Certainly, discourse features may only be symptoms or fragmentary enactments of larger problems: inequality, class differences, sexism, racism, power, and dominance of course involve more than text and talk. Yet discourse plays a crucial role in their ideological formulation, in their communicative reproduction, in the social and political decision procedures, and in the institutional management and representation of such issues (e.g., in laws, meetings, media coverage, informal daily talk about them, their reformulation in documents). As soon as we know more about the discursive representation and management of such problems and conflicts, we have the design for the key that can disrupt, disclose, and challenge the mechanisms involved. Thus a subtle analysis of the ways indirect forms of ethnocentrism and racism still exhibit themselves in our newpapers may lead journalists to at least change their selection of topics, to pay attention to the representation of actors in news events, to have due regard to subtleties of style, and even to adopt a special code for reporting about ethnic minorities and ethnic relations. This is one example among many. Although we may in this way change only some surface manifestation of a deeper or more complex problem, we at least have done more than just describe the words in the world.

It hardly needs to be reminded here that, besides these limitations to what we can do, there are other caveats to heed. Examples of theoretically ill-understood and methodologically wrong applications can be mentioned by any linguist and social scientist. Language programs conceived within sociolinguistic endeavors to eliminate linguistic "deficiencies" are well known for their weak sociolinguistic theory and for their wrong social perspective on the problems involved. Without a sound discourse analysis, which takes all the relevant discursive and contextual parameters into account, and without an adequate and critical social analysis of the power structures and group or ethnic differences and conflicts involved, we will of course yield the wrong assessment and hence misguided advice. Similar examples may be given for other domains of educational settings, for the news media, for legal discourse and interaction, or for the documents of public information. Yet, despite such warnings, we may also have some confidence, inspired by the rapid advances in the domain of discourse analysis. The chapters in this volume were written to show that, indeed, such advances, as they have been documented in the previous volumes, can be intelligently and critically put to actual use.

CHAPTER **2**

Interpersonal Conflict

Janet Beavin Bavelas, L. Edna Rogers, and Frank E. Millar

INTRODUCTION

This chapter focuses on methods for studying conflict as discourse between persons. Interpersonal conflict is a ubiquitous experience—sometimes stimulating and constructive, but potentially painful and threatening. For this is not conflict in the abstract, as political and other social conflicts may be. Interpersonal conflict is an activity we engage in directly, something we do with other people. Indeed, the first and most important contribution that a discourse analysis can make to this particular social issue is to equate interpersonal conflict with discourse between people. Most interpersonal conflict is verbal, not physical; the conflict is the argument itself. Thus, to analyze such dialogue is to approach and study the phenomenon most directly. In linguistic terms, interpersonal conflict is a speech event; it is performative in that saying equals doing. The argument, quarrel, insults, or disagreement are the conflict. In other words, people do not relate, then talk; rather, they relate in talk (Duncan, 1967, p. 249); the relationship is the exchange of messages (Bateson, 1972, p. 275). We should therefore study how people conflict (and not only why they conflict, with what outcomes, or how they feel about it). In this chapter, we describe some of the methods available for studying how people conflict.

The authors have reviewed relevant disciplines (communication, linguistics, psychiatry, psychology, and sociology) for methods and examples that fit three defining criteria: (1) A direct conflict should be identified and studied, (2) it should be interpersonal, that is, occurring between individuals, and (3) actual discourse should be recorded and analyzed. Surprisingly, only a handful of studies met these three simple criteria.

Traditionally, linguists tend to approach discourse as a cognitive (individual) phenomenon rather than as a social (interpersonal) process. The other social sciences virtually ignore discourse itself, seldom even recording what was said, much less analyzing it for sequential patterns.

Thus, there are two reasons for applying scholarly methods to problems of social or practical import, such as interpersonal conflict. The first is obvious—to contribute our knowledge to the understanding and possible solution of a problem. The second is the converse—to contribute the problem to our knowledge, that is, to affect scholars and scholarly thinking. Traditional disciplinary boundaries have, in our opinion, been responsible for the striking paucity of research on the discourse of interpersonal conflict. Every discipline provides rich, unique tools for studying human behavior. Yet each discipline ends by studying topics as defined by that discipline and not as they naturally occur. This treatens to imprison us doubly, isolating us from natural phenomena and from other disciplines, each in its own ivory tower. Important problems have a compelling identity, a vitality of their own that invades disciplinary isolation. Such problems may introduce us to new ways of seeing and doing.

STUDIES OF INTERPERSONAL CONFLICT

Our focus in the following is more on methodology than on substantive findings. This set of selected studies represents the variety of available methods, arranged roughly in order from less to more complex procedures and phenomena. We conclude with a number of suggestions for other possibilities that would seem worth trying.

Brenneis and Lein (1977); Lein and Brenneis (1978)

The straightforward method of studying conflict discourse to be found in these two articles could serve as a prototype for a wide variety of initial investigations. They arranged for a conflict to occur by asking children to role-play an argument about, for example, who is strongest or whose ball it is. The children seem to have gotten quite absorbed in their roles and to have generated spontaneous and lengthy disputes, which were tape-recorded. An example may awaken memories of your own childhood (or your own children):

(1) (Brenneis & Lein, 1977, p. 55)
    Bob: You're skinny.
    Tom: You're slimmy.

2 Interpersonal Conflict

  Bob: You're scrawny.
  Tom: You're . . . I don't know.
  Bob: You're weakling.
  Tom: You're the slimmiest kid in the whole world.
  Bob: You're the weaklingest . . . .
  Tom: You're baloney (etc.).

These classic quarrels were produced by children in grades one to eight, from three speech communities (white American, New England; black American children of migrant harvesters; and rural Hindi-speaking Fiji Indian children).

 Lein and Brenneis approached this material inductively. They first identified content categories (e.g., threats, commands) and stylistic categories (e.g., volume, speed); these categories describe an individual's utterances. More important, individual utterances were organized into patterned argument sequences, involving the productions of both participants. Three sequential patterns were found: repetition, inversion, and escalation. An example of the repetition pattern is:

(2) (Lein & Brenneis, 1978, p. 300)
  Alan: I'm the strongest.
  Joey: I'm the strongest.
  Alan: I am.
  Joey: I am.

Inversion is evident in the following, especially in the last four statements:

(3) (Brenneis & Lein, 1977, pp. 56–57)
  Dave: I am, you dumb-dumb.
  Larry: I'm not no dumb-dumb, dodo.
  Dave: Yes, you are.
  Larry: No, I'm not.
  Dave: Yes, you are.
  Larry: No, I'm not.

Perhaps the most common pattern was that of escalation, either in content:

(4) (Brenneis & Lein, 1977, p. 62)
  Ann: I can lift up our whole family. I bet you can't lift that up with one finger.
  Joey: I can lift the whole world up with one finger.
  Ann: Well, I can lift up the whole universe. So why don't you just be quiet about that?

or stylistic escalation, typically by volume:

(5) (Lein & Brenneis, 1978, p. 305)
    Bill: Me. (p)
    Ken: Me. (mf)
    Bill: ME. (f)
    Ken: ME!! (ff)
    Bill: ME!!! (fff)

Clearly, then, these verbal conflicts are sequentially organized. Lein and Brenneis concluded that, for all the groups they compared,

> it is evident that arguments are rule-governed, socially organized and frequently quite complex events. Even in situations which one might initially expect are emotionally loaded and therefore likely to get out of hand, children are observing cultural conventions and each other quite closely. Overtly competitive as they are, arguments are also cooperative performances; children build arguments together. . . . Arguments do not represent the breakdown of interactional conventions and are not loosely linked individual diatribes. They rather have their own rules. (1978, p. 308)

Brenneis and Lein's findings run counter to the intuition that conflict equals chaos. Their observations, which are upheld in some of the studies to be described below, suggest that verbal conflict can be a speech event of remarkable regularity and coordination.

Camras (1977)

Again, conflict between children was studied, using a method with interesting similarities and differences from that of Lein and Brenneis. Camras created a spontaneous conflict between pairs of American middle-class kindergartners by presenting them with a desirable object (a caged gerbil) that only one could play with at once. The ensuing interaction was filmed, providing a permanent record of the side view of each child as well as their spoken interaction. Camras identified episodes of conflict both by verbal outcries (*My turn!, No!*) and by pushing and holding of the prized object. Then—and this is the offbeat aspect—the facial expressions of the paticipants were categorized and analyzed, especially aggressive expressions such as lowered brows, face thrust forward, or lips pressed together with tightened mouth corners. One pattern observed was as follows: Child A has the object, and B tries to take it. Child A displays oblique brows, and B not only desists but now waits before attempting to take the object again. If A did not display any aggressive facial expression, B would make the attempt sooner.

The advantages of this study are that it focused on the dyadic (rather than monadic) unit, that is, the relation between one child's facial expression and the other's response to the conflict; it extended stylistics from paralanguage (e.g., volume) to facial expression and found systematic patterns, as did Lein and Brenneis; and it showed that conflict could be created for observation—elicited rather than enacted. Obviously, including the verbal language of conflict would have been even more satisfying. Also, the reliance on standard, nonsequential statistical methods (analysis of variance) took a heavy toll in intelligibility, serving to obscure rather than to reveal the pattern of discourse.

Labov (1972)

Suppose you don't happen to be a black, inner-city adolescent, and you overhear the following exchange:

(6) (Labov, 1972, p. 141)
    A: Eat shit.
    B: Hop on the spoon.
    A: Move over.
    B: I can't, your mother's already there.

Or this dialogue between John and Willie, with Rel as observer:

(7) (Labov, 1972, p. 145)
    John: Who father wear raggedy drawers?
    Willie: Yeh the ones with so many holes in them when-a-you walk they whistle?
    Rel: Oh . . . shi-it! When you walk they whistle! Oh shit!

A nonmember of this culture might expect an escalation into physical conflict to follow quickly from these insults to the other person, his family, and their poverty. However, as Labov shows, these are ritual insults, part of a complex and coordinated pattern of verbal conflict called "sounding," a speech event he studied among young American black males in south-central Harlem. His team used a variety of techniques, principally direct observation through long-term interaction with several adolescent peer groups. Conversations were tape-recorded in buses on trips and in group sessions, providing a great deal of spontaneous interaction for analysis. There was no necessity to arrange for or to instigate conflict via sounding, as it occurred frequently whenever a group was together.

What is sounding? It consists of a dialogue, performed for an audience of peer observers, in which the participants trade insults. The most common targets of insults are the other person's mother, self, or house, which are typically characterized as ugly, disgusting, immoral, or poor, using certain fixed syntactical forms. For example, "Your mother raised you on ugly milk" (Labov, 1972, p. 136); "Your mother so low she c'play Chinese handball on a curve [curb]" (1972, p. 157); "When I came across your house, a rat gave me a jay-walkin' ticket" (1972, p. 137).

These "sounds" are typically delivered in a competitive sequence like (6) above and are freely evaluated by the audience, as with Rel's appreciation of Willie's metaphor in (7). In his elegant analysis of their forms and syntax, Labov proposed "rules" for sounding as a speech event. It is a highly structured and coordinated competition, performed for an audience, with winners and losers (the latter being those who are "topped" or who cannot keep up the series). The key difference between a ritual and a personal insult is that the ritual attribution must be so outlandish as to be clearly untrue in the eyes of both participants. That is, while it is true that these boys (and their homes) are poor, it is part of their shared knowledge that the following never happened: "When I came to your house, seven roaches jumped me and one search me" (1972, p. 137). To say directly that the other person is poor or hungry, that his father is old or stutters, or any other true statement is to descend to personal insult. Such exchanges quickly become a different kind of conflict, often ending in hard feelings and a strident argument, including protestations of unfairness from the audience:

(8) (Labov, 1972, p. 151)

> Boot: At least my father ain't got a gray head! His father got a big bald spot with a gray head right down there and one long string . . .
> David: Because he'old, he's old, that's why! He's old, that's why! . . .
> Boot: . . . and one long string, that covers his whole head, one, one long string, about that high, covers his whole head.
> David: [with tears in his eyes] You lyin' Boot! . . . You know 'cause he old, tha's why!
> Ricky: [to Boot] Aw man, cut it out.

Thus statements about a simple truth such as the father's gray hair and baldness violate the rules of sounding, whereas the obviously exaggerated untruths do not: "He got a head like a water-pump . . . a mailbox . . . like the front of a bus" (1972, p. 132), or "His mother was so dirty, when she get the rag [to] take a bath, the water went back down the drain" (1972, p. 133). Again, verbal conflict follows an organized and rather sophisticated interpersonal pattern.

Watzlawick, Beavin, and Jackson (1967)

The coordinated discourse of conflict described so far has interesting similarities to the structure of the fictional arguments in Albee's (1962) play, *Who's Afraid of Virginia Woolf?*, as analyzed by Watzlawick *et al.* The main protagonists are a long-married couple, George and Martha, in circumstances quite different from Lein and Brenneis' or Labov's real subjects; the setting is a small New England university town, where George is a professor and Martha the president's daughter. Yet their unremitting verbal battles resemble Brenneis and Lein's children in elaborate forms of escalation:

(9) (Albee, 1962, p. 14)
    George: . . . chewing your ice cubes . . . like a cocker spaniel. You'll crack your big teeth.
    Martha: THEY'RE MY BIG TEETH!
    George: Some of them . . . some of them.
    Martha: I've got more teeth than you've got.
    George: Two more.
    Martha: Well, two more's a lot more.
    George: I suppose it is. I suppose it's pretty remarkable . . . considering how old you are.
    Martha: YOU CUT THAT OUT! (Pause) You're not so young yourself.
    George: (With boyish pleasure . . . a chant) I'm six years younger than you are . . . I always have been and I always will be.
    Martha: (Glumly) Well . . . you're going bald.

Or, in a more demanding exchange, performed in front of their guests:

(10) (Albee, 1962, p. 101)
    George: Monstre!
    Martha: Cochon!
    George: Bête!
    Martha: Canaille!
    George: Putain!

As in sounding, they admire their game and expect others to, and they have rules for what is ritual (including her sexual conduct) and what is off-limits (their imaginary son). Thus the playwright, too, portrays interpersonal conflict not as chaos but as a speech event with pattern and structure. The analysis by Watzlawick *et al.* focuses on how the characters form an interpersonal system, which is manifested through and understandable entirely by their interaction.

Gottman (1979):
Couples Interaction Scoring System

The methods to be described next are examples of more elaborately developed coding systems. These are applicable to a wide variety of dialogues, although they have usually been applied to marital interaction.

Gottman analyzes longish sequences of couples' discussions on conflictive topics, principally by applying the eight content codes given in Table 2.1. These content codes are partially derived from the work of Hops, Wills, Patterson, and Weiss (1972) and were further refined by Gottman using a combination of logical and empirical analyses. We have applied them to two sample couples' conflicts in Tables 2.3 and 2.4 in the following section. In addition to the verbal content, the nonverbal behaviors of speaker and listener are also coded at each point, though only as positive, neutral, or negative.

There are two other interesting aspects to Gottman's work. Dialogues are coded by "thought units" rather than the more usual message or utterance units. Any given conversational turn may contain one to several of these thought units, as in the third utterance in Table 2.4, which is first a disagreement (*No*) and then an example of mindreading (*You would have been scared too*). A second noteworthy aspect is the statistical analysis applied, called lag sequential analysis. The lag sequential technique provides information about the probability of given behaviors following a selected criterion behavior at different time-ordered behavioral steps (lags) in an ongoing interaction (Sackett, 1979). Lag profiles can be created that provide information about the interconnectedness of message sequences so that multiple-event patterns can be identified. Such patterns can then be used to test research hypotheses concerning the dynamics of discourse and specified outcome variables, such as the resolution or nonresolution of conflict. Few studies of conflict have employed this technique, with the notable exceptions of the work of Gottman, of Margolin and Wampold (1981), and of Notarius, Krokoff, and Markman (1981) on marital conflicts.

Rogers and Farace (1975):
Relational Communication Control System

In 1936, Bateson proposed that a relationship evolves through cumulative interaction into two general forms: symmetrical, where the partners' behaviors mirror each other (e.g., competition); or complementary, where the behaviors differ but complement each other (Bateson, 1958). The two complementary positions have been called "one-up" and "one-

Table 2.1

Content Codes in the Couples Interaction Scoring System[a]

Content code	Example statement
AG: agreement	You're right. I never saw it that way before. I'm sorry for the way I acted.
DG: disagreement	No, you're wrong. No, because we have to go to Mom's. Please don't smoke.
CT: communication talk	We're getting off the topic. Let's wrap this up in 5 minutes. I'm afraid I don't understand what you're saying.
MR: mindreading	You're lying. You always get mad in these situations. You spent a lot of time with that woman at the party last night.
PS: problem-solving and information exchange	You had your way last time so it's my turn to decide. We're taking the kids to the park this Sunday at 2 p.m. I just want us to be more happy.
SO: summarizing other	It seems to me that what you're saying is that I drink too much. To put it in a few words, you're tired of the way things are. What we're both saying is that we want to move to British Columbia.
SS: summarizing self	So, all I'm saying is that I do not want to take all the responsibility for disciplining the children.
PF: expressing feelings about a problem	Most people are selfish about how they spend their time. We have a problem with the kids. I'm very nervous right now.

[a] Partially derived from Hops, Wills, Patterson, and Weiss (1972) and from Gottman (1979). Examples are based on those given by Gottman (1979, pp. 82–86).

down,'' indicating that one person defines the nature of the relationship and the other person accepts that definition. Sluzki and Beavin (1965) proposed that the symmetrical or complementary nature of the relationship would be manifested in the interactants' discourse, specifically in the grammatical and response form of sequential messages. Following these premises (see Rogers, 1981), Rogers and Farace (1975) designed a coding scheme for these aspects of dialogue. They were particularly interested in the "command" (Bateson, 1951) or "relationship" (Watzlawick *et al.*, 1967) level of a message, rather than in its content. That is, they assumed that any message not only conveys information but seeks to define or redefine the nature of the interactants' relationship.

Rogers and Farace's system is typically applied to a couples' open-ended discussion of topics they consider conflictive or problematic for their relationship (Millar & Rogers, 1976). Coding moves from the individual message unit to the "transact" (the relation between contiguous messages) and then to sequential patterns in the couples' interactions. First, each individual message is assigned a three-digit code. The first number designates the speaker. The second designates the grammatical form as (1) assertion, (2) question, (3) talkover, (4) noncomplete, or (5) other. The third digit describes the response functions of the message relative to the immediately preceding message of the other speaker, that is, as (1) support, (2) nonsupport, (3) extension, (4) answer, (5) instruction, (6) order, (7) disconfirmation, (8) topic change, (9) initiation–termination, or (10) other. Thus the wife (coded 1 for speaker) may make an assertion (coded 1 for grammatical form) that does not support the husband's previous proposal (coded 2 for nonsupport in response to previous speaker): 112.

Each of these 50 possible message types is then categorized according to how it defines the nature of the relationship: as an attempt to assert a definition of the relationship, a one-up movement (↑); as a request for or acceptance of the other's definition of the relationship, a one-down movement (↓); or as a nondemanding, nonaccepting, least-constraining movement, a one-across maneuver (→). The assignment of these control directions for each of the message types is given in Table 2.2. For example, the wife's nonsupportive assertion described above would be a one-up manuever.

Finally, by combining the control directions of contiguous messages, the minimum unit for describing relationship is created; this smallest unit is a transact. In a complementary transact, the control directions are opposite (↑ ↓ , ↓ ↑). The definition of their relationship offered by one interactant is accepted by the other. In a symmetrical transact (↑ ↑ , ↓ ↓ , →→) the control directions are the same. Each conversant behaves toward the other as the other has behaved toward him or her. In transitory transacts (↑ →, → ↑ , ↓ →, → ↓), the directions are different but not complementary, with one conversant choosing the minimally constraining one-across maneuver.

This general scheme has been applied to interpersonal conflict by defining such conflict as three consecutive one-up moves (↑ ↑ ↑); see

Table 2.2
Control Directions of Message Types

Response Code		Assertion	Question	Talkover	Noncomplete	Other
Support	1	↓	↓	↓	↓	↓
Nonsupport	2	↑	↑	↑	↑	↑
Extension	3	→	↓	↑	→	→
Answer	4	↑	↑	↑	↑	↑
Instruction	5	↑	↑	↑	↑	↑
Order	6	↑	↑	↑	↑	↑
Disconfirmation	7	↑	↑	↑	↑	↑
Topic change	8	↑	↑	↑	↑	↑
Initiation—termination	9	↑	↑	↑	→	↑
Other	10	→	↓	↓	→	→

Millar, Rogers, and Bavelas (1984). One interactant attempts to define the relationship; this is rejected by an opposing claim from the other, which is in turn opposed by the initial speaker. The conflict pattern then represents the first step toward a potential symmetrical escalation. In this coding system, a simple disagreement is a pair of symmetrical transacts, and a conflict is a double symmetrical transact. The coding system is illustrated in Tables 2.3 and 2.4, where conflicts thus defined can be seen.

Wiener and Mehrabian (1968); Bavelas and Chovil (1985)

All of the above methods have studied arguments, quarrels, insults, disagreements, and other means by which conflict is manifested as discourse. These are, as noted at the outset, speech events or performatives in which the conflict is the discourse and vice versa. Two other methods that do not fit this model, because the discourse studied in fact avoids such direct conflict, are here mentioned. Both of these approaches study the effect of an experimentally created potential for conflict involving another person on the subject's subsequent written or spoken message. This kind of data is worth considering if, as these studies suggest, one response to potential conflict among adults is that their language becomes more indirect or tangential. That is, one pattern of conflict discourse may be a coordinated disengagement that avoids direct conflict.

Table 2.3
An Interspousal Conflict

W: What did you expect of me when we got married?
H: Well, uh, . . . I really didn't have any expectations of you.
W: I expected you to take care of me.
H: Haven't I? (asked challengingly)
W: Yes. Have I complained?
H: Yeah.
W: No! No.
H: Silently!
W: No. No, no, . . . no.

		Rogers–Farace relational control codes		
Gottman's CISS content codes	Message type	Control direction	transact	triad
W: Q/PS[a]	123	↓		
H: (Blurp), PF	214	↑	↓ ↑	
W: PS	113	→	↑ →	↓ ↑ →
H: Q/PS	222	↑	→ ↑	↑ → ↑
W: AG, Q/PF	111/	↓	↑ ↓	→ ↑ ↓
	122[b]	↑	↓ ↑	↑ ↓ ↑
H: DG	214	↑	↑ ↑	↓ ↑ ↑
W: DG, DG	112	↑	↑ ↑	↑ ↑ ↑
H: MR	212	↑	↑ ↑	↑ ↑ ↑
W: DG, DG, DG	112	↑	↑ ↑	↑ ↑ ↑

[a]With CISS, questions are always double-coded, first as a question, then by a content code.
[b]Messages may be double-coded with the Rogers–Farace system.

Wiener and Mehrabian (1968) proposed that language can be characterized by (and coded for) a greater or lesser degree of "immediacy," where "non-immediacy" is a more distant separation of the speaker from the object of speech. Non-immediacy is, for example, saying "you and I" rather than "we"; or referring to "those people" rather than to "these people." Wiener and Mehrabian (1968, Chap. 5) and Conville (1975) found that non-immediacy increased (compared to a control group writing messages under positive conditions) in the language of experimental subjects who had to address or describe a person toward whom they had negative feelings.

In another program of research, such indirectness was measured differently, but with analogous results (Bavelas, 1983; Bavelas & Chovil,

2 Interpersonal Conflict

Table 2.4
An Engaged Couple's Conflict

M: I think, I think that two or three years ago we'd been scared to death to a, to even consider it. So . . .
F: You would have been scared to death.
M: No, you would have been scared too.
F: [No. I wouldn't have been scared too. . . .][a]
M: [You sure would have!]
F: Ahhh . . . anyway . . . I . . . you know, I'm really kinda glad that, that happened. Because I think, it, uh, you know, it just kinda moves us, moves us out, out of where we were and, you know, you know, we'll move into something, something different.
M: Yup.

			Rogers–Farace relational control codes	
Gottman's CISS content codes	Message type	Control direction	transact	triad
M: MR	213	→		
F: MR	112	↑	→↑	
M: DG, MR	212	↑	↑↑	→↑↑
F: DG, DG	132	↑	↑↑	↑↑↑
M: MR	232	↑	↑↑	↑↑↑
F: (Blurp), PF, PS	113	→	↑→	↑↑→
M: AG	211	↓	→↓	↑→↓

[a]The brackets represent a successful talkover in the Rogers–Farace transcription procedures.

1985; Bavelas & Smith, 1982). The concept of "disqualification"—saying something without really saying it—was borrowed from psychiatric studies of distressed families (e.g., Haley 1959; Sluzki, Beavin, Tarnopolsky, & Verón, 1967) and applied to the language used by normal adults in response to experimentally induced conflicts. The degree of disqualification was defined as the degree to which a message leaves unclear its content, sender, receiver, or context. For example, an experimental subject is asked to imagine a situation in which a friend has sent a gift so bizarre that it is not possible to tell whether it is a joke or serious and then to reply in writing to the question, "How do you like the gift I sent you?" One subject wrote the following: "Yes I received your gift. They say a person gives what he would like to receive. Hopefully one day, I'll be able to return the favor some way or another. Have a nice day" (Bavelas & Chovil, 1985). Applying the four above criteria of disqualification, this message is unclear in content because the sentences do not hold together well and because of its possibe double meanings. It avoids giving the sender's opinion by use of the construction *They say*. It refers very little to the friend who sent the gift and, indeed, after the first sentence seems to be addressed to anyone in general; therefore it is not clearly addressed to the receiver of the message. Finally, it obviously changes context by not answering the question asked and giving other information instead. All messages written under such conditions were more disqualified than control-group messages.

As already emphasized, both the non-immediacy and the disqualification research seem quite far from natural conflict discourse. However, they are included here for two reasons. First, they illustrate the possible use of experimental manipulation in eliciting and analyzing discourse. More important, they could be adapted to dyadic exchanges to establish whether, in some circumstances, adults use a special language for conflict, one that continues the dialogue without direct confrontation (see also Brown & Levinson, 1978; Goguen & Linde, 1981). Given the apparent ability of children to build arguments together, as documented by Lein and Brenneis and by Labov, it should not surprise us that adults may avoid arguments together, by systematically deflecting their language away from the sensitive topic.

SUMMARY AND SUGGESTIONS

The studies reviewed above lead us to conclude that conflict discourse is not always bad, simple, or the same, and that it can be quite fruitfully analyzed. In the following, the many options suggested by our wider review of the literature are outlined in the hope that readers will find among them some directions of interest in this still underresearched area.

Kinds of Dyads and Groups

Whenever people interact, there is interpersonal discourse to observe, and some of this may be conflictive. This includes families (husband–wife, parent–child, siblings, in-laws); dating couples; friends, gangs, peer and social groups (from parties to meetings to playgrounds); work groups and teams; or even strangers in some situations (e.g., formal adversaries such as lawyers or political opponents, labor negotiators, juries, buyers and sellers in bargaining situations, or partisans at sports events). Fiction or published correspondence may also provide already complete data.

Ways of Obtaining Conflict Data

We have seen that conflict can be successfully role-played by participants. Rausch, Barry, Hertel, and Swain (1974) have formalized this for marital conflict in their "Improvisation Scenes." Or, if "real" conflict is desired, it can be found by selecting relationships and situations such as those suggested above (distressed couples, political campaigns, ritual insults or conflicts, situations involving bargains, complaints, blame).

In addition to enacting and finding conflict, we can deliberately elicit it by experimentally arranged circumstances. The task itself may elicit conflict, as did Camras' (1977); some of Watzlawick's (1966); the "Color Matching Test" (Goodrich & Boomer, 1963; Ryder & Goodrich, 1966); the Prisoners' Dilemma paradigm (Rapoport, 1970; Terhune, 1968); the "Acme–Bolt Trucking Game" (Deutsch & Krauss, 1962); SIMFAM game technique (Straus, 1968; Straus & Tallman, 1971); the "Inventory of Marital Conflict" (Olson & Ryder, 1970); or even watching a film (Hall & Williams, 1966). Most commonly used, because of its naturalness, is discussion of a topic on which disagreement is known to exist, for example, by "Revealed Differences Technique" (Strodbeck, 1951); by unrevealed differences (Ferreira, 1963; Ferreira & Winter, 1965); or by asking the couple to indicate problem areas of their relationship for discussion (e.g., Margolin & Wampold, 1981; Millar & Rogers, 1976; Twentyman & Martin, 1978; Weiss, Hops, & Patterson, 1973).

Media

Although spoken conflict has appropriately dominated research, it may be that other possibilities have been thus neglected. Consider the nonverbal aspects of face-to-face (or telephone) interaction, and especially written material, such as notes, letters, memos, and newspaper or periodical dialogues in a series of letters to the editor, rebuttals, and so forth.

Research Methods

The full variety of methods recommended by, for example, Labov (1975) have been used and should be further explored: Interviews with and judgments of native users (although these may be less satisfactory for interpersonal than for individual linguistic events); induction from observation on an ad hoc basis; induction using established coding systems with emphasis on generalizability; and hypothesis-testing experiments when the state of our knowledge, based on earlier stages, justifies. The pay-off of each method will of course differ, from purely descriptive categorization to rules analysis to system structures. Used to supplement rather than to compete with each other, a combination of such methods—especially in multidisciplinary efforts—would enrich not only the topic but the investigators.

ACKNOWLEDGMENT

We wish to acknowledge the financial assistance of the University of Victoria and the Social Sciences and Humanities Research Council of Canada and the bibliographic assistance of Sandra Kades and Brad Dishan.

REFERENCES

Albee, E. (1962). *Who's afraid of Virginia Woolf?* New York: Atheneum.
Bateson, G. (1951). Information and codification: a philosophical approach. In J. Ruesch & G. Bateson (Eds.), *Communication: The social matrix of psychiatry* (pp. 168–211). New York: Norton.
Bateson, G. (1958). *Naven* (2nd ed.). Stanford: Stanford University Press.
Bateson, G. (1972). *Steps to an ecology of mind*. New York: Ballantine.
Bavelas, J. B. (1983). Situations that lead to disqualification. *Human Communication Research, 9,* 130–145.
Bavelas, J. B., & Chovil, N. (1985). How people disqualify: Experimental studies of spontaneous written disqualification. *Communication Monographs* (in press).
Bavelas, J. B., & Smith, B. J. (1982). A method for scaling verbal disqualification. *Human Communication Research, 8,* 214–227.
Brenneis, D., & Lein, L. (1977). "You fruithead": A sociolinguistic approach to children's dispute settlement. In S. Ervin-Tripp & C. Mitchell-Kernan (Eds.), *Child discourse* (pp. 49–65). New York: Academic Press.
Brown, P., & Levinson, S. (1978). Universals in language usage: Politeness phenomena. In E. N. Goody (Ed.), *Questions and politeness: strategies in social interaction* (pp. 56–289). Cambridge: Cambridge University Press.
Camras, L. A. (1977). Facial expressions used by children in a conflict situation. *Child Development, 48,* 1431–1435.
Conville, R. L. (1975). Linguistic nonimmediacy and attribution of communicator's attitudes. *Psychological Reports, 36,* 951–957.
Deutsch, M., & Krauss, R. M. (1962). Studies of interpersonal bargaining. *Journal of Conflict Resolution, 6,* 52–76.
Duncan, H. D. (1967). The search for a social theory of communication in American sociology. In F. Dance (Ed.), *Human communication theory* (pp. 236–263). New York: Holt, Rinehart and Winston.
Ferreira, A. J. (1963). Decision-making in normal and pathologic families. *Archives of General Psychiatry, 8,* 68–73.
Ferreira, A. J., & Winter, W. D. (1965). Family interaction and decision-making. *Archives of General Psychiatry, 13,* 214–223.
Goguen, J. A., & Linde, C. (October, 1981). *Linguistic methodology for the analysis of aviation accidents*. (Contract No. NAS2-11052). Palo Alto, CA: U.S. Ames Research Center, NASA.
Goodrich, D., & Boomer, D. S. (1963). Experimental assessment of modes of conflict resolution. *Family Process, 2,* 15–24.
Gottman, J. M. (1979). *Marital interaction: Experimental investigations*. New York: Academic Press.
Haley, J. (1959). An interactional description of schizophrenia. *Psychiatry, 22,* 321–332.
Hall, J., & Williams, M. S. (1966). A comparison of decision-making performances in established and ad hoc groups. *Journal of Personality and Social Psychology, 3,* 214–222.

Hops, H., Wills, T. A., Patterson, G. R., & Weiss, R. L. (1972). *Marital interaction coding system.* Unpublished manuscript, University of Oregon and Oregon Research Institute.
Labov, W. (1972). Rules for ritual insults. In D. Sudnow (Ed.), *Studies in social interaction* (pp. 120–169). New York: Free Press.
Labov, W. (1975). *What is a linguistic fact?* Lisse: Peter de Ridder Press.
Lein, L., & Brenneis, D. (1978). Children's disputes in three speech communities. *Language in Society, 7,* 299–323.
Margolin, G., & Wampold, B. E. (1981). Sequential analysis of conflict and accord in distressed and nondistressed marital partners. *Journal of Consulting and Clinical Psychology, 49,* 554–567.
Millar, F. E., & Rogers, L. E. (1976). A relational approach to interpersonal communication. In G. R. Miller (Ed.), *Explorations in interpersonal communication* (pp. 87–103). Beverly Hills, CA: Sage Publications.
Millar, F. E., Rogers, L. E., & Bavelas, J. B. (1984). Indentifying patterns of verbal conflict in interpersonal dynamics. *The Western Journal of Speech Communication, 48,* 231–246.
Notarius, C. I., Krokoff, L. J., & Markman, H. J. (1981). Analysis of observational data. In E. E. Filsinger & R. A. Lewis (Eds.), *Assessing marriage: New behavioral approaches* (pp. 197–216). Beverly Hills, CA: Sage Publications.
Olson, D. H., & Ryder, R. G. (1970). Inventory of marital conflicts (IMC): An experimental interaction procedure. *Journal of Marriage and the Family, 32,* 443–448.
Rapoport, A. (1970). Conflict resolution in the light of game theory and beyond. In P. Swingle (Ed.), *The Structure of Conflict* (pp. 1–43). New York: Academic Press.
Rausch, H. L., Barry, W. A., Hertel, R. K., & Swain, M. A. (1974). *Communication, conflict, and marriage.* San Francisco: Jossey-Bass.
Rogers, L. E. (1981). Symmetry and complementarity: Evolution and evaluation of an idea. In C. Wilder-Mott & J. H. Weakland (Eds.), *Rigor and Imagination: Essays from the Legacy of Gregory Bateson* (pp. 231–251). New York: Praeger.
Rogers, L. E., & Farace, R. V. (1975). Analysis of relational communication in dyads: New measurement procedures. *Human Communication Research, 1,* 222–239.
Ryder, R. G., & Goodrich, D. (1966). Married couples' responses to disagreement. *Family Process, 5,* 30–42.
Sackett, G. P. (1979). The lag sequential analysis of contingency and cyclicity in behavior interaction research. In J. Osofsky (Ed.), *Handbook of infant development* (pp. 623–649). New York: Wiley.
Sluzki, C. E., & Beavin, J. (1965). Simetría y complementaridad: una definición operacional y una tipología de parejas (Symmetry and complementarity: An operational definition and a typology of dyads). *Acta psiquiátrica y psicológica de América latina, 11,* 321–330. (Reprinted in English in P. Watzlawick and J. H. Weakland (Eds.), *The Interactional View* (pp. 71–87). New York: W. W. Norton, 1977).
Sluzki, C. E., Beavin, J., Tarnopolsky, A., & Verón, E. (1967). Transactional disqualification: Research on the double bind. *Archives of General Psychiatry, 16,* 494–504.
Straus, M. A. (1968). Communication, creativity, and problem-solving ability of middle- and working-class families in three societies. *American Journal of Sociology, 73,* 417–430.
Straus, M. A., & Tallman, I. (1971). SIMFAM: A technique for observational measurement and experimental study of families. In J. Aldous, T. Condon, R. Hill, M. Straus, & I. Tallman (Eds.), *Family problem solving. A symposium on theoretical methodological and substantive concerns* (pp. 379–438). Hindale, IL: Dryden.
Strodtbeck, F. L. (1951). Husband–wife interaction over revealed differences. *American Sociological Review, 16,* 468–473.

Terhune, K. Q. (1968). Motives, situation, and interpersonal conflict within prisoner's dilemma. *Journal of Personality and Social Psychology Monograph Supplement, 8,* 1–24.

Twentyman, C. T., & Martin, B. (1978). Modification of problem interaction in mother–child dyads by modelling and behavior rehearsal. *Journal of Clinical Psychology, 34,* 138–143.

Watzlawick, P. (1966). A structured family interview. *Family Process, 5,* 256–271.

Watzlawick, P., Beavin, J., & Jackson, D. D. (1967). *Pragmatics of human communication. A study of interactional patterns, pathologies, and paradoxes.* New York: Norton.

Weiss, R. L., Hops, H., & Patterson, G. R. (1973). A framework for conceptualizing marital conflict: A technology for altering it, some data for evaluating it. In L. A. Hamerlynck, L. C. Handy, & E. J. Mash (Eds.), *Behavior Change: Methodology, Concepts and Practice* (pp. 309–342). Champaign: Research Press.

Wiener, M., & Mehrabian, A. (1968). *Language within language: Immediacy, a channel in verbal communication.* New York: Appleton-Century-Crofts.

CHAPTER 3

Ideological Structures in Discourse

Gunther Kress

TEXT AND DISCOURSE

In recent discussions of language structure beyond the level of sentence, the terms 'text' and 'discourse' have tended to be used without sharp distinction. On the whole, discussions with a more sociological basis or aim tend to use the term 'discourse' (Corsaro, 1981), while those with a more linguistic basis or aim tend to use the term 'text' (van Dijk, 1978). Where the materiality, form, and structure of language are at issue, the emphasis tends to be textual; where the content, function, and social significance of language are at issue, the study tends to be of discourse. I say "tends" because the matter is not hard and fast; also, there have been proposals, such as that of van Dijk (1978, 1981), to establish a distinction between the two terms that does not coincide with the one sketched above.

In this essay, the distinction is drawn firmly, on theoretical grounds, with each term having its own quite specific and distinctive area of reference. Discourse is a category that belongs to and derives from the social domain, and text is a category that belongs to and derives from the linguistic domain. The relation between the two is one of realization: Discourse finds its expression in text. However, this is never a straightforward relation; any one text may be the expression or realization of a number of sometimes competing and contradictory discourses.

The notion of discourse advanced here is that of 'mode of talking', a notion that attempts to capture the quite commonplace insight that is pointed to in expressions such as 'legal discourse', 'racist discourse', 'medical discourse'. Its most explicit theoretical discussion exists in certain French philosophical work, for instance that of Foucault (1970,

1971, 1980). In essence it points to the fact that social institutions produce specific ways or modes of talking about certain areas of social life, which are related to the place and nature of that institution. That is, in relation to certain areas of social life that are of particular significance to a social institution, it will produce a set of statements about that area that will define, describe, delimit, and circumscribe what it is possible and impossible to say with respect to it, and how it is to be talked about. So, for instance, matters such as gender, authority, race, professionalism, science, or the family will have specific discourses associated with them (Muecke, 1983). Discourse, in this sense, is not neutral with respect to language; certain syntactic forms will necessarily correlate with certain discourses. This correlation is explored in detail in Kress and Hodge (1978). For instance, in discourses of power and authority, social agency will be assigned in particular ways, and this will be expressed through particular transitivity forms; or specific modal forms will systematically express relations of power. In this way a given discourse, say sexist discourse, will display certain quite characteristic linguistic features, expressive of causality or agency, power, gender, as well as linguistic features serving to focalize or topicalize specific aspects of the discourse.

However, although any given discourse is highly specific concerning the statements possible within its terms and of certain linguistic features, it is not text. In its expression in text, these specific aspects of a discourse constitute one determinative and constitutive factor of the text: Certain of the range of linguistic features that make up the text are determined, selected, by the characteristics of the discourse. Consequently, the presence of any linguistic feature in a text always points to some aspect of the discourse of which the text is an expression. The systematicness of features of the discourse also guarantees the systematicness of the selection of all the linguistic features of the text.

A second factor in the determination and constitution of the form of any text derives from the category of 'genre'. The presence of a range of linguistic features does not of itself determine the form of the text; that is determined by the formal features of particular genres. At any given point in history and in any given social group, certain genres are available for the expression of specific discourses. Each generic form has particular possibilities and limitations, which are an inherent part of that genre. Hence the expression of a discourse within a specific genre carries with it the meanings, potentialities, and limitations of that genre. For instance, the generic form 'editorial' did not exist prior to the emergence of newspapers in their present form in the mid-nineteenth century. But once in existence, this genre immediately endows the discourse that it presents with a meaning beyond that expressed by the linguistic features of the text. It has a modal effect (see Kress and Hodge, 1978) which affects the manner in which the text is read. So the expression of sexist discourse in the genre editorial will carry a different modality from its expression in a short story.

The form of a text is consequently a factor of the conjunction of the linguistic features specified by the discourse, and of the formal aspects of the genre together. It is clear from this that the relation between text and discourse is not an entirely straightforward one. It could be said that the relation between discourse and text is one of emergence; discourse emerges in and through texts. Discourse is never simply the aggregate of texts but is rather, on the one hand, the (abstract) structure of an aggregate, which is, on the other hand, affected and obscured by the effect of genre.

Further, any particular text may be the result of the expression of a number of discourses, differing, and often contradictory. Hence a text is rarely "of one piece" in terms of the linguistic features that it contains, or of the discourses that it expresses.

LANGUAGE AND IDEOLOGY

'Ideology' is one of the less settled categories of philosophical and sociological discussions of the last century or more. Its meanings range from the relatively innocuous "system of ideas" or "worldview" to more contested ones such as "false consciousness" or "ideas of the dominant, ruling class." It might therefore seem pointless or distractive to introduce such a term into considerations of theories of language. There are, however, quite powerful reasons for doing so. Any theory of language that is serious about the social function and effect of language cannot make do with asocial categories such as "worldview." Rather, it has to focus quite deliberately on the relations of language to the material condition of its uses and of its users. And here it is essential to accept the category 'ideology' as the term that covers concerns with forms of knowledge and their relation to class structure, to class conflict, and class interest, to modes of production and of economic structure, and with forms of knowledge in specific social practices. Ideology is concerned equally with dominant and with oppositional forms of knowledge in a society, with accommodative strategies, and with knowledge deriving from the historical and social positions of its users (Mannheim, 1955; Parkin, 1971; Sumner, 1975, pp. 4–6).

Ideologies, in the sense here outlined, find their clearest articulation in language (though it is important to insist that ideologies find articulation in a vast range of differing social practices). Hence a powerful way of examining ideological structure is through the examination of language. Conversely, the forms of language are illuminated by an analysis of the ideologies at work in given societies. The connection between language and ideology exists at many levels: at the lexical level and at the grammatical–syntactic level (see for instance the work of Halliday, in Kress, 1976; Kress & Hodge, 1978; Vološinov, 1973; Whorf, 1956). In Saussurian linguistics this connection is not and cannot be made. As Eagleton has said,

> language cannot be, for Saussure, as it can be for Vološinov and Baxtin, a terrain of ideological struggle. Such a recognition would involve, precisely, the displacement and rearticulation of formal linguistic difference at the level of other theoretical practices. If the dictionary informs us that the opposite of capitalism is totalitarianism, we will need more than the *Course of General Linguistics* to illuminate that particular diacritical formulation (1980, p 165).

The relation between language and ideology depends on the category of discourse. Any linguistic form considered in isolation has no specifically determinate meaning as such, nor does it possess any ideological significance or function. It is because linguistic forms always appear in a text and therefore in systematic form as the sign of the system of meaning embodied in specific discourse that we can attribute ideological significance to them. The defined and delimited set of statements that constitute a discourse are themselves expressive of and organized by a specific ideology. That is, ideology and discourse are aspects of the same phenomenon, regarded from two different standpoints.

To summarize: The systematic organization of content in discourse, drawing on and deriving from the prior classification of this material in an ideological system, leads to the systematic selection of linguistic categories and features in a text. Hence the presence of a linguistic feature in a text is always the sign of the presence of one term from a discursive and ideological system appearing in the context of the copresence of other terms from that system. A linguistic feature or category therefore never appears simply by itself—it always appears as the representative of a system of linguistic terms, which themselves realize discursive and ideological systems. The linguistic term in a discourse and in a text therefore derives a specific meaning from its place in a system of other linguistic terms. That is, the system gives specific meaning to terms in the system.

Ideological significance can be "read off" from the linguistic items in a text: The linguistic feature appears as the sign of a term in an ideological system and this term has a quite precise meaning deriving from its place in a system of other terms. However, beyond this, texts can also be read for their ideological content because of the iconic nature of linguistic forms. While most lexical forms do stand in an entirely conventional relation to their referents in the world (with exceptions such as onomatopoeia), most or perhaps all syntactic forms and processes have an "expressive" relation to their referents. For instance, in the relation between an active and a passive clause, the shift of emphasis (indicated by first position) from agent to goal directly expresses the relative significance assigned by the speaker or writer to the respective entities. So, for instance, in *The Chairman has advised me that* . . . , *The Chairman* occupies first position and has the emphasis conveyed by that; in the equivalent passive clause *I have been advised by the Chairman that* . . . , that emphasis now attaches to *I*. Hence the form of the clause in each voice contributes to the meaning; and the (actual or understood) relation between active and passive clauses similarly signals a specific meaning. The absence of the agent in many passive clauses (e.g., *I have been advised that* . . .) is another example of the expressiveness of syntactic forms and processes. The whole of the syntactic system of a language functions in the same manner. Hence a syntactic form signals not simply the prior presence of a specific ideological selection, it also signals or expresses the meaning or content of that ideological choice. And while a single linguistic form has a wide range of possible meanings (i.e., it is not clear from a passive clause in isolation why precisely the object has been made emphatic), when this form appears in the context of the systematic selection of the whole range of linguistic forms occurring in a text, then the meaning of each form becomes quite specific.

Ideological content is expressed in linguistic forms in two ways. First, as the sign of ideologically determined selections made by the speaker or writer—in other words, as an index of ideological activity. Second, as the expression of ideological content expressed by a linguistic form in the context of other forms in a text. This content becomes specific because of the copresence of the other forms in a text that narrows and determines the meaning of any given linguistic form. It needs to be said here that selection or choice of a linguistic form may not be a "live" process for the individual speaker: If discourses are the organizations of ideological materials in discursive forms, and if these discourses exist in an already established repertoire of discourses in a social group, then the individual speaker will not in fact be creating the discourse but rather will simply reproduce the discourse that she or he has previously learned. However, as discourse and text are distinct categories, and as discourse must be realized in a specific genre, it is possible for the speaker to use established discursive rules, but to give them a relatively novel implementation in text. Indeed, as there is not a direct, homologous relation between the social unit 'discourse' and the linguistic unit 'text', a text may be the location of a number of often contradictory or disparate discourses. Hence it is in text rather than in discourse that language users can exercise creativity; while discourses are relatively fixed, texts are relatively unstable and unpredictable. The unpredictability of texts is a major cause of linguistic change.

EXEMPLIFICATIONS

A first example consists of the verbal text of a television news broadcast dealing with one set of disturbances during the 1981 tour of New Zealand by the South African Rugby Union team, the Springboks. The broadcast was part of a 6:30 P.M. television newsbroadcast ("Eyewitness News") on an Adelaide commercial station, Channel 10:

	Verbal text	Picture on the screen
1	Newsreader: The first match of	Head of newsreader
2	the highly controversial Spring-	
3	bok tour of NZ produced two	
4	victors today: the South Africans	
	and the police. The Springboks	Slow motion background picture
5	had the easier of the clashes an-	of punch
6	nihilating a Poverty Bay rugby	
7	side 24 to 6. But the NZ police	
8	forces guarding the ground at	
9	Gisbourne had to cope with	
10	dozens of angry protesters who	
11	chanted antiapartheid slogans,	
12	blew whistles to disrupt the	
13	match, and made two attempts	
14	to invade the pitch. Here's to-	
15	day's special satellite report:	
16	Reporter 1: Things began	March head-on; close up of
17	peacefully enough with a march	Maori face, shot from behind
18	through the town. But the calm	police lines
19	wasn't to last for long. Squads	Back fence
20	of police hurried to the vulner-	
21	able back fence but reinforce-	
22	ments weren't there quickly	
23	enough. The demonstrators	

3 Ideological Structures in Discourse

24 stormed the fence, with only a	
25 handful of police trying to hold	
26 them back. Many managed to	
27 get up a slippery bank and began	
28 tearing the fence down. Violent	Close up of fights; Focus on
29 clashes followed. More clashes,	punch being thrown
30 this time more bitter, erupted.	
31 The confrontation was to last	
32 several hours. Several people	
33 claimed to have been injured in	
34 the brawls. As some lay on the	Injured person
35 ground, emotion subsided. The	Arrest
36 demonstration ended late this	
37 afternoon after 13 had been	
38 arrested.	Arrest
39 Reporter 2: Elsewhere around	Head of Reporter 2 in front of
40 the country many other people	demonstration
41 were arrested. Demonstrations	
42 such as this one in Auckland	
43 this evening spanned the length	
44 and breadth of the nation today	
45 as the antitour groups branded	
46 today NZ's day of shame. JW	
47 reporting from NZ for Eyewit-	
48 ness News.	

This text is organized in three main sections, from line 1–15 (the newsreader's introduction); 16–38 (one reporter's past-tense narrative account); and 39–48 (another reporter's generalizing summary). This formal, material organization of the text has its own specific meaning within the wider genre of television news report. That is, the authority of the newsreader's text is reinforced and confirmed by the modality of actuality (the "eyewitness") conveyed by the texts of the two reporters "on the spot." In other words, the fact that the discourse is realized in the genre of news report has specific effects and creates certain meanings beyond those conveyed by the other linguistic features of the text alone. I am ignoring here the effects of the visual text: In fact, the report must be read as the conjunction of the meanings of the verbal and visual codes, as a single text. As will be seen, the verbal and visual codes of this single text give expression to divergent discourses of authority.

Beyond this material organization of the text, the discourse produces a different structure, reflecting the ideological organization of this area of social life. This content-structure finds its expression not in these formal divisions of the text, but in the selection and organization of syntactic forms within the discourse, and their presence in the text overall. The content-structure I am referring to deals with the manner in which the events are portrayed causally. Here in this text, events either appear in a transactive form (see Kress & Hodge, 1978, pp. 7-8), that is, portrayed as either arising directly as the result of some agent's action and with a direct effect on a goal (where both agent and goal may be either animate or inanimate), or in a nontransactive form, arising without such action, that is, as either a self-caused action or an action that happens in some unspecified way. Clearly the mode in which an action is presented, either as transactive or as nontransactive, is not a matter of truth or of reality but rather a matter of the way in which that particular action is integrated into the ideological system of the speaker, and the manner in which such an action is therefore articulated in a specific discourse.

Generally speaking, in this text, transactive clauses (in the active voice) occur with the demonstrators (or some lexical substitutes of them) as agents: (In the examples that follow I have supplied the subject nouns of embedded subjectless clauses); *protestors chanted slogans, . . . blew whistles, . . . disrupt the match, . . . invade the pitch; the demonstrators stormed the fence, . . . (began) tearing the fence down.* Transactives where the agent may have been other than demonstrators occur in passive clauses where the agent has been deleted: *people claimed to have been injured, 13 people had been arrested, many other people were arrested.*

Nontransactive clauses predominate in this text: *NZ police force had to cope with angry protestors; Things began peacefully enough, police hurried to the back fence, violent clashes followed; More clashes . . . erupted, the confrontation was to last several hours, emotion subsided,* and so on. It is clear enough that the selection of transitivity features is systematic: The ideological–discursive structures are realized in a certain form in the text, and the presence of transactive or nontransactive clauses in the text is not a matter of chance but of the expression of an ideological system and of a specific discourse of authority.

Other aspects of the text reveal the operation of selection. The choice of lexical items is guided by the metaphor of a military clash, a battle; and this metaphor permits the casting of one side as 'enemy' and the other as 'friend or protector'. So the police *guard the ground,* which the protestors attempt to *invade, storm.* In this way the newscast audience's perceptions or readings of the text are structured so that they will not only regard the report as "simply reporting the facts as they were" but will also structure their interpretation of the relevance of the text overall (van Dijk, 1979, pp. 113-126).

Of course the visual part of the text is crucial to the reader's interpretation. In the case of this news broadcast, it fully supports and maintains the structuring of the verbal text. Camera shots of the demonstrators are taken head on, so that they are seen as advances on the police and, by implication, on the viewer. So in these respects—selection of lexical items, syntactic forms, and the structuring of the visual text—the same ideological and discursive system is operating. It leads to the production of an ideologically unified and congruent text.

In another respect the visual part of the text goes beyond the ideology coded in the verbal part, or it is, at the very least, more potent in its effect. The camera angles produce an identification of viewer–police–reporter vis-à-vis the enemy–demonstrator. The visual code operating in the text locates the viewer more precisely and more decisively than the verbal, without any need to use overt moralistic, political, or ideologically charged labels. In this way antiracist, antifascist human beings are presented as violent and aggressive. It is a potent moment in the media illusion of "facts" unmediated by "politics" or "ideology."

The same item of news received a noticeably different treatment on another station's broadcast on the same evening. This was on the Australian Broadcasting Commission's Channel 2—a government-funded station. In that broadcast both the visual and verbal text were structured so as to produce a distanced report: Camera shots were from side-on to the marchers, to the police, and to the scuffles; and in the verbal text, transactive and nontransactive clauses were used to report actions of both the antiapartheid groups and of the police.

As mentioned above, all aspects of the syntactic (and textual) system of a language can be and are brought into play to express the ideological meanings articulated in discourse. In the two newspaper reports below, the ideological distinction is a fine one, but it is nevertheless present. Both papers, *The Sun* and *Daily Mirror,* are afternoon tabloids. The former is owned by the J. Fairfax group, the latter by Rupert Murdoch's News Limited. Both are nearly identical in format and are aimed at the same market. In the reports, the distinction is articulated by three features mainly: by transitivity (as in the television text just discussed), by thematic structure (Kress, 1976), and by the overall sequential ordering of items in the text.

      PM TO HOLD TALKS ON MPs PAY RISE
      (from the *Daily Mirror*)
1   The Prime Minister, Mr. Fraser, will have top priority talks with

      senior Cabinet ministers tomorrow on the backlash against MPs' pay rise.
2   Mr. Fraser returns to Canberra from his 17-day US tour late tonight.
3   He will be briefed early tomorrow by the Deputy Prime Minister, Mr. Anthony, and departmental advisers.
4   The Deputy Liberal Leader, Sir Phillip Lynch, who is also in Canberra, is expected to join the talks.
5   Other Cabinet ministers in other cities are likely to be contacted by telephone.
6   The angry reaction to a 20 per cent pay jump in politicians' salaries has provoked massive union unrest and public criticism.
7   Mr. Fraser will be looking at ways of countering a revolt among Government MPs who want to reject the rises.
8   The Australian Democrats' leader, Senator Chipp, has said his party would move in the Senate to slash the new pay levels.
9   The public storm coupled with parliamentary moves could force Mr. Fraser to call for the rises to be rescinded.
10   Briefings tomorrow will prepare the way for a Cabinet meeting on Tuesday.
11   Staff said he had intended to rest at The Lodge in Canberra tomorrow to recover from his US trip and the long flight home.

PAY POSER FOR FRASER (from *The Sun*)

1   Despite efforts by some Federal MPs to reduce the level of their 20 per cent pay increase, the move will fail unless the Prime Minister intervenes.
2   Mr. Fraser returns to Canberra late tonight from a 17-country overseas trip, during which Federal Cabinet agreed that the basic salary of MPs should rise by $6,000 to $36,000.
3   The size of the increase has angered MPs in all political parties, but they do not have the numbers to defeat the necessary legislation when it is introduced to Parliament in the Budget session starting on August 18.
4   The MPs opposed to the size of the increase believed it should be reduced to that which had been awarded to wage and salaries earners in the national wage case.
5   This would reduce it to about $2,000.
6   While overseas, Mr. Fraser has not commented directly on Cabinet's decision to accept a 20 per cent increase.
7   But it is believed he is concerned about what it has done for the Government's image in trying to keep the lid on wage demands.

3 Ideological Structures in Discourse

8   It is understood he believes Cabinet should have accepted a smaller increase to set an example in wage restraint for the rest of the community.
9   To moderate the size of the increase, Mr. Fraser will have to raise the issue in Federal Cabinet, which is due to start a lengthy series of meetings in Canberra next week to finalize the Budget.
10 If he is successful in arguing to reduce the size of the rise it would embarrass the Government.

Although Mr. Fraser acted swiftly and unilaterally to cut the salary increases that had been accepted by his cabinet during his absence, this is not reflected in the use of transitivity in either of the two reports. In the *Daily Mirror* report Mr. Fraser appears as the subject noun of non-transactive clauses, *Mr. Fraser returns to Canberra, Mr. Fraser will be looking at ways;* as the object noun in transactive clauses, both in the active voice, *The public storm could force Mr. Fraser,* and in the passive voice; as the subject noun of the passive clause *He will be briefed;* and as the subject noun of relational clauses (Kress & Hodge, 1978, p. 8), *Mr. Fraser will have talks*. Hence, syntactically Mr. Fraser is not presented as agent.

In terms of the thematic structure, Mr. Fraser (through lexically identical terms) appears as theme in four out of the eleven *Daily Mirror* sentences. Other individuals also occur in thematic position: *The Deputy Liberal Leader, Other cabinet ministers, The Australian Democrat leader, Staff said*. In two sentences, an abstract version of "the people" appears in thematic position: *The angry reaction, The public storm*.

The main actions or events are reported in nouns (both nominalizations and lexical nouns): *talks, backlash, reaction, pay jump, union unrest*. Those actions that are expressed in the verbs are mainly concerned with mental processes, interactions, or communications: *briefed, is expected, join, contacted, provoked, looking at, move, prepare*.

The overall textual structure has its effects in that the headline plus the first three sentences have Mr. Fraser (in some form) as theme. Hence although he occurs only four times in thematic position, the opening three sentences focus on him and therefore give relatively greater prominence to this item. That is, the Prime Minister is presented as the most relevant individual. The reader is likely to respond to this structure and read the report in that light. There is thus an interesting tension between some aspects of the textual–linguistic structure of this report. As far as the transitivity choices are concerned, Mr. Fraser is nonagentive; as far as the thematic structuring is concerned, Mr. Fraser is focal.

The majority of verbs in the text do not express the significant actions but are concerned with the expression of meanings, pointing to interaction, relation, mental processes. The major actions are reported either in nouns or nominalizations. From an ideological point of view this presents the Prime Minister (through a syntactic–textual metaphor, so to speak) as the most significant individual, but nevertheless, as acted on, nonactive himself, responding rather than initiating, within a network of interactive relations. The main actions of people in government are, according to this metaphor, not real actions, but the mediation, facilitation, interrelation between individuals, groups, and abstract categories.

The Sun article differs in significant respects from the previous one. In terms of transitivity, Mr. Fraser does not appear as the subject noun of a transactive clause. He occurs as subject noun of nontransactive clauses: *the Prime Minister intervenes, Mr. Fraser returns, Mr. Fraser has not commented, he is concerned, he believes, Mr. Fraser will have to raise the issue*. Unlike in the *Daily Mirror* report, Mr. Fraser does not appear as the object of an action, either as the subject noun of passive clauses, or directly as the object noun of a transactive clause. In ideological terms, this points to a difference in the placing of the office of Prime Minister—or of the individual incumbent—in comparison with the *Daily Mirror* report. Whereas in the latter the Prime Minister is shown as affected by the action of others, of individuals, and of abstract notions, and is therefore shown as integrated into a system of relationships, in this report he is shown syntactically and textually as an isolated individual. The notion of government and of its activities presented here is substantially different from that presented in the *Daily Mirror* report.

That conception of government is further borne out by the manner in which thematic items are selected in *The Sun* text. Mr. Fraser appears only once in thematic position; not in the headline (where he is in thematic position in an "affected" role, in a quasi-object position); not in the first sentence; but just the once in the second sentence. And whereas most of the other thematic positions in the *Daily Mirror* piece are taken by individuals or groups of individuals, this is also not the case in *The Sun* report. Hence attention is moved away from the action or effect of individual or collective political agents. This blurring of authority and causality in *The Sun* text is marked and reinforced by a high incidence (compared to the *Daily Mirror* text) of agentless passive clauses: *when it is introduced, it should be reduced, that which had been awarded, it is believed, it is understood*. The deleted or missing agents of these clauses are of two kinds: the potent actors in this political world *(it should be reduced)*, and the possessors of knowledge *(it is understood)*. Hence some actions are presented as caused or known about, but caused by actors or known by knowers who remain hidden. To the extent that there is action, other than that by these unknown agents, it is generally due to the effect of abstractions, *The size of the increase has angered MPs;* or the action of collectives; *Cabinet . . . finalize(s) the Budget, MPs . . . defeat the necessary legislation, Cabinet . . . accept(s) a 20 per cent increase.*

In terms of an overall discursive congruence, *The Sun* text does not show the marked tension between the thematic focus on one individual as seemingly potent actor and the downplaying of that same individual's actual potency through his representation in transitivity choices. To that extent this article is more unified, even though the picture of governmental processes that it represents is much more diffuse and vague than the *Daily Mirror*'s. The question arises, therefore, whether the *Daily Mirror* text contains a single discourse, or whether two distinct discourses about governmental processes have been expressed in the one single text. That is, it may be the case that in any text two or more distinct ideologies and their respective discourses may be realized, drawing on differing aspects of the syntactic–textual system to achieve this; or, in the case of texts consisting of verbal and visual (or other nonverbal) media, utilizing the two distinct modes to code the distinct ideologies and discourses. It seems that this is so, in the *Daily Mirror*'s text, with thematic structures realizing one discourse on political process, and transitivity structures realizing another.

Obvious examples to illustrate this point are likely to be multicode texts. In the case of the newscast, it seems to be the case that the verbal and visual parts of the text largely support each other and express the same ideology, though with one code being a much clearer expression of one kind of discourse than the other. In such a case the verbal text provides an anchorage for the visual text (Barthes, 1979), constraining its meanings and making them more explicit, or, in other cases, perhaps in the majority, the two codes can express differing ideologies and discourses. Here I briefly discuss an advertisement for a Berlei bra (Figure 3.1).

As has been pointed out frequently, the language used about women differs from that used about men. In other words, there exists a sexist discourse. Within and through sexist discourse, both sexes have been assigned conventionalized, stereotyped sex roles that have certain language uses associated with them. Two types of sexist discourse are characterized by assigning differing attributes to women, depending on either their sexual potency (women as sex objects) or their role as part of the (re-productive) labor force. This text presents both versions of women, drawing on the differing modes of talking about women just mentioned, and using the verbal and the visual code in the manner suggested above.

They say that having a baby makes a woman beautiful.

Perhaps this is why.

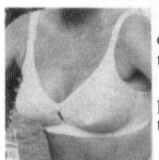

Having a baby is a very special experience and so Berlei have developed two very special bras.

Maternity bras that combine the practical aspects that a mother needs with the prettiness that every woman deserves.

Available in beautiful lace or soft smooth Trilobal Tricot, the Berlei maternity bra shows the way with a new improved Super Clip that can be undone with one hand, and a patented* sling support that supports the breast even when feeding baby. Just two of a range of maternity bras for every pre and post-natal situation.

Trust Berlei to respond to a woman's needs.

Berlei Maternity.
For the Woman in every Mother.

Figure 3.1   An example of competing discourses in both verbal and visual texts.

The headline makes an initial distinction between the two versions of women: Having a baby makes a woman beautiful; here 'woman' is presented as a category not of itself associated with beauty, woman has to be made beautiful by having a baby; the *they say* makes this someone else's judgment, not necessarily "ours." The third sentence of the text draws on the caricature version of "women's talk": *Having a baby is a very special experience . . . two very special bras.* The fourth sentence reintroduces the distinction of the headline, this time in a more defined form: *the practical aspects that a mother needs* versus *the prettiness that every woman deserves.* "Motherhood" is clearly one version of being a woman that is distinct from that of woman as sex object. The difference between *needs* and *deserves* further brings out the dependent nature of woman as sex object. This distinction is continued systematically in *beautiful lace or soft smooth Trilobal Tricot (beautiful, lace, soft, smooth* all being marked as +feminine in the covert gender system of English) as compared to the technical detail and mechanical specificity of *a new improved Super Clip that can be undone with one hand,* and *a patented* sling support that supports the breast* and *every pre and post-natal situation.* The last line again makes the point of the distinction between the asexual category 'mother' and the sexually potent category 'woman': that is, it has to be asserted that the asexual *Mother* can contain the sexually potent *Woman.* The syntax reinforces the sexist message, though weakly and implicitly: *Trust Berlei to respond to a woman's needs,* that is, the male agent supplying the female object's needs.

These two ideologies and discourses—woman as an object of sexual desire and woman as domestic labor and agent of reproduction—are both articulated in the same text. A reconciliation of the two discourses is attempted through the conjunction and adjunction of elements of the two ideologies. The text is crossed by two differing, competing discourses. In the verbal text, an attempt is made to resolve the contradiction, though not completely successfully. The picture that is part of the advertisement also attempts a resolution, though the same dichotomy exists in the picture: Woman as drudge, asexual or antisexual, is foregrounded—but set against an exotic backgound symbolizing the sexually desirable female. The two discourses are expressed in the visual text also, quite clearly and distinctly. The reconciliation of the differences may be somewhat more effective visually than it is verbally: The simultaneity of perception allows the perceiver to absorb the image as a whole, and to respond to its "factualness" or "naturalness" without detailed analysis. Nevertheless, the distinction between foreground and background clearly expresses the two distinct discourses. And, interestingly, woman as agent of reproduction is the foregrounded discourse.

ACKNOWLEDGMENTS

I wish to thank David Aers, Jill Brewster, Roger Fowler, Gareth Jones, Noel King, Stephen Muecke, Grace O'Neale, and Teun van Dijk for comments and help on this essay.

BIBLIOGRAPHY

Aers, D., & Kress, G. (1982). The politics of style: Discourses of law and authority in *Measure for Measure. Style, XVI* (1), 22–37.
Barthes, R. (1979). The rhetoric of the image. In S. Heath (Ed.), *Image—Music—Text* (pp. 32–51). London: Fontana.
Corsaro, W. (1981). Communication processes in studies of social organization: Sociological approaches to discourse analysis. *Text, 1* (1), 5–63.
Eagleton, T. (1980). Text, ideology, realism. In E. W. Said (Ed.), *Literature and society* (pp. 149–173). Baltimore: John Hopkins University Press.
Foucault, M. (1970). Las meniñas. In *The Order of Things*. London: Tavistock.
Foucault, M. (1971). Orders of discourse. *Social Science Information, 10* (2), 7–30.
Foucault, M. (1980). Prison talk. In C. Gordon (Ed.), *Power/Knowledge* (pp. 37–54). New York: Pantheon.
Fowler, R., Hodge, R., Kress, G., & Trew, T. (1978). *Language and control*. London: Routledge & Kegan Paul.
Kress, G. (Ed.). (1976). *Halliday: System and function in language*. London: Oxford University Press.
Kress, G. (1982). *Learning to write*. London: Routledge & Kegan Paul.
Kress, G. (1983a). Linguistic processes and the mediation of 'reality': The politics of newspaper language. *International Journal of the Sociology of Language, 40*, 43–57.
Kress, G. (1983b). Linguistic and ideological transformations in newspaper language. In H. Davis & P. Walton (Eds.), *Language, Image, Media* (pp. 120–138). Oxford: Basil Blackwell.
Kress, G., & Hodge, R. (1978). *Language as ideology*. London: Routledge & Kegan Paul.
Kress, G., & Trew, T. (1978a). Transformations and discourse: Study in conceptual change. *Journal of Literary Semantics, 7* (1), 29–48.
Kress, G., & Trew, T. (1978b). Ideological transformations of discourse: Or how the *Sunday Times* got *its* message across. *The Sociological Review, 26* (4), 755–776.
Mannheim, K. (1955). *Ideology and utopia*. New York: Harvest Books.
Muecke, S. (1983). Available discourses on Aborigines. *Australian Journal of Cultural Studies, 1*, 87–99.
Parkin, T. (1971). *Class, inequality, political order*. St. Albans: Paladin.
Sumner, C. (1975). *Reading ideologies*. London: Academic Press.
van Dijk, T. A. (1978). New developments and problems in text linguistics. In J. Petöfi (Ed.), *Text vs. sentence* (Vol. 2) (pp. 509–523). Hamburg: Buske Verlag.
van Dijk, T. A. (1979). From text grammar to interdisciplinary discourse studies. La Jolla Conference on Cognitive Science. U. of California at San Diego.
van Dijk, T. A. (1981). Relevance assignment in discourse comprehension. *Discourse Processes, 2*, 113–126.
Vološinov, V. N. (1973). (L. Matejka & I. R. Titunik, Trans.). *Marxism and the philosophy of language*. New York: Academic Press.
Whorf, B. (1956). *Language, thought, and reality*. Cambridge, MA: Massachusetts Institute of Technology Press.

CHAPTER **4**

Political Discourse Analysis

Gill Seidel

APPROACHES TO POLITICAL DISCOURSE ANALYSIS

An interest in analyzing political text is shared by many disciplines. Studies have focused on different constitutive elements using a variety of methods. Some of these bear little relation to any linguistic theories. This is clearly the case with content analysis, the mapping and counting of themes used to test hypotheses, which is still predominant in sociology, social psychology, political science, and media studies. Apart from content analysis, other work on political text, more properly linguistic (though also concerned with the extralinguistic dimensions), and largely French, may be summarized under a number of headings.[1]

1. Discourse analysis with particular reference to paraphrase and synonymy (a Harrisian model); for example, Pêcheux (1969); Pêcheux, Henry, Poitou, & Haroche (1979); Maldidier (1971).
2. Discourse analysis with particular reference to argumentation and syntax (a Hallidayan model); for example, Trew (1979a); Seidel (1980, 1982).
3. Discourse analysis focusing on enunciation (theories of Benveniste, and Culioli and Fuchs); for example, Courdesses (1971); Fiala (1977); Bachmann, Courdesses, and Le Guennec (1978); Veron (1978); Michard-Marchal and Ribéry (1979, 1982); Achard (1978).
4. Lexical studies and lexicometrics (a statistical model); for example,

---
[1] For an earlier but still useful typology and summary of trends, see Guespin (1971, 1976); Robin (1973); and Bachmann *et al.* (1978); and for work in political lexicology in Spain and in the German Democratic Republic, see Cabre Castellvi (1983) and Techteimer (1983).

Cotteret and Moreau (1969); Groupe de St. Cloud (1975); Tournier (1976, 1982); Bergounioux *et al.* (1982).
5. Narrative functions (structuralist model); for example, Faye (1972a, 1972b, 1973).
6. Rhetorical studies; for example, Guilhaumou (1981).
7. Semiotics; for example, Barthes (1957).
8. Case grammar; for example, Slakta (1971).
9. Anthropological–sociolinguistic studies (sociolinguistic model); for example, Comaroff (1975); Parkin (1975); Marcellesi (1971); O'Barr and O'Barr (1976); Seidel (1978); Carbó (1982b, 1984).

My aim in this essay is to provide a brief critical discussion of some of these trends. My main illustrations are taken from work concerned with the persistent asymmetries in our society: the construction of class, "race," and gender.

It is my contention that discourse of any kind—text as a suprasentential unit of meaning, an extension of the syntactic and logical structuring of a sentence—is a site of struggle. It is a terrain, a dynamic linguistic, and, above all, semantic space in which social meanings are produced or challenged. This is most clearly, but not exclusively, the case with political discourse, since the theory and practice of politics and political talk is seen to be primarily concerned with power. This of course assumes a conflict, not a consensus model of society, and a model of language use seen as part of social action and concerned with the relation between action and structure. Political discourse analysis, particularly in France, also focuses on the ideological meaning in text. To study ideology in text is to study the ways in which meaning (signification) serves to sustain relations of domination (Thompson, 1982).

Discourse analysis may be seen as a unifying focus for both linguistics and sociology in the way that the linguistics of a sentence was not (Achard, 1978). Discourse, including political discourse, clearly has a pragmatic dimension in that it has as its main investigative focus the study of sign systems, or codes, in terms of user relations. In other words, it is concerned with what kind of language users use, that is, their consistent semantic and syntactic options in terms of the interactional strategies of individuals, groups, and classes. Traditional studies of syntax, semantics, language change, and variation were not concerned with actual language users.

The theorization in this area, for which the groundwork was laid by Vološinov (1973) and Bakhtin more than 50 years ago, has injected into pragmatics and linguistics a political awareness and a theory of social action, largely Marxist, that may be seen as part of the development of socially relevant and socially realistic linguistics (Hymes, 1977).

For Vološinov, it was a question of speech genres (Frew, 1980). He argued that there was a structured set of discourses defined as practices that are coherent organizations of content and interaction. "Each period and each social group has its own repertoire of speech forms for ideological communication in human behaviour. Each . . . genre has its own corresponding set of themes" (Vološinov, 1973, p. 20). His emphasis on forms of communication as social practice (Boutet, 1980), and what he quaintly termed "language-etiquette" and "speech-tact," that is, what is seen as appropriate to a situation, relates the production of meaning both to discourse structure and to the hierarchic organization of society (Vološinov, 1973, p. 21). These hierarchic arrangements have been seen almost exclusively in terms of class antagonisms.

To what extent political discourse does, in fact, constitute a genre (like literary discourse), or a domain (like economic discourse), or a field (like scientific discourse) is highly questionable. Summaries like that of Desideri and Marcarino accept the genre designation and its *sous-genres* (political meeting, electoral manifesto, tract, etc.) as unproblematic (Desideri & Marcarino, 1980, pp. 99–122). I do not share this reductionist view. Neither politics nor political discourse can be defined as a closed entity. Politics is ubiquitous, and therefore any narrow definition of the political, or one concerned solely with particular events, rests on a mystifying closure. The *Langage et Société* group at the Maison des Sciences de l'Homme in Paris led by Pierre Achard considers the political as one of the discursive instances, not excluding others (rationalist, technical, economic, racist, etc.). These subdivisions also bring conceptual problems.

Another difficulty, indeed a theoretical blindspot, of political discourse analysis in the Vološinov tradition carried out from a classical Marxist perspective is its overarching concern with class divisions and their contrasted semantic potential and its consequent neglect of gender divisions as the most constant feature of subordination in our society.

The implications for feminist research have wider ramifications than might first appear: The disparity between analysis of society in terms of class and the underdevelopment of work on the structure of gender means that women too, almost inevitably, come to use existing class and functionalist theories that are characterized by the invisibility of women's subordination. These concerns, both political and academic, have been sensitively explored in a number of women's publications.[2] Clearly, feminist intellectual work is explicitly both an intellectual and a political engagement.

---

[2] These include the Women's Study Group, Centre for Contemporary Studies, at the University of Birmingham, 1978; *Signs,* Spring 1982, 7, (3) Special Issue: Feminist Theory; Spender (1981).

Arguably the same is true of some Marxist work in academia, despite its over-formalization. It is the political engagement that shapes the intellectual agenda and its specific criteria of relevance, as in the definition of the 'social' and 'social facts' in a socially constituted linguistics (Edwards & Seidel, 1979). But because the feminist agenda is that of a subordinate group with a different meaning potential that the dominant theoretical model cannot encompass and has the power to exclude by virtue of its dominance, it is inevitably trivialized or ignored. It is the dominant class (and I refer here to the class of men) that has the power to make meanings stick (Thompson, 1982). There are important structural analogies with the politics of naming (Kramer, 1975).

This raises the whole question of objective and subjective knowledge and meaning (whose knowledge?, whose meaning?). The question is crucial. It is also a particular focus of political discourse analysis in the Marxist tradition in which discourse is not seen as a product of a subject operating freely in the language system—it is not *parole*—but as a system of codes that are acquired, determined, and socially distributed in terms of class and symbolic class capital (Pêcheux, 1975, p. 144).

In this theoretical perspective, the invisibility of women's subordination is confirmed and formalized. For feminists, therefore, the dominant conceptualization in this area (Marxist or functionalist) is fundamentally flawed.

I should now like to offer some short illustrations of the work subsumed under the first three headings in the preceding summary, though these are by no means mutually exclusive. This is demonstrably the case, for example, with work on enunciation, sociolinguistic studies of pronouns (Carbó, 1978; Seidel, 1975, 1978), and lexicometric studies using factor analysis (Geffroy, Guilhaumou, & Salem, 1976, 1981), all of which may share a common concern: the investigation of shifters.

DISCOURSE ANALYSIS WITH PARTICULAR REFERENCE TO PARAPHRASE AND SYNONYMY

A heavily theorized account of discourse has been developed by Michel Pêcheux at the Laboratoire de Psychologie Sociale, University of Paris VII, (1969, 1975; Pêcheux *et al.*, 1979; Robin, 1973) as a tool for ideological struggle. He states as his objective the need to provide "the basis for a scientific analysis of "discursive processes" by articulating through historical materialism the study of ideological superstructures, psychoanalytical theory and linguistic research" (Pêcheux, 1975, p. 234). As part of this design, and drawing on Althusser's work on the theory of ideology, he has reformulated the Saussurian dichotomy *langue–parole* as *langue/processus discursifs*. This shift, foreshadowed in the work of Vološinov and Bakhtin (Bennett, 1979, pp. 75–82) and their critique of Saussure (see also Guespin in Gardin, Baggioni, & Guespin, 1980), takes into account the distinct systems of linguistic value that exist in a single language community, in *langue* (Haroche, Henry, & Pêcheux, 1971). In other words, it focuses on the different meanings that words and expressions (signifiers) can have according to the ideological position of the users and the determining effects of the sociohistorical conditions (or 'ideological formations') in which the utterances are produced that are themselves constitutive of meaning. Discursive processes are thus seen as part of an ideological class relation (Pêcheux, 1975, p. 82; Pêcheux *et al.*, 1979, p. 23–24).

In linguistic terms, a 'discursive process' is described as the system of relations of substitution, paraphrase, synonymy, and metonymy between the signifiers (Pêcheux, 1975, pp. 145–146). In other words, it is part of a "matrix of meaning" in which a system of relations are produced in discourse in terms of the mechanisms of selection and combination (Woods, 1977, p. 61).

Pêcheux's method of automatic discourse analysis (AAD) is based on a Harrisian model of equivalences (Harris, 1952). The AAD does, however, retain the connectors absent in Harris as markers of discursivity. Sentences are reduced to premodalized utterances (*énoncés élémentaires*). The linguistic analysis, the computer program, and the configuration of semantic domains are described and exemplified in an English translation in Aitken, Bailey, and Hamilton-Smith, 1973; and in French in Robin, 1973, and *Langages,* No. 37, March 1975.

The power of this method has been illustrated in its application to different readings of a controversial politically ambiguous text, the Mansholt report, in terms of an analysis of the paraphrases and linked arguments and preconstructs elicited from a group of 50 mature managerial students in 1973 (Pêcheux *et al.,* 1979). It cannot, however, be applied to a heterogeneous corpus. The students were provided with a short extract containing a number of central themes. The text was read to them twice, and they also had access to a hard copy. They were asked to write a "full and objective" summary of about 10 lines. They were told that the investigators were primarily concerned with the transmission of information and the form in which it was transmitted. At the end of the exercise, half the group were reminded that the text emanated ostensibly from a left-wing trade union source (CFDT, the French Democratic Confederation of Labor), and the other half were prompted toward a right-wing source (Giscardians, and Gaullists in the government). They were also invited to suggest other likely sources. Only a minority came up with left-wing signatories. The students were subsequently divided into two groups according to their own political positions, in order to confront the different right–left paraphrases. These two sets of paraphrases may be regarded as two images of the same text and as a materialization of an ideological and political hypothesis (Pêcheux *et al.*, 1979, p. 34).

Three main ambiguities were being explored in this experiment: first, the political ambiguity of the Mansholt report itself; second, the ambiguity of the political positions designated by "right" and "left" in France in the spring of 1973; and third, the class ambiguity of this group of technical managers who were imbued with an elitist ideology, yet had ended up on a retraining course at the age of 30 as a result of unemployment.

The semantic domains are divided into four classes in which the "right" and "left" paraphrases are compared via syntactic analysis and the relations and intersections traced between the domains. These domains are (1) the causes of the crisis, (2) the policy of economic reorganization, (3) the policy of consumption, and (4) the policy of cultural development.

In terms of the first domain, the respective "right" (*droite* abbreviated D) and "left" (*gauche* abbreviated G) results are displayed in Tables 4.1 and 4.2.

It is the question of predicates that highlights some of the differences between the right and left corpora. For example, *a lack of raw materials* or *natural growth (manque)* in D13 (right corpus) could be seen as substituting for *diminution, limitation,* or *restriction,* through which a second more overtly political argument is being rehearsed in the left corpus. The argument thus moves from *a natural state of shortage* to the introduction of a *restriction* by means of a political agent.

The question of agency is also the focus of Trew's work, as we shall see, which also involves syntactic analysis. The great strength of AAD is its internal methodological consistency and its homogeneous class concerns. If, however, one has difficulty with the overriding class concerns and Althusserian problematic, then one is led inevitably to question the entire theoretical and methodological apparatus.

DISCOURSE ANALYSIS WITH PARTICULAR REFERENCE TO SYNTAX

Other linguists and philosophers analyzing text share a similar concern with the choices of words and constructions within a single language community in which contrasting styles of speech and writing express different analyses and experiences seen as part of a social process and

4 Political Discourse Analysis

Table 4.1
Causes of the Crisis: The "Right"

D11

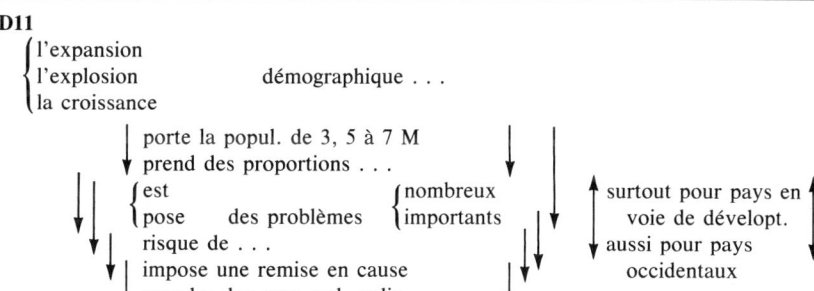

$\left\{\begin{array}{l}\text{l'expansion}\\ \text{l'explosion}\\ \text{la croissance}\end{array}\right.$ démographique . . .

    ↓ porte la popul. de 3, 5 à 7 M
       prend des proportions . . .
    ↓↓ $\left\{\begin{array}{l}\text{est}\\ \text{pose}\end{array}\right.$ des problèmes $\left\{\begin{array}{l}\text{nombreux}\\ \text{importants}\end{array}\right.$ ↓↓ ↑ surtout pour pays en ↑
       risque de . . .   voie de dévelopt.
    ↓| impose une remise en cause   ↓↓ ↓ aussi pour pays
    ↓ prendre des mes. pol. radic.   occidentaux

Menacer (explosion démographique, pays en voie de développement et industrialisés).
menacer (x y) : x menace y

D12

$\left\{\begin{array}{l}\text{arrêt}\\ \text{freinage}\end{array}\right.$ naturel de la croissance

PRC* / s'arrêter (croissance)/
s'arrêter (x) : x s'arrête

* PRC = preconstruct (*préconstruit*)

D11 (English)

$\left\{\begin{array}{l}\text{expansion}\\ \text{explosion}\\ \text{growth}\end{array}\right.$ demographic

    ↓ increases the pop. to 3, 5, 7 M.
       assumes the order of . . .
     $\left\{\begin{array}{l}\text{is}\\ \text{poses}\end{array}\right.$ problems $\left\{\begin{array}{l}\text{many}\\ \text{important}\end{array}\right.$ ↑ especially for developing ↑
     risks   countries
     necessitates a calling into question   also for western
     takes radical political measures   ↓ countries ↓

to threaten (demographic explosion, developing and industrialized countries)
threaten (x, y) : x threatens y

D12

$\left\{\begin{array}{l}\text{stoppage}\\ \text{slowing down}\end{array}\right.$ natural growth

PRC / to stop growth
to stop (x) : x stops

50   Gill Seidel

Table 4.2
Causes of the Crisis: The "Left"

G11

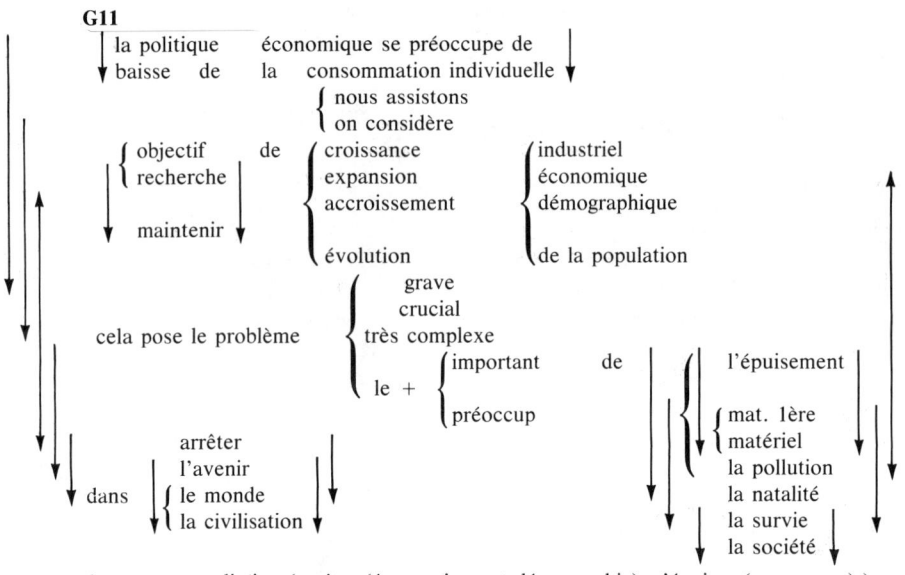

être en contradiction (croître (économique et démographie), s'épuiser (ressources))
être en contradiction (P1 P2) : P1 est en contradiction avec P2 *
  * P = proposition

G11 (English)

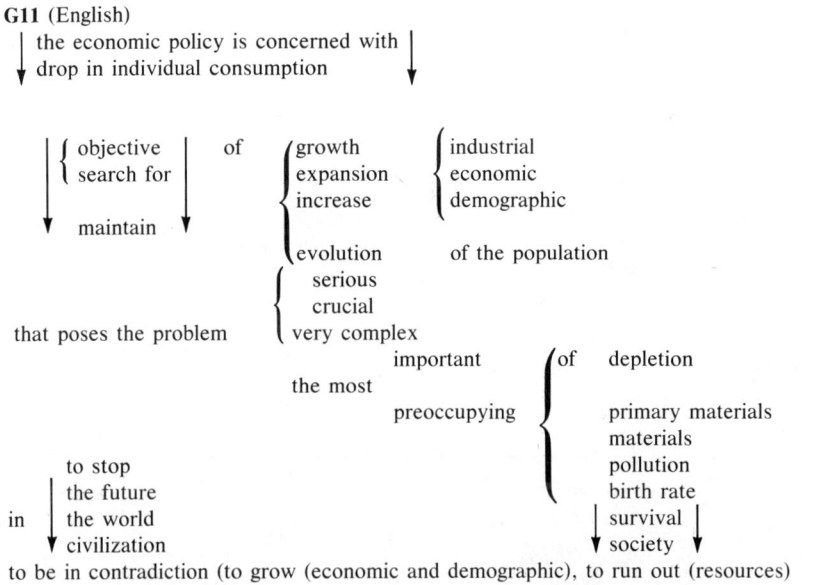

to be in contradiction (to grow (economic and demographic), to run out (resources)
to be in contradiction (P1, P2) : P1 is in contradiction with P2

4 Political Discourse Analysis

Table 4.2 (continued)

G12	
on ne peut pas	$\left\{\begin{array}{l}\text{espérer une stabilisation}\\ \text{conserver le taux de croissance}\\ \text{freiner l'explosion}\end{array}\right.$

IMPOSS / espérer (∅ stabiliser (∅ économie et démographie)) /
espérer (x P) : x espère que P

G12 (English)	
it is not possible	$\left\{\begin{array}{l}\text{to hope for a stabilization}\\ \text{to maintain the growth rate}\\ \text{to halt the explosion}\end{array}\right.$

IMPOS / to hope (∅ stabilize (∅ economy and demography)) /
to hope (x P) : x hopes that P

expressing structured social differences. The concern with syntax and its relation to political and social discourses that serves to legitimate a social order, or to challenge it, has been illustrated by Trew (1979a, 1979b) at the University of East Anglia. Trew has adapted a Hallidayan model of language (Halliday, 1967a, 1967b, 1968, 1979) that explicitly addresses itself to the relation between linguistic choice and the semiotic constraints of the speech situation. His examples illustrate his main preoccupation, not with class, as in the case of Pêcheux, nor with the representation of gender, as in the work of Michard-Marchal and Ribéry, but with the reporting of "race."

He is concerned with the theoretical processes involved in the representation and linking of particular events (like "race riots" or the shooting of Africans by police in former Rhodesia) to a network of causal relations that form part of our judgment and perception. This is commonplace in philosophical discussions, but it tends to be conducted at a very abstract level. Put very crudely, Trew is focusing on who (the principal participant) is reported to have done what (the focal process) to whom or what (the affected), and, most important, how these processes and participants are categorized, as this marking of agency and its mediation affects the way in which we see social and political relations. In doing so, he is applying a politically sensitive philosophical framework shaped by Foucault, using linguistic concepts derived from Halliday. Examples are headlines from the *Times* and the *Guardian:*

RIOTING BLACKS SHOT DEAD BY POLICE AS ANC LEADERS MEET (from the *Times*)
  Eleven Africans were shot dead and 15 wounded when Rhodesian police opened fire on a rioting crowd of about 2,000.

POLICE SHOOT 11 DEAD IN SALISBURY RIOT (from the *Guardian*)
> Riot police shot and killed 11 African demonstrators and wounded 15 others.

The following table shows both the similarities and the differences (Trew, 1979a, p. 100).

	Agent	Process	Affected	Circumstance
Times		Passive		
Headline	police	shoot dead	rioting blacks	(as) ANC leaders meet
Report	—	shoot dead	eleven Africans	(when) Rhodesian police opened fire on a rioting crowd
Guardian		Active		
Headline	police	shoot dead	11	(in) Salisbury riots
Report	riot police	shoot and kill	11 African demonstrators	

In the *Times* the effect of the linguistic facts pointed out is to shift the focus away from those who did the shooting, and on to the victims categorized as *Africans* or *blacks*. Both newspapers clearly locate the events in the context of *riots*. The agents who did the shooting are characterized as *police* (and not, for example, as *murderers* or *racists*). In subsequent news stories, with the emphasis on the split in the African National Council, there is a weakening of the expression of causal links between the shooting and the shooters:

SPLIT THREATENS ANC AFTER SALISBURY'S RIOTS (from the *Times*)
> After Sunday's riots in which 13 Africans were killed and 28 injured, a serious rift in the ranks of the African National Council became apparent today.

The exclusion of the killing from the headlines is striking. In subsequent tables, Trew summarizes the series of linguistic transformations that have taken place in the *Times* and sets out the sequence of linguistic events that has the effect of offering a new explanation of the event described originally. He illustrates how linguistic theory can be used in that discourse is a point of intersection between ideological and linguistic processes, with a determinate relation between the two. He argues that the ideological character of a discourse consists in the systematic patterns and organization of certain linguistic characteristics, including, most importantly, the systematic patterns of classification of process and participants and the presentation of agency and interaction. In his view, ideology is best understood by an analysis of the processes of which texts are a part. But ideological difference is not seen to consist merely of variation in which the ideological conflict is played out between various modes and their range of linguistic expression. Paradoxically, this lexical variation needs also to take theoretical account of the case of the same word being used with different meanings because it is embedded within different linguistic systems expressing different ideologies or theories. This is discussed elsewhere with reference to the lexical item *pouvoir* (power) in the French political tracts, left and right, of May 1968 in terms of polysemy in Seidel, 1975. There is also overt ideological conflict manifested linguistically in ways that mark particular terms as acceptable or not (Trew, 1979b, pp. 154–155).[3]

It has been suggested that Trew's analysis is reductionist and ahistorical. In my view, it offers a powerful illustration in accessible language of how students of linguistics and of the media can analyze some of the ideological determinants in discourse, and how it is intricated in social processes and in stages in the reproduction and transformation of ideology.

DISCOURSE ANALYSIS FOCUSING ON ENUNCIATION

Marchal and Ribéry (1982) apply the linguistic model developed by Culioli and Fuchs at the University of Paris VII to investigate the semantic disymmetries in the linguistic representation of gender (Culioli, 1971, 1976, 1978; and Culioli, Fuchs, & Pêcheux, 1970; Fuchs, 1971, 1979, 1980). Gender has been inadequately conceptualized in the human sciences as presently constituted (Guillaumin, 1978a, 1978b; Mathieu, 1971, 1977; Roberts, 1981; Spender, 1981). In order to investigate the ideological representations of gender in the social sciences, Marchal and Ribéry

---

[3] One example, not from Trew, would be the dispute about the appropriateness of *chairperson* to denote either a woman or man in the chair, which would have the function of displacing the use of *chairman* as a generic. Another example would be the acceptable naming (the ideological acceptability) of the withdrawal or cessation of work as a *day of action*, a *strike*, or *industrial sabotage*. This dispute paradigm is frequently in evidence. This was also the case in the differential reporting of the national steel strike in Britain in 1980 in the *Telegraph* editorials and the national strike bulletins (Seidel, 1980). The same phenomenon may be observed in the dominant nonlexicalization of the British engagement in the Falklands as *war*, or more currently, the embittered discussions focusing on the meaning of *uneconomic pits* in the national miner's strike in Britain.

develop the work on enunciation processes and apply it to a central corpus of three contemporary texts. These are texts of Pierre Clastres (1966, 1976), Maurice Godelier (1978), and Pierre Bourdieu (1972). All three were analyzed to show how the same speaker talks of both sexes. The analysis takes account of the properties constructed by the determinations of the predicates, all lexicalizations relating to 'woman' and 'man', the values of the quantifying operations, and an examination of the relations of localization in relation to 'woman' or 'man' (Michard-Marchal & Ribéry, 1982, p. 34). The investigation focuses on the modal and aspect values, which are also semantic, because it is these that basically attribute the properties of animate and inanimate (Fuchs & Léonard, 1979).

The Clastres text, stemming from a reflection on language, considers the sexual division of all modes of social behaviour of an Amerindian people of South America, the Guayaki. Very systematically, the analysis shows that the properties of the notions of 'woman' and 'man' highlighted by the linguistic analysis underlie the totality of assertions, which justifies the over-all reasoning. With particular reference to the Clastres text, which provides the widest range of enunciation phenomena, Michard-Marchal and Ribéry arrive at detailed conclusions (1982, pp. 174–175) from which I have extrapolated the following:

1. 'Woman' is generally constructed as nonanimate: The enunciations carry the minimum determination markers.
2. The property most frequently assigned to 'man' is that of agent. It carries the maximum marks of determinacy. 'Woman' is rarely constructed as agent. The markers of determination for 'women' are the same as those ascribed to animate as well as nonanimate notions that are constructed as sparking off automatic processes in the same way as instruments, machines, or natural elements. Men are categorized as involved in processes (*faire*) relating to practices. Women, on the other hand, are seen more as involved in states (*être*), like motherhood and wifehood.[4] The power relation is thus obscured in the enunciation process (Michard-Marchal & Ribéry, 1982, p. 75).
3. The notions 'man' and 'woman' are present in enunciations in which 'woman' alone was the "source-notion."[5] This is modalized by

---

[4] Carbó (1982a, 1982b, 1984) has made similar observations with regard to the opposition 'indigenous'–'white' in her work on Mexican parliamentary debates concerning Mexico's indigenous population.

[5] See Fuchs and Léonard (1979); the term "source-notion" is defined in Chapter IV. It is a representation of a cognitive order (comprising physical and cultural properties) that is nonverbalized and only coincides with a syntactical subject in the framework of an active predicate.

making 'man' a constraining subject. These modalities are always given a value, and the orientation man→woman is irreversible.

The researchers compare the results of their linguistic analyses to historical studies of linguistic changes in language practices at the time of the rise of the bourgeoisie and its accession to power (Bisseret, 1974). Just as the bourgeoisie, as members of the dominant class, consider themselves as the norm and construct individuals of the dominated class as something different or marked (the hegemonic class is always unmarked), individuals of a sexed group construct the group to which they belong as different from the other sexed group. And as in traditional class relations, discourses construct one of the sexed groups as the norm to which the other group is compared and measured. In the same way, whites are seen simply as existing (unmarked), whereas blacks or Chinese are seen as different, and the asymmetrical relational factor is obscured (Guillaumin, 1978b, p. 16). Michard-Marchal and Ribéry conclude that any language practice includes the viewpoint of enunciative subjects to the extent that their more or less conscious attitudes are determined by social relations.

I have drawn upon different illustrations of discourse analysis that are rigorous and systematic, though they vary in their conceptualization of the social. Students of political discourse analysis in search of a method should be guided by their own view of the adequacy of the sociopolitical representations on which the different theories and methodologies rely. In my view, no method, however rigorous, can remain closed, abolishing the need for new explanations in order to transcend the closure of discourse and the closure of the political. The French language is particularly sensitive to this emphasis: To foreclose the political is tantamount to dwelling exclusively on *la politique* (politics) as opposed to the more open and dynamic *le politique* (the political) (Debray, 1981). The mapping of the relation between struggles against these three oppressions, those of sexism, racism, and capitalism, and their construction in discourse, remains both an overall political objective and a politically inspired academic agenda (Seidel, 1984, 1985; in preparation).

ACKNOWLEDGMENTS

I should like to thank Teresa Carbó, Annie Geffroy, and Claire Michard-Marchal for their comments on an earlier draft.

BIBLIOGRAPHY

Achard, P. (1978). Une partie intégrante de la sociolinguistique: L'analyse du discours. *Langage et Société,* (6), 3–26.

Aitken, A. J., Bailey, R. W., & Hamilton-Smith, N. (Eds.). (1973). *The computer and literary studies*. Edinburgh: Edinburgh University Press.

Bachmann, C., Duro-Courdesses, L., & Le Guennec, N. (1978). *Discours politique et situation sociale*. Publication du Groupe Communication et Travail, UER des Sciences de l'Expression et de la Communication. Paris: Université de Paris-Nord.

Barthes, R. (1957). *Mythologies*. Paris: Seuil.

Bennett, T. (1979). *Formalism and Marxism*. London: Methuen.

Bergounioux, A., Launay, M. F., Mouriaux, R., Sueur, J-P., & Tournier, M. (1982). *La parole syndicale: Etude du vocabulaire confédéral des centrales ouvrières francaises, 1971–1976*. Etude réalisée par le 'Groupe de Saint-Cloud'. Paris: Presses Universitaires de France.

Bisseret, N. (1974). Langage et identité de classe: les classes sociales "se" parlent. *Année Sociologique, 25*.

Bloch, M. (Ed.). (1975). *Political language and oratory in traditional society*. London: Academic Press.

Bonnafous, S. (1980). *Les motions du congrès de Metz (1979) du parti socialiste: Processus discursifs et structures lexicales*. Thèse de 3ᵉ cycle, Université de Nanterre.

Bonnafous, S., & Willems, D. (1982). Etat présent des études sur le discours gaulliste. *Mots, (4)*, 171–180.

Bourdieu, P. (1972). *Esquisse d'une théorie de la pratique; trois études d'ethnologie Kabyle*. Paris: Droz.

Bourdieu, P. (1981). La représentation politique: Eléments pour une théorie du champ politique. *Actes de la Recherche en Sciences Sociales, 36–37*, 3–24.

Boutet, J. (1980). Quelques courants dans l'approche sociale du langage. *Langage et Société, 12*, 33–70.

Cabre Castellvi, M. T. (1983). Les recherches de lexicologie politique en Espagne, in *Actes du 2ᵉ Colloque de Lexicologie Politique*, Saint-Cloud, 15–20 septembre 1980. Paris: Klincksieck.

Carbó, T. (1978). Acerca de las posibilidades del analisis de textos políticos: Luis Echeverría en la Réunion Nacional sobre Asentamientos Humanos (1 de abril de 1976). Unpublished paper presented at a seminar on discourse theory at the Centro de Estudios Lingüísticos y Literarios de El Colegio de Mexico, June 1978. (to appear in *Revue d'Etudes Mexicaines*, Perpignan.)

Carbó, T. (1980). Notas para la lectura de una carta de la Union Nacional de Veteranos de la Revolución (1936). Unpublished paper, Instituto Nacional de Antropologia y de Historia, Mexico City.

Carbó, T. (1982a, November). El debate indigenísta en Mexico: Un ejemplo de analisis de discurso parlamentario. Paper presented to the Symposium on Theory and Discourse Analysis in Contemporary Thought, Unidad Académica de los Ciclos Profesional y de Posgrado de CCH, Universidad Autónoma de México.

Carbó, T. (1982b, August). Los indigenos Mexicanos como objeto de debate parlamentario: 1920–1930. Paper presented to the Tenth World Congress of Sociology (Sociolinguistics Section), Mexico.

Carbó, T. (1984). *Discurso político: Lectura y análisis*. Mexico: CIESAS, Cuadernos de la Casa Chata, No. 105.

Centre for Contemporary Cultural Studies (CCCS),Women's Study Group. (1978). *Women take issue: Aspects of women's subordination*. Birmingham: CCCS.

Clastres, P. (1966). L'arc et le panier. *L'Homme, 6 (2)*.

Clastres, P. (1976). L'arc et le panier. In *La société contre l'État* (Chap. 5). Paris: Editions de Minuit.

Comaroff, J. (1975). Talking politics: Oratory and authority in a Tswana chiefdom. In

Bloch (Ed.), *Political language and oratory in traditional society* (pp. 141-160). London: Academic Press.
Cotteret, J. M., & Moreau, R. (1969). *Le vocabulaire du Général de Gaulle.* Paris: Armand Colin.
Courdesses, L. (1971). Blum et Thorez en mai 1936: Analyses d'énoncés. *Langue Française, 9.*
Courtine, J-J. (1980). Quelques problèmes théoriques et méthodologiques en analyse du discours, à propos du discours communiste adressé aux chrétiens. *Langages, 62,* 9-127.
Culioli, A. (1971). A propos d'opérations intervenant dans le traitement formel des langues naturelles. *Mathématiques et Sciences Humaines,* (34), 7-15.
Culioli, A. (1976). *Transcription du Séminaire de DEA.* Stencilled paper, Université de Paris VII, Département de Recherches Linguistiques.
Culioli, A. (1978). *Transcription du Séminaire de DEA de 1977-1978.* Photocopied manuscripts, Université de Paris VII, Département de Recherches Linguistiques.
Culioli, A., Fuchs, C., & Pêcheux, M. (1970). *Considérations théoriques à propos du traitement formel du langage.* Document de Linguistique Quantitative, (7).
Debray, R. (1981). *Critique de la raison politique.* Paris: Gallimard.
Desideri, P., & Marcarino, A. (1980). *Testualità e tipologia del discorso politico: Bibliografia.* Rome: Bulzone.
Ebel, M., & Fiala, P. (1983). *Sous le consensus, la xénophobie. Paroles, arguments, contextes (Suisse, 1961-1981).* Lausanne: Institut de Sciences Politiques, Mémoire et Documents, 16.
Edwards, A. D., & Seidel, G. (1979). Social facts and socially-constituted linguistics. *Sociolinguistics Newsletter,* (Research Committee on sociolinguistics of the International Sociological Association), *10* (2).
Ezcurra, A. M., & de Lella, C. (1980). *La U.P.I. en Puebla:* Manipulación ideológica de las III Conferencia General del Episcopado Latinoamericano. Lima: Celadec; Mexico: Centro de Estudios Ecuménicos.
Faye, J-P. (1972a). *Langages totalitaires.* Paris: Hermann.
Faye, J-P. (1972b). *Théorie du récit.* Paris: Hermann.
Faye, J-P. (1973). *La critique du langage et son économie.* Paris: Editions-Galilée. (Série, *Langue 1.*)
Feminist Theory. (1982). Special Issue, *Signs, Journal of Women in Culture and Society, 7* (3).
Fiala, P. (1977). *Recherches sur les discours xénophobes, Cahiers du Centre de Sémiologie de Neuchâtel,* (26).
Fowler, R., Hodge, B., Kress, H., Trew, T. (1979). *Language and control.* London: Routledge & Kegan Paul.
Frew, J. (1980). Discourse genres. *Journal of Literary Semantics, 9,* 73-81.
Fuchs, C. (1971). *Contribution préliminaire à la construction d'une grammaire de français.* Thèse de doctorat de 3e cycle, Université de Paris VII.
Fuchs, C. (1979). Référenciation et paraphrase: Variations sur une valeur aspectuelle in *Mélanges de syntaxe et sémantique, DRLAV, 21.* Paris: Centre de Recherches de l'Université de Paris VII.
Fuchs, C. (1980). Paraphrase et théories du langage. Contribution à une histoire des théories linguistiques contemporaines et à la construction d'une théorie énonciative. Thèse de doctorat d'état.
Fuchs, C., & Léonard, A-M. (1979). *Vers une théorie des aspects, les systèmes du français et de l'anglais.* Paris and the Hague: Mouton. (*Connaissance et Langage,* 6.)
Gardin, B., Baggioni, D., & Guespin, L. (1980). *Pratiques linguistiques, pratiques sociales.*

Paris and Rouen: Presses Universitaires de France and Publications de l'Université de Rouen.

Geffroy, A., Guilhaumou, J., & Salem, A. (1976). Factor analysis and lexicometrics: Shifters in some texts of the French Revolution (1779–1794). In A. Jones & R. F. Churchouse (Eds.), *The computer in literary studies* (pp. 177–193). Cardiff: University of Wales.

Geffroy, A., Guilhaumou, J., & Salem, A. (1981). Personnes du discours et figures du pouvoir dans *L'Ami du Peuple* de Leclerc (1793). (Colloque de Saint-Cloud 1980), *Bulletin du Centre d'Analyse du Discours,* (5), 105–148.

Godelier, M. (1978). Pouvoir et langage. *Communications,* (28).

Groupe de Saint-Cloud, Geffroy, A., Lafon, P., Tournier, M. (1975). *Des tracts en Mai 68. Mesure de vocabulaire et de contenu.* Parties I et II. Paris: Fondation Nationale des Sciences Politiques, and Armand Colin.

Guilhaumou, J. (Ed.). (1981). La rhétorique du discours, objet d'histoire (XVIIIe–XXe siècles). *Bulletin du Centre d'Analyse du Discours,* (5).

Guespin, L. (1971). Problématique des travaux sur le discours politique. *Langages,* (23).

Guespin, L. (1976). Typologie du discours politique. *Langages,* (41).

Guespin, L. (1980). Pour une théorie globale du langage. In B. Gardin, D. Baggioni, & L. Guespin (Eds.), *Pratiques linguistiques, pratiques sociales.* Paris and Rouen: Presses Universitaires de France and Publications de l'Université de Rouen.

Guillaumin, C. (1978a). Pratique du pouvoir et idée de nature, (I) L'appropriation des femmes. *Questions Féministes,* (2), 5–30.

Guillaumin, C. (1978b). Pratique du pouvoir et idée de nature, (II) Le discours de la nature. *Questions Féministes,* (3), 5–30.

Gumbrecht, H. U. (1979a). Historische Text—Pragmatik als Grundlagenwissenschaft der Geschichtsschreibun. *Lendemains,* Part 6.

Gumbrecht, H. U. (1979b). Persuader ceux qui pensent comme vous. Les fonctions du discours épidictique sur la mort de Marat. *Poétique,* (39), 363–384.

Halliday, M. A. K. (1967a). Notes on transitivity and theme in English, Part 1. *Journal of Linguistics, 3* (1), 37–81.

Halliday, M. A. K. (1967b). Notes on transitivity and theme in English, Part 2. *Journal of Linguistics, 3* (2), 199–244.

Halliday, M. A. K. (1968). Notes on transitivity and theme in English, Part 3. *Journal of Linguistics, 4* (2), 179–215.

Halliday, M. A. K. (1979). *Language as social semiotic: The social interpretation of language and meaning.* London: Arnold.

Haroche, C., Henry, P., Pêcheux, M. (1971). La sémantique et la coupure sausurienne: Langue, langage, discours. *Langages,* 6 (24) 93–106.

Harris, S. Z. (1952). Discourse analysis. *Language, 28,* 1–30.

Hymes, D. (1977). *Foundations in sociolinguistics.* London: Tavistock.

Ipola, E. de (1982). *Ideología y discurso populista.* Mexico: Folios Ediciones.

Kadima-Tschimanga (1982). La société sous le vocabulaire: *Blancs, Noirs et Evolués,* dans l'ancien Congo Belge. *Mots* (5), 25–50.

Kramer, C., Thorne, B., & Henley, N. (1978). Review essay: Perspectives on language and communication. *Signs: Journal of Women in Culture and Society, 3* (3), 638–651.

Kramer, C. (1975). Women's speech; Separate but Unequal? In B. Thorne, & N. Henley (Eds.), *Language and sex: Difference and dominance* (pp. 43–56). Rowley, MA: Newbury House.

Lehmann, M. (1978). Langue, idéologie et dictionnaire: le discours sur *femme* et *fille* dans le *Petit Larousse illustré* de 1906 à 1978. *Bulletin du Centre d'Analyse du Discours,* (3), 1–175.

Maldidier, D. (1971). Le discours politique de la guerre d'Algérie: approche synchronique et diachronique. *Langages,* (23).
Marcellesi, J-B. (1971). Linguistique et société. *Langue Française,* (9).
Mathieu, N-C. (1971). Notes pour une définition sociologique des catégories de sexe. *Epistémologie Sociologique,* No. 11, 1971, pp. 19–39.
Mathieu, N-C. (1977). Masculinité/fémininité. *Questions Féministes,* (1).
Michard-Marchal, C., & Ribéry, C. (1979). Rapports de sexage et opérations énonciatives. *Langage et Société, 8,* 31–54.
Michard-Marchal, C., & Ribéry, C. (1982). *Sexisme et sciences humaines, Pratique linguistique du rapport de sexage.* Lille: Presses Universitaires de Lille.
Nasr, M. Abou-Chdid. (1980). *L'idéologie nationale arabe dans les discours de Gamal Abdel Nasser, 1952–1970.* Thèse de 3ᵉ cycle, Université de Paris IV.
Nasr, M. Abou-Chdid. (1981). Analyse des champs sémantiques de la notion de *umma arabiyya* (nation arabe) dans le discours Nassérien. *Mots,* (2), 13–36.
O'Barr, W., & O'Barr, J. (Eds.). (1976). *Language and politics.* The Hague: Mouton.
Parkin, D. (1975). The rhetoric of responsibility: Bureaucratic communications in a Kenya farming area. In Bloch (Ed.), *Political language and oratory in traditional society* (pp. 113–116). London: Academic Press.
Paquot, A., Zylberberg, J. (1982). L'incantation québecoise, *Mots,* (4), 7–28.
Pêcheux, M. (1969). *Analyse automatique du discours.* Paris: Dunod.
Pêcheux, M. (1975). *Les vérités de la palice.* Paris: Maspero. (*Language, Semantics and Ideology* (1982), H. Nagpal, Trans. London: Macmillan.)
Pêcheux, M., & Wesselius, J. (1973). Students and workers in May 68 student tracts. In A. Aitken, R. Bailey, & N. Hamilton-Smith (Eds.), *The computer and literary studies* (pp. 135–151). Edinburgh: Edinburgh University Press.
Pêcheux, M., Henry, P., Poitou, J-P., & Haroche, C. (1979). Un exemple d'ambiguïté idéologique: Le rapport Mansholt. *Technologies, Idéologies et Pratiques, 1* (2).
Pêcheux, M., Léon, J., Bonnafous, S., & Marandin, J-M. (1982). Présentation de l'analyse automatique du discours (AAD 69): Théories, procédures, résultats, perspectives. *Mots,* (4), 95–123.
Peschanski, D. (1981). *Discours communiste et grand tournant. Etude du vocabulaire de l'Humanité (1934–1936).* Thèse de 3ᵉ cycle, Ecole Normale Supérieure de Saint-Cloud.
Reichardt, R. (1982). Pour une histoire des mots—Thèmes socio-politiques en France (1680–1920). *Mots,* (5), 189–202.
Robin, R. (1973). *Histoire et linguistique.* Paris: Armand Colin.
Roberts, H. (Ed.). (1981). *Doing feminist research.* London: Routledge & Kegan Paul.
Rubango, N. (1981). Vocabulaire politique de la presse zaïroise contemporaine. *Mots,* (3), 35–45.
Sefchovitch, S. (Ed.). (1978). *El discurso politico.* Simposio de México, 7–11 Noviembre 1977, *Pensamiento Universitario,* 9, Universidad Nacional Autónoma de Mexico.
Seidel, G. (1975). Ambiguity in political discourse: A sociolinguistic investigation into a corpus of French political tracts of May 68. In Bloch (Ed.), *Political language and oratory in traditional society* (pp. 205–226). London: Academic Press.
Seidel, G. (1978). Verbal strategies and the politics of ambiguity, *Travaux de Lexicométrie et de Lexicologie Politique,* (3), 101–122. (extract from D. Phil. thesis, Sussex 1977, in French translation).
Seidel, G. (1980). Continuities in right-wing thought and language—scapegoating and union-bashing: A feminist perspective. International Conference on Language and Power, Bellagio, Italy.
Seidel, G. (1982). Le fascisme dans les textes de la Nouvelle Droite. *Mots,* (3), 47–61.

Seidel, G. (1984). Le discours d'exclusion: Les mises à distance, le non-droit. *Mots,* (March) (8), 5-16.
Seidel, G. (1985a). The concept of culture in the English and French New Right. In R. Lentàs (Ed.), *The ideology of the New Right.* Oxford: Polity Press/Blackwell.
Seidel, G. (1985b). *The holocaust denial.* Leeds: Beyond the Pale Collective.
Seidel, G. (in preparation). *Right, left: The politics of language.*
Seidel, G. (Ed.). (in preparation). *La droite, genre masculin.* Paris.
Sigal, S., & Veron, E. (1981). Péron: Discurso político e ideología. In A. Rouquié (Ed.), *Argentina hoy.* Mexico: Siglo XXI, Editores.
Simonin-Grumbach, J. (1975). Pour une typologie des discours. In *Langue, discours, société.* Paris: Seuil.
Slater, C. (1981). *Defeatists and their enemies: Political invective in France 1914-1918.* Oxford: Oxford University Press.
Spender, D. (1980). *Man made language.* London: Routledge & Kegan Paul.
Spender, D. (1981). *Men's studies modified: The impact of feminism on the academic disciplines.* Oxford: Pergamon Press.
Slakta, D. (1971). L'acte de *demander* dans les cahiers de doléance. *Langue Française,* (9).
Techteimer, B. (1983). Des études de lexicologie politique sur l'allemand faites en RDA in *Actes du 2ᵉ Colloque de Lexicologie Politique,* Saint-Cloud, 15-20 septembre 1980. Paris: Klincksieck.
Thompson, J. B. (1982, August). Critical discussion of recent work in English on ideology and discourse analysis. Paper presented at the Tenth World Congress of Sociology, Mexico.
Thorne, B., & Henley, N. (Eds.). (1975). *Language and sex: Difference and dominance.* Rowley, Mass: Newbury House.
Tournier, M. (1976). *Un vocabulaire ouvrier en 1848. Essai de lexicométrie.* Thèse d'état, Ecole Normale Supérieure de Saint-Cloud, Université de Paris III.
Tournier, M. (1982). Les vocabulaires politiques à l'étude aujourd'hui (1962-1982). *Raison Présente, 62,* 79-101.
Trew, T. (1979a). Theory and ideology at work. In R. Fowler, B. Hodge, H. Kress, & T. Trew (Eds.), *Language and control* (pp. 99-116). London: Routledge & Kegan Paul.
Trew, T. (1979b). "What the papers say": Linguistic variation and ideological difference. In R. Fowler, B. Hodge, H. Kress, & T. Trew (Eds.), *Language and control* (pp. 117-156). London: Routledge & Kegan Paul.
Veron, E. (1978). Sémiosis de l'idéologie et du pouvoir. *Communications, 28,* 7-20.
Veron, E. (1978). Le Hibou. *Communications, 28,* 69-125.
Viollet, C. (1984). *Pratiques argumentatives et discours oral.* Thèse de 3ᵉ cycle, Université de Paris VII.
Vološinov, V. N. (1973). *Marxism and the philosophy of language* (L. Matejka & I. R. Titunik, Trans.). London: Seminar Press.
Woods, M. (1977). Discourse analysis: The work of Michel Pêcheux, *Ideology and Consciousness,* (3), 57-79.

CHAPTER **5**

Power

Roger Fowler

LANGUAGE AS SOCIAL PRACTICE

'Power' is not a very satisfactory technical term, but its everyday usage will be adequate to get us going. Let us say that power is the ability of people and institutions to control the behavior and material lives of others. It is obviously a transitive concept entailing an asymmetrical relationship: X is more powerful than/has power over Y. It is also a very general concept: an abstraction picking out one feature in an indefinitely large number of very diverse kinds of relationship. When we talk about power we may be referring to relationships between parents and children, employers and employees, doctors and patients, a government and its subjects, and so on. Features of the relationships, including those that contribute to having or not having power, are remarkably diverse. It will clearly not be possible to discuss more than a handful of the specific types of relationships involved.

These power relationships are not natural and objective; they are artificial, socially constructed intersubjective realities. People—those with power, mostly—may behave as if these relationships are inevitable and immutable; but they are part of the process called by Berger and Luckman, in the title of their book (1976), "the social construction of reality." From our point of view, the most important insight, recognized to some extent by Berger and Luckman, is that language is a major mechanism in this process of social construction. It is an instrument for consolidating and manipulating concepts and relationships in the area of power and control (as well as other areas of social and ideological structure). We can summarize this by characterizing language as a social practice. Not only is it used to enforce and exploit existing positions of authority and privilege in the obvious ways (commands, regulations, etc.); the use of language continuously constitutes the statuses and roles upon which people base their claims to exercise power, and the statuses and roles which seem to require subservience.

Language is a reality-creating social practice. We insisted on this view in *Language and Control* (Fowler, Hodge, Kress, & Trew, 1979) not only because it emphasizes the necessity of studying language in relation to power, repression, and inequality but also because it corrects the prevalent misformulation in traditional sociolinguistics. The latter theorizes language and society as distinct entities. Social institutions, roles, statuses, and inequalities are regarded, incorrectly, as originating independently of language. Sociolinguists do not generally concern themselves with the means by which social formations arise, and therefore they tend to take for granted such matters as socioeconomic class and official institutions. Variations in linguistic structure are observed and correlated with differences in social structure: Upper-class speakers in New York have more /r/s in their speech, black American speech does not use the copula *is* (and its variants), scientific English uses many passives with deleted agents, and so on. Social structure and linguistic structure are shown to covary systematically and predictably. This kind of correlational sociolinguistics has been developed to a high degree of precision and ingenuity by Labov (1972b) and Trudgill (1974). Although it is very informative about the details of speech of different classes of speakers in different communities, it tends to be complacent and uncritical, accepting "official" versions of society and not seeing language as an instrument of inequality.

There is an illusory egalitarianism in correlation sociolinguistics. Research such as Labov's seems to demonstrate that members of different social groups speak different varieties. Attacking notions of linguistic inequality and verbal deficit implied by social theorists such as Basil Bernstein, Labov attempts to show that black American English is as adequate to conceptual and social needs as is middle-class English (1972a). But even if all varieties are as good as one another (cf. the technically correct assertion in most linguistic textbooks that "there are no primitive languages"), it is an indisputable fact that some varieties and items are associated with situations of prestige, success, and authority, and some with situations of powerlessness and deprivation. Seeing language as a practice that contributes to inequality, rather than as an innocent medium that simply reflects inequality, forces linguists to be more critical and gives social purpose to their own investigations. (For further discussion see Dittmar, 1976; Fowler *et al.*, 1979, Chap. 10; Hudson, 1980.)

THE PRONOUNS OF POWER AND SOLIDARITY

Brown and Gilman's pioneering study of pronoun usage (1960/1972) is much bolder than the correlational research I have just alluded to in its willingness to interpret the varying distribution of linguistic items in semantic and ideological terms. This is an account of the second-person pronouns used in addressing single individuals in some familiar European languages. Whereas modern English invariably uses *you* (apart from specialized, archaic religious uses of *thou* and *thee*), French, German, Spanish, Italian, Russian, and other languages provide a choice: between *tu* and *vous* in French, *du* and *Sie* in German. Anyone who has learned one of these languages knows that this is not a free choice: Whether you say *tu* or *vous* depends on your relationship with the person you are speaking to. Brown and Gilman tried to establish what kinds of relationships determined choice of pronoun for the different languages. Parents address their children as *tu*, soldiers address officers as *vous*, and so on. Rather than simply listing such dyads in the communities concerned, Brown and Gilman postulated two abstract underlying social principles from the intersection of which the social semantics of any particular system could be generated. These they call "power" and "solidarity": the former has the dimensions "superior", "inferior", and "equal", the latter "solidary" and "non-solidary." Given the theoretical terms, we can predict pronoun usage: equal and non-solidary (e.g., businessmen from two firms) predicts *vous;* equal and solidary (siblings of similar age, lovers, manual workers in the same trade) predicts *tu*.

'Power' in Brown and Gilman's scheme matches our commonsense usage of the term: It is an abstraction from such relationships as 'older than', 'stronger than', 'richer than'. 'Solidarity' is based on similarities that make for like-mindedness or similar behavior dispositions. According to Brown and Gilman, solidarity can exist either between individuals who are equal on the power scale, or between nonequals (superior and "old family retainer" or "elderly female servant whom he has known from childhood"). The idea of solidarity between nonequals seems to me to be based on a quaintly optimistic social theory, but fortunately I do not need to make any further reference to it.

For present purposes we assume that Brown and Gilman's categories are broadly acceptable, apart from the detail just mentioned. In specific communities, they will generate particular social configurations, relationships between individuals that are power-asymmetrical or solidary, and between institutions and individuals. They will also generate systems of linguistic items, like the pronouns, by means of which the social distinctions are articulated in discourse. Names and address forms, for example, can predictably be related to the same basic set of sociosemantic distinctions (see Brown and Ford, 1964; Ervin-Tripp, 1972). We shall see below that power and solidarity are articulated in many different parts of linguistic structure, not just obvious, observable closed systems like personal pronouns and titles.

DIRECTIVE AND CONSTITUTIVE LINGUISTIC PRACTICES

In *Language and Control* we drew attention to the two types of linguistic process by which social control is exercised by the powerful; we called them "directive" and "constitutive" (Fowler *et al.*, 1979, pp. 35–36). Directive practices include explicitly manipulative speech acts (Cole & Morgan, 1975; Searle, 1969) such as commands, requests, and proclamations, and interpersonal practices which, while not speech acts, nevertheless carry clearly recognized social meanings in the area of power, like the pronominal usages just discussed. Directive linguistic practices are very clearly visible in face-to-face conversation, especially in genres of discourse that are directly implicated in the power structure, such as interviews (Fowler *et al.*, 1979, Chap. 4), and in written official discourse directed to a larger community (1979, Chap. 2). There is nothing more to be explained about directive practices here; they will reappear in the linguistic checklist below.

Constitutive practice needs a little more comment. Its basis is the idea of the social construction of reality introduced above. In this case, what are being constructed are the institutions, roles, and statuses that preserve the hierarchic structure of society, guarding the exploitive opportunities of the ruling classes and keeping the lower orders in voluntary or involuntary subservience. The role of language in this is to continuously articulate ideology, to insist on systems of beliefs that legitimate the institutions of power. Language shares this task with other semiotic systems (dress, the arts, sport, decor, etc.), but it is the most important system of signs in society, so richly impregnated is it with conventional meanings (cf. Barthes, 1967).

There is not enough space to explain in detail here how language constructs ideology, but the basis of the mechanism may be mentioned and illustrated at the level of vocabulary. One of the fundamental principles of modern linguistics, enunciated by Ferdinand de Saussure (see 1974 edition), is that linguistic signs are arbitrary: There is no essential connection between ideas or things outside language and the words that designate them. Saussure and others (Leach, 1964; Sapir, 1949; Whorf, 1956) have assumed that this semiotic arbitrariness allows different cultures to chop up 'the world' into unpredictably variable conceptual categories. Certainly semiotic arbitrariness is a precondition for differences in the way the world gets coded. In support of this claim, the difficulties of translating between languages and the marked differences between languages in particular areas of vocabulary such as kinship terminology and color terminology have been cited. In the light of recent psycholinguistic research, color terminology turns out to be a bad example for the thesis of linguistic relativity: Some colors are more nameable than others, apparently because the way in which human beings are biologically equipped to perceive color makes some colors more salient than others. These nameable colors are examples of natural categories that are very likely to be coded in different languages; other natural categories have been proposed in the fields of shapes, dimensions, directions, logical categories (see Clark & Clark, 1977, Chap. 14). As far as natural categories are concerned, then, the terminology is still arbitrary, but the concepts named are ones that arise necessarily because of the way human beings are constructed. The vast remainder of the vocabulary, however, is fully arbitrary in the Saussurean sense that meanings are not natural but rather chopped out of the flux of experience according to the needs of the community of speakers.

Thus the vocabulary of a language could be considered a kind of lexical map of the preoccupations of a culture. Whatever is important to a culture is richly lexicalized: Detailed systems of terms develop for the areas of expertise, the features of habitat, the institutions and relationships, and the beliefs and values of a community. Possessing the terms crystalizes the relevant concepts for their users; using them in discourse keeps the ideas current in the community's consciousness, helps transmit them from group to group and generation to generation. In this way ideology is reproduced and disseminated within society—ideology in the neutral sense of a worldview, a largely unconscious theory of the way the world works accepted as commonsense (see Fowler, 1981, Chap. 1).

As we shall see below, it is not only lexical processes that are responsible for articulating ideology: Syntactic structures such as transitivity (see Trew, 1979a, 1979b) and various syntactic transformations (Fowler *et al.*, 1979) may articulate social meanings, and even features of pronunciation are value laden.

IDEOLOGY IN SOCIOLINGUISTIC VARIETIES

The above argument for the reality-constituting power of language concurs with M. A. K. Halliday's theory of "language as social semiotic" (to quote the title of one of his books, 1978). In many respects, Hallidayan systemic–functional linguistics is the most suitable for our purpose (see also Halliday, 1978; Kress, 1976). Halliday claims that "the particular form taken by the grammatical system of language is closely related to the social and personal needs that language is required to serve." (Halliday, 1970, p. 142). Obviously this extreme statement of linguistic functionalism has to be tempered to accommodate natural categories, and the universal constraints on syntactic forms claimed by Chomsky, but Halliday's argument, like mine, is that the major part of linguistic structure can be explained as responding to the needs of the society that uses the language—including, most importantly, the ideological needs referred to in the previous section.

The major finding of dialectology and sociolinguistics is that languages are not unitary: that different groups, and different speech situations, employ different "varieties" of English, Norwegian, and so on (on Norwegian, see Blom & Gumperz, 1972 for an exemplary study). If it is difficult to talk about "varieties" in some cases of sociolinguistic variation, at least we can see that certain linguistic items appear characteristically in certain contexts—*curtilage* in estage agents' house descriptions, *axilla* in doctors' notes on patients (see Hudson, 1980). Sociolinguistic variation is to be expected when a language serves a hierarchically stratified society, further divided into many areas of specialized interest and expertise, like ours. Halliday's claim is that sociolinguistic varieties ('registers')[1] are not simply different sets of linguistic forms but different "ranges of semantic potential" (1978). The language of different groups, and of individuals in different social roles, articulates characteristically different social meanings; and of course this is the case because different groups need to affirm different ideologies, and, as we have seen, linguistic practice is the most powerful way of articulating experience, beliefs, and values.

This notion of differential ideology within a language can easily be related to power and its necessary antithesis, solidarity. A solidary group or dyad is based on "like-mindedness," as Brown and Gilman so acutely express it; in our terms, on community of ideology: a shared system of beliefs about reality. Linguistic practice, the continual speaking and writing of the value-laden sociolinguistic variety, and the repeated utterance of characteristic single linguistic items, affirms and reconstitutes the group's values and the individual's status and roles. By these means, the inner coherence of the group in maintained and its boundaries clearly defined (outsiders do not use the characteristic forms).

---

[1] 'Register' is Halliday's term: It is not equivalent to 'variety', but I do not want to get into a tangle explaining details of terminology unnecessarily.

5 Power

Examples are obvious but far from trivial. Professional groups like lawyers, doctors, sports commentators, and disc jockeys have extensive technical terminologies that are not just the tools of their trade but also badges of identity and hurdles for the novice. The educated middle class is taught formal and complex syntax for writing and reading, whereas others do not achieve these skills. Working-class men express solidarity with their peers, and an ideology of masculinity, by accents that are markedly those of the region and not of the transregional middle-class variety, whereas their wives overcorrect in the direction of middle-class norms, expressing admiration for the values of a higher class and by linguistic practice seeking to achieve the attendant opportunities (Trudgill, 1974).

These expressive practices relate to power because (1) solidarity entails exclusivity, reluctance to admit to a subcommunity whose values are prized; (2) variety-differentiated groups are not simply horizontally distinct, but also vertically stratified: They are tied to economic and constitutional circumstances that confer power and opportunity differentially. A lawyer earns more money than a laborer, is authorized to intervene in the latter's affairs, has greater skill and opportunity to promote his own interests in public, and so on. Language—the mysterious jargon of the law, the elaborate syntax—is an important instrument in maintaining the power differential between the two classes, the authority of the one and the powerlessness of the other.

The power advantage enjoyed by the professional classes (doctors, lawyers, teachers, etc.) is linguistically managed both by directive devices (naming, commands, etc.) and by constitutive structures. Here the linguistic construction of ideology works toward having the realities of the two classes accepted as natural, unchangeable. Lawyers and laborers speak differently because they occupy different worlds, and in order that they should continue to occupy different worlds. It is to the advantage of the lawyers that linguistic practice manages the reproduction of this situation: so there is an affirmation of the rightness of distinct worldviews. Of course from my point of view this has to be regarded as an undesirable situation and one that a critical linguist ought to expose.

Finally, the most massive and pervasive linguistic practice working to maintain power differentials is the imposition of ideology by official and public institutions. The French Marxist theorist Louis Althusser has identified the instruments of this process: what he calls "ideological state apparatuses" such as the church, the law, education, which, along with "repressive state apparatuses" (the armed forces, the police), work to reproduce the existing power structure (1971). The ideological state apparatuses have the function of legitimating the existence and behavior of the ruling authorities. They perform this function by bathing society in official discourse: laws, reports, parliamentary debates, sermons, textbooks, lectures. In this practice the state-controlled agencies are happily joined by commercial enterprises that benefit from acquiescent public attitudes: banks, estate agents, manufacturers, and especially concerns that control the dissemination of ideas—publishers of books, magazines and newspapers, radio and television companies. All these are specialists in the production of ideological discourse, working in language, visual images, behavioral sign systems such as dance and sport. This discourse functions in exactly the constitutive fashion described earlier: By constructing and reiterating certain selected signs, it insists upon a set of concepts that make up a certain reality—one that is favorable to the groups for whom the ideology is constructed. These processes have been identified and attacked in many studies of advertising, political language, and news reporting: Orwell's trenchant expositions in *1984* (1949/1959) and "Politics and the English Language" (1946/1960) are well known and suggestive pioneering commentaries. There has been a flood of popular writings on the media following the example of Orwell, but it is only recently, with the maturity of semiology and linguistics, that we have begun to be able to analyze with some precision the sign structures that can present warped versions of reality (Barthes, 1972; Trew, 1979a, 1979b; Williamson, 1978).

LINGUISTIC CHECKLIST

So far, there have been few studies of language concentrating on its implication in the power structure of society. (Some sociolinguistic studies of other aspects of discourse may, with caution, be reinterpreted to shed light on language and power.) Ideally we need a series of studies of the linguistic practice of power in different genres of discourse; in the meantime, the beginning has to be informal and fragmentary. Often useful at this stage of a developing branch of descriptive linguistics is an informal checklist of items, or categories of structure, that seem to figure frequently in the practices under investigation. The checklist is designed to direct students' attention toward parts of language that will probably repay close examination. I should emphasize that it has been compiled on the basis of my own fragmentary observations and reinterpretations of other people's work, and that the structure of the list is not significant—it has no special theoretical status for the linguistics of power. For similar checklists see Fowler, 1981, Chap. 2; Fowler *et al.*, 1979, Chap. 10; Leech and Short, 1981, pp. 75–82.

Lexical Processes

What concepts are furnished with names in the discourse of a particular social group is of the utmost importance, since vocabulary reflects and expresses the interests of the group. Provision of a term for a concept is called 'lexicalization'. Other relevant lexical processes include 'overlexicalization' and 'underlexicalization' (Halliday, 1978, Chap. 9). Overlexicalization is the availability of many words for one concept, and it indicates the prominence of the concept in a community's beliefs and intellectual interests (e.g., words for God in a Christian community). It is a special case of a more general process, the presence in a sociolinguistic variety of extensive sets of lexical items for systems of related concepts: technical jargons, the slangs of in-groups, and the like. Underlexicalization is a converse process: lack of a term that would neatly encode a concept; this is communicatively and socially significant when a speaker laboriously expresses a concept that is not fully in his power by a circumlocution.

Several distinctions between vocabulary items that have been traditionally noticed by stylisticians are of relevance to the topic of language and power. Referentially, words may be abstract (*cognition, democracy*) or concrete (*spade, brick*), general (*food, material*) or specific (*rice, silk*). Etymologically, the origins of words may be foreign (*beige, Angst, semiology*) or native (*read, kinsman*). Morphologically, lexical items may be complex (*revisionism, childishness*) or simple (*apple, red*). It would be broadly true to say that, for each of these oppositions, the first category is associated with more formal settings and relationships, with learning and with institutional power.

Transitivity

This is Halliday's—rather untraditional—term for the kinds of processes and participants that occur in clauses (see Kress, 1976, Chap. 11). A somewhat different analysis of the same phenomena has been proposed by Fillmore (1968), and students might find it useful to adopt aspects of and terms from both theories. Halliday and Fillmore focus on the predicates (usually verbs and adjectives) that communicate action, processes, states, and so on, and the roles performed by the entities participating in these processes (usually designated by nouns). There are some fundamental distinctions made at the level of transitivity, between, for instance, agents deliberately performing actions—*John opened the door* or *John ran*, objects undergoing processes—*The door opened* or *John fell*, instruments being used to effect actions—*A key opened the door*, experiencers undergoing mental states and mental processes—*Alice was sad* or *Andrew listened attentively*, and so on.

Transitivity has in recent years been of increasing interest to students of literary stylistics. Halliday and others have claimed that, in fictional writings, different choices of transitivity structure in clauses will add up to different worldviews, perceptibly different presentations of the world of the fiction (Cluysenaar, 1976, pp. 90–92; Fowler, 1977, pp. 103ff; Halliday, 1971; Leech & Short, 1981, Chap. 6). A predominance of, say, agent-action structures or of experiencer-mental processes will give rise to a characteristic perception of the fictional world as, perhaps, a world of controlled activity or an introspective, reflective world, respectively. But there is no reason to believe that these effects of transitivity are restricted to literary fictions. They are in fact a fundamental part of the linguistic constitution of reality; therefore they contribute to the formation of relations and differentials of power. (For preliminary studies see Fowler et al., 1979, Chaps. 2, 6, 7.)

In analyzing transitivity, it is important to note not only what roles of participants go with what predicates, but also what kinds of entities are categorized as performing certain roles. For instance, a newspaper reporting street disturbances might implicitly blame the young people of the area by consistently characterizing them as agents while exculpating the police by not attributing agency to them. Or a government might play down its responsibility by sheltering behind abstract terms used as pseudoagents: ***Circumstances*** *dictate the raising of taxes* thoroughly mystifies the practice of power.

Syntax

Traditional stylistics assumes that alternative syntactic phrasings are available to express essentially the same meaning, with perhaps minor but stylistically significant variations of focus, perspective, or emphasis (see Leech & Short, 1981, Chaps. 1, 4 and Refs.). This view may be supported by the early version of transformational–generative grammar; it is very difficult, however, to give a precise theoretical linguistic characterization of this insight. It seems, nevertheless, to be one of the necessary main working assumptions of the sociolinguistics of language and power. My invented example *Circumstances dictate the raising of taxes* mystifies not only by the pseudoagency of *circumstances,* but also by the syntactic options taken in the remainder of the sentence. In this example, the salient feature is the deletion of nouns designating participants: *dictate* has no object, *raising* no subject, *taxes* is not linked to any specification of who is taxed. It is very easy to imagine syntactic paraphrases that would spell out the participants, for example, *Circumstances dictate that we should raise your taxes,* without altering the statement substantially—and equally easy to imagine why a government would prefer the nonspecifying syntax.

It is impossible to treat all the relevant areas of syntactic variability here. I map out three broad categories and mention some important structures in each.

Deletion. There are numerous conventions for leaving out parts of constructions. In *ellipsis,* a truncated second sentence relies for its interpretation on the implication that some words from a preceding sentence are relied on to complete the meaning (Halliday & Hasan, 1976, Chap. 4):

> *Who are you talking about?*
> *[I'm talking about] John.*
> *Where did he go?*
> *[He went] to the station.*

Elliptical styles are clearly linked to ranges of sociolinguistic values (different according to context): these include brusqueness, emphasis (power) and intimacy, shared knowledge (solidarity).

Two sociolinguistically important constructions that permit deletion are nominalization and passive. Nominalization is a rendering of the content of a verb in the form of a noun: *raising* is an example in the sentence invented earlier. Nominalizations are endemic in authoritarian discourse of all kinds: official publications, academic writing, legal language: **Failure** to display this notice will result in **prosecution, Nominalization is a rendering**. . . . Nominalizations have two ideologically practical consequences. First, they are a source of new nouns, codings of experience that can be transmitted to the appropriate social groups by propaganda or education. Second, they permit deletion of both agency and modality (words like *must, shall:* see below), thus making mysterious the participants, obligations, and responsibilities spoken of by the discourse. Passive permits agent-deletion, though not deletion of modality, so it is possible to fail to specify the cause of an event—*John was murdered*. Passives and nominalizations are prominent, and interact, in varieties of language that practice an ideology of impersonality, such as scientific writing and constitutional documents (see Fowler & Kress, 1979, Chap. 2).

Sequencing. A passive allows a different ordering of participant nouns than its active equivalent: *Brutus killed Caesar → Caesar was killed by Brutus*. It is one of a number of reordering transformations that are used to determine the order in which information is released to an addressee, and to focus attention on topics of relatively great importance. Topical importance may be signaled by taking a noun phrase out of its normal position and placing it in an unusual and therefore especially noticeable position, for instance an object noun phrase at the beginning of a sentence: *Fords I find particularly reliable*. Interruptions of sequence by parenthetically inserted phrases are also worth studying. All of these facilities for syntactic reordering are strictly speaking rhetorical; that is, devices for manipulating the addressee's attention.

Complexity. In popular attitudes and in sociolinguistics, syntactic complexity has traditionally been seen as related to social distinctions involving power and prestige. For example, Basil Bernstein's well-known and controversial theory of restricted and elaborated speech codes imputes syntactic complexity to the middle class and simplicity to the working class (Bernstein, 1971). This theory is so loosely and tendentiously formulated that it offers no useful basis for further work. But there is no doubt that complex syntax is a property of the discourse of knowledge and authority.

Syntactic complexity can be crudely measured in words per sentence, but it is much more revealing to study what kinds of clauses and phrases occur in what relationships. An important fundamental distinction is between subordination and coordination of clauses. A high ratio of subordinate clauses per sentence implies complexity of logical relationships among the clauses that modify one another; coordination (*and . . . and, then . . . then*) implies a sequence of separate propositions all of the same kind. There is an old distinction between hypotactic and paratactic styles founded on subordination and coordination, respectively: The latter is traditionally associated with naive or primitive modes of discourse, for instance, medieval chronicles, children's storytelling, simple descriptive language. Complexity of noun phrases in terms of what and how many premodifiers and postmodifiers occur is also an index of stylistic and cognitive complexity.

Modality

The term 'modality' subsumes a range of devices that indicate speakers' attitudes to the propositions they utter, and to some degree to their addressees. These attitudes fall into the areas of validity—the speaker expresses greater or less confidence in the truth of his propositions; predictability—the future events referred to are more or less likely to happen; desirability—practical, moral, or aesthetic judgments; obligation—speaker's judgment that another person is obligated to perform some action; permission—speaker allows addressee to perform some action. The connection of these last two modal meanings with power is obvious, but the first three are also significantly implicated: Frequent and confident judgments of validity, predictability, and (un)desirability are an important part of the practices by means of which claims to authority are articulated and legitimated authority is expressed.

Modality is signified in a range of linguistic forms: centrally, the modal auxiliary verbs *may, shall, must, need,* and others; sentence adverbs such as *probably, certainly, regrettably;* adjectives such as *necessary, unfortunate, certain.* Some verbs, and many nominalizations, are essentially modal: *permit, predict, prove; obligation, likelihood, desirability, authority.*

The other side of the coin is the modality of deference. An inferior addressing a superior has many constructions available for signaling deference, lack of overconfidence, acquiescence: softeners such as *sort of, you know;* tentative and unconfident use of past tense—*I was wondering if . . . ,* tag questions—*The gallery opens at ten, doesn't it?,* rising intonation patterns signaling unassertiveness, and so on (see Halliday in Kress, 1976, Chap. 13; Lakoff, 1975.)

Speech Acts

J. L. Austin and J. R. Searle have shown how utterances not only communicate propositional meanings but also achieve actions through speech: promising, requesting, commanding, warning, and more (Austin, 1962; Cole & Morgan, 1975; Searle, 1969). These speech acts work in relation to the communicative contexts in which they are uttered; unless the circumstances are appropriate, they misfire, as when, for example, I appear to promise but promise something my addressee does not desire, or warn when I have not the status relative to my addressee to permit warning. Many of the conditions for the successful performance of speech acts relate to the socially ascribed roles and statuses of speakers and hearers, so it is understandable that speech acts are centrally implicated in establishing and maintaining power relationships.

For some speech acts, utterance of exactly specified words is essential (baptizing, naming ships, etc.), but for others considerable variability in phrasing is possible. Such variations are of the utmost importance for the articulation of power relationships. There are, for example, many finely discriminated forms for making a request, graded according to degrees and nuances of politeness or peremptoriness (see Fowler & Kress, 1979, Chap. 2; Searle, 1975.)

Implicature

The term, introduced by H. P. Grice (1975), refers to unstated propositions "between the lines" of discourse. Grice shows how implicatures are produced, often by apparent breaches of conventions for the cooperative conduct of conversation (e.g., apparently irrelevant remarks that become relevant when interpreted in the light of some unstated proposition). Two points can be made about implicature in this context. First, an implicature is not accidental, but the product of an intentional act. Presumably there are conventions governing who has the "right to implicate" in terms of status and authority. Second, the propositions that are implicated in any context may be consistent with one another and add up to a semantic system, a set of ideological commitments invoked to underpin the discourse—this would be a way in which one speaker imposes an ideology on another. On underlying propositions as a referential basis for discourse, see Labov and Fanshel (1977).

Turn Taking

Schegloff and Sacks and their associates have shown that conversation is not a disorderly free-for-all but an ordered sequence of contributions or turns. There are tacit conventions for the sequencing of turns; for holding the floor, for interrupting, for opening and closing conversations. Quite clearly, the question of who speaks when is closely bound up with power relationships among participants, and the linguistic constructions that control the ordering are well worth studying. Coulthard (1977) gives a clear introduction to these techniques, and to an extension of the analysis to discourse within one power-laden context, the classroom (see Sinclair & Coulthard, 1975).

Address, Naming, and Personal Reference

The exemplary relevance of practices in this area has already been established (above, p. 63 and References); I mention it again here for the sake of completeness.

Phonology

Sounds and sound patterns, unlike, say, pronouns, are intrinsically meaningless; but any linguistic forms can have social values attached to them, and this is certainly the case with phonology. Accent is traditionally and popularly associated with social class: Research by Labov (1972a, 1972b) and Trudgill (1974) shows how closely and predictably the distribution of phonemes correlates with social stratification, and how speakers use phonological forms to constitute themselves as members of certain status-conferring classes.

One accent of British English, "Received Pronunciation," is strongly associated with the ruling classes and with powerful professional groups such as doctors, lawyers, teachers: Received Pronunciation is (but decreasingly) an unacknowledged prerequisite for entry to such professions.

5 Power

A BRIEF EXAMPLE

To show convincingly the relationship between language and power in a given sample of discourse would require a great deal of research and much space for exposition. The difficulty is not in describing the linguistic construction of the texts (though that is a complex skill) but in relating textual structure to social theory and to social context. The fact is that there is no invariant relationship between textual structure and significance in context—you cannot argue that such a structure has such a social meaning but can only describe the text and its context and suggest interrelations. Experienced discourse analysts are aware of tendencies for certain structures and certain contexts to correlate, for example, nominalizations and legal discourse, but this does not affect the principle: Nominalizations prominent in a discourse can signify anything; that is, one cannot "read off" a specific significance by observing a specific structure. The social context of the discourse needs an initially independent description into which the linguistic description is to be reintegrated.

I have taken a shortcut here by treating a piece of discourse the social, economic, and political parameters of which are pretty familiar to anyone who knows a little about the British Health Service and about British newspapers. It is a report in the *Sunday Times,* February 5, 1978, concerning the delays encountered by large numbers of people waiting for surgical treatment in hospitals. It quotes a brief Parliamentary statement of November 22, 1977, by the then Secretary for Social Services, David Ennals, to the effect that only people who do not have an urgent need for surgery have to wait, while "urgent cases" receive prompt treatment. In a piece of "investigative journalism," the *Sunday Times* reanalyzes the statistics on the basis of which the claim was made, interviews a number of politicians, doctors, and others involved, and suggests that the situation is worse than Mr. Ennals claimed: that there is inadequate surgical provision in general, and that patients are waiting long periods for operations though suffering from acute and painful conditions. The connections between this discourse and power differential are clear, once mentioned. Mr. Ennals was at that time a cabinet minister; his words were uttered in the House of Commons and reported in *Hansard* (the official printed record of Parliamentary proceedings); the *Sunday Times* is a respected serious newspaper. Many of the other protagonists are also in positions of great power: surgeons, administrators, politicians. By contrast, the countless elderly patients who must wait years for surgery are profoundly powerless: Ill within an inadequate system, they can do nothing to speed their treatment; only the surgeons have the authority to decide which patients get early treatment, while others die or suffer chronic pain.

The point I want to make about the discourse practice encountered here is that, although the newspaper is ostensibly critical of the validity of Mr. Ennals' claim and explicitly sympathizes with and appears to promote the patients' interests, its language characterizes the patients as inherently powerless and the surgeons and politicians as inherently powerful, and so it tends to reproduce the power differential as if it were natural. This is a very characteristic contradiction in well-intentioned public discourse, and linguistic criticism can be helpful in showing how it comes about.

The layout of the article foregrounds a contrast between claim and reality:

This is how Ennals told MPs the lists are shrinking
Mr. Ennals: In the majority of cases there is little wait if the matter is urgent. That should be recognised. Most of those who are having to wait are non-urgent cases. When a case becomes urgent, it goes to the top of the list.

This report describes the reality—seen through the eyes of surgeons who must take life or death decisions
A cold, bleak Thursday in Northampton. Inside a cramped office at the sprawling 19th century general hospital, surgeon John Chapman is deciding who shall be called in from his waiting list for operations the next week. He scans through 400 or so cards—one for each patient. It is a job as grim and depressing as the weather outside.

"I couldn't even tell you if some of these are still alive," he says. "This chap"—pulling one card from the pile—"he'd be 93 by now and he's been waiting for 3½ years for surgical corrections to waterworks trouble. He's probably in severe discomfort, getting out of bed several times a night to relieve himself. There's always the possibility that a complication might mean I would have to admit him as an emergency."

In the last two or three weeks, emergency cases have squeezed out a significant number of urgent admissions to Northampton General. Even then, some of these have had to wait in casualty while a consultant found a bed by sending another patient home prematurely. "We have literally had to throw people out of the hospital who weren't quite ready to go home in order to cram in another emergency sitting in casualty," says Chapman. "It's ridiculous."

He pulls another card from the pile: a 70-year-old woman who had an emergency colostomy operation 18 months ago (insertion of a bowel outlet in the abdomen). She should have been readmitted 15 months ago for the operation to be reversed. Now Chapman books her down for the week after next.

"The lady hasn't been in great pain, but to cope with a colostomy at her age of life is quite traumatic and she has had to wait 15 months longer than necessary. She is very embarrassed, and even now I can't say categorically I will get her in the week after next."

Chapman picks another card at random. This time it carries a red sticker, telling him that a GP believes the patient now needs "very urgent treatment." It is another elderly patient with a suspected tumour, who goes on to next week's list. [This is about the first one-fourth of quite a long article.]

Mr. Ennals' statement has the characteristic impersonality of official discourse and the characteristic modality of authoritarian discourse. To dispose of modality first, of the seven clauses, five are marked as unquestioned assertions (*is, is, are, becomes, goes*) and two contain modals of obligation (*should be, having to*). There is no equivocation: This is how the situation necessarily is. Impersonality begins with the pseudolocative *in the majority of cases*, which mystifies a set of complex relationships between patients, their illnesses, and their official medical histories by expressing these relationships as a single locative phrase, a phrase that is pointless here as far as the literal meaning of *in* is concerned, but which serves in this register of officialese to obscure relationships that are embarrassing to the discourse. But the main vehicle of impersonality is nominalization. Patients and their predicaments are coded in the highly abstract words *case, wait, matter,* and *list*. The treatment of *case* is particularly striking. This word is specifically associated with the context of medical records, but that conventional association does not mitigate the rather unpleasant fact that it is an extremely impersonal expression for referring to an individual suffering from an illness so severe that it requires surgery; the highly general *matter* for the illness works in the same way. To return to *case,* it is foregrounded by three repetitions in a text of only 42 words and finally replaced by the inanimate pronoun *it,* thus achieving a remarkable transformation of a human individual into a depersonalized object. I am suggesting that impersonality of style works as depersonalization of reference to people here; and this is one of the principal ideological features carried by the language of the main text: Though the waiting patients receive gestures of sympathy, they are dehumanized by the language and coded in powerless roles in clause structure.

In the main text, some of the linguistic features that contribute to mediation of this power asymmetry are the lexical classification of participants, their characteristic roles in clause structure, and the types of predicates they accompany.

The noun phrases that refer to the category of patients (and marginally, their families), excluding anaphoric pronouns, are as follows. I have arranged them in an order that reflects my intuitive judgment of how *individuating* they are—going from the most specific to the most general and abstract:

Participants A: Patients.   82-year-old Elizabeth Cooper, Miss Cooper, a 70-year-old woman, the lady, this chap, a niece, breadwinner, family, people, these, patient(s) (9 times), case(s) (4 times plus complex noun phrases), urgent cases waiting more than a month, nonurgent cases waiting more than a year, cases awaiting urgent treatment, those who have had to wait for urgent treatment more than a month, those who have had to wait (3), urgent waiting cases, urgent cases (2), nonurgent cases, urgent admissions, emergency admissions, emergency cases, emergency (2), waiting lists, lists (3), waiting figures, lengthening queues, overall total, total figure, number (these quantitative expressions occur several times).

The article is in an important sense about patients, but it treats them in an extremely impersonal way. Only one individual is referred to by name; four other noun phrases refer to specific persons in terms such as *the lady* (dismissive?); two refer to family roles; one refers generally to *people;* the most frequent noun phrase, *patient(s)*, places the people concerned in the category that is most relevant to the article, but note that it is a term that generalizes away from reference to the individual and so contributes to a context in which there are very few personal references. (There is an important point about "naturalness" to be acknowledged here. Although it may seem natural, even inevitable, to speak repeatedly about "patients," given the subject matter of the text, this does not neutralize the stylistic or ideological effect of the usage but merely makes it less noticeable: It is a general term used insistently to refer to individual humans). The next group of noun phrases are based on *case*, and the same observations apply as to *patient*, even more pertinently, since *case* is more general, applying to legal cases and other types of situation. Another notable feature of *case* is the fact that it provides the basis for an extensive technical system for classifying types of patient. In *Language and Control* we noted how easily nominalized forms breed systems of technical lexicalizations in official discourse (Fowler et al., 1979, pp. 40–41). What happens here is that the compound noun phrases based on *case, waiting, list,* and related terms multiply to make very visible the parameters of the classifying system, inserting the structure of the system between the individuals to whom the text refers and the reader's perception of those individuals. As the remainder of the list of patients shows, the purpose of the system is to subject the patients to quantification, to sort them into categories that can be counted: a process which is far removed from writing of the particularities of their conditions.

Participants B: Other. (David) Ennals (10), (John) Chapman (7), (Maurice) McLain (2), Dr. Maurice Miller, Dr. Gerald Vaughan, Secretary for Social Services, the Hon. Gentleman, chairman, the minister, an opposition health spokesman, surgeon(s) (3), consultant (4), a GP, colleagues (2), politicians, (health) administrators (4), doctors, general surgeons, orthopaedic surgeon(s) (2), nurses, anaesthetists, back-up staff, MPs (8), the Commons, Parliament, health authorities, Ennals' department.

Participant list B is quite different from Participant list A. Five individuals are referred to by name, others by a role term such as *chairman, an opposition health spokesman*. There are numerous precise occupational labels for categories of people: *nurses,* and so on. Even the less personal categories, such as *Parliament,* point to sets of specific individuals in such a way that one could discover who those people are, which is not possible with, for instance, *non-urgent cases,* which is an artificial product of the classification system with completely anonymous members.

A differential pattern between A and B emerges when we examine how they relate to predicates. The A nouns often relate to state predicates, including mental states:

1. are alive, is 93, 's in severe discomfort, n't quite ready, n't been in great pain, is very embarrassed, needs, housebound, has given up hope, relies on, could cry.

Class A nouns are agents of actions very rarely, and these are usually actions that affect only the patient himself:

2. getting out, relieve himself, cope with, eases the pain.

Other apparent actions of A really refer to processes relating A to the waiting lists (3, below) and should therefore be grouped with predicates that indicate states and changes of state of the waiting lists (4, below):

3. been waiting, wait, had to wait, goes on to, waiting, having to wait, goes to, wait, wait, on the waiting list, awaiting, had to wait, waits, have been waiting.
4. number of A down/up/decreasing (many references), lengthening queues of A, on his list, rise in number of A.

Class A nouns are also the objects of actions of which B nouns are agents; sometimes in passive constructions:

5. be called in, admit A, squeezed out A, sending A home, throw A out, cram in A, be readmitted, books A down, gets A in, take A, marked for, cut A, reduce A, decides A, promised A, told A.

A telling list. Some of the verbs designate violent physical actions: *squeezed out, cut*. Though a sympathetic reader might excuse these because they are used metaphorically, the words and their connotations *are* in the text, and some are not metaphorical (*throw out, cram in*): The worldview of the *Sunday Times,* and of the surgeons from whom these words are quoted, accepts that patients can be subjected to violent physical manipulation.

As might be expected, B predicates are much more active, including the actions just mentioned, the physical manipulations by John Chapman of his card index, and other activities:

1. call in, scans through, pulling from, admit, found, sending home, throw out, cram in, pulls from, books A down, get A in, picks, take A, set ourselves, spending, dealing with, spend, share.
2. speech acts: says, say, answering, told, declared, added, assure, present a picture, misled, told, say, told, explained, asked, explain, told, asked, said, said, points out, guarantee, promised.
3. mental processes (rather than states) involving judgment or reflection: deciding, believes, inferred, was selective, chose, compared, inferred, identify, thought, expect, seek consolation, believe, decides.

Mere states are few: *quietly indignant, depressing.* Finally, B nouns are almost never objects of actions: rarely and self-pityingly, MPs are misled, surgeons are cajoled.

The picture emerges of a large number of specific surgeons, politicians, administrators, and the like who are being active and vociferous, if ineffectual; and of countless anonymous patients who have no opportunity for action or even personal recognition. The latter are, linguistically, on the receiving end of official actions, but all that happens to them is that they get classified and quantified. I do not think that this is quite the story that the *Sunday Times* wished to tell: But in writing about the inadequacy of the system, the text uses language that strongly encodes a power differential between the classes of participants.

Two further points can be made about this analysis, in conclusion. First, I have concentrated on only part of the linguistic structure of the text, albeit the important areas of lexicalization and transitivity. Other aspects also deserve attention in a full characterization of the discourse: Here it would be particularly valuable to look at modality, at the syntactic structure of sentences, including a more thorough analysis of nominalizations, and at the etymologies of words and the sociolinguistic registers with which vocabulary items are associated. No doubt my reactions to this text were partly influenced by features other than the ones I analyzed explicitly. It is worth emphasizing that, though some features may be especially informative in a given text and context, the character of discourse is the product of linguistic organization at all levels.

Finally, it is no accident or rarity that this text is an example of the indirect and contradictory way in which discourse can constitute an ideology, in this case an ideology of power. Although the writer of the article would doubtless claim that he has exposed a hospital system whose inadequate resources seriously underserve the needs of patients, and which desperately requires more funds and procedural reform, his language unwittingly reproduces the attitudes that block reform. This conventional middle-class discourse, quite ordinary in its stylistic character, is impregnated with discriminatory assumptions. The general point to be made is that such language is widely current; that it is the standard mode for discussing matters of public concern in serious media contexts. It would take a major, bold, and self-conscious shift of discourse for a newspaper writer to avoid this mold. I would hope that linguistic criticism of the kind illustrated here helps make such shifts possible.

REFERENCES

Althusser, L. (1971). Ideology and ideological state apparatuses. In *Lenin and philosophy* B. Brewster, Trans. London: New Left Books.
Austin, J. L. (1962). *How to do things with words*. London: Oxford University Press.
Bach, E., & Harms, R. T. (Eds.). (1968). *Universals in linguistic theory*. New York: Holt, Rinehart and Winston.
Barthes, R. (1967). (A. Lavers, & C. Smith, Trans.) *Elements of semiology*. London: Jonathan Cape.
Barthes, R. (1972). (A. Lavers, Trans.) *Mythologies*. London: Jonathan Cape.
Berger, P. L., & Luckman, T. (1976). *The social construction of reality*. Harmondsworth: Penguin.
Bernstein, B. (1971). *Class, codes and control* (Vol. 1). London: Routledge & Kegan Paul.
Blom, J.-P., & Gumperz, J. J. (1972). Social meaning in linguistic structure: Code-switching in Norway. In J. Gumperz & D. Hymes (Eds.), *Directions in sociolinguistics* (Chap. 14). New York: Holt, Rinehart and Winston.
Brown, R., & Ford, M. (1964). Address in American English. In D. Hymes (Ed.), *Language in culture and society* (Chap. 26). New York: Harper and Row.
Brown, R., & Gilman, A. (1972). The pronouns of power and solidarity. In P. P. Giglioli (Ed.), *Language and social context* (Chap. 12). Harmondsworth: Penguin.
Clark, H. H., & Clark, E. V. (1977). *Psychology and language*. New York: Harcourt Brace Jovanovich.
Cluysenaar, A. (1976). *Introduction to literary stylistics*. London: Batsford.
Cole, P., & Morgan, J. L. (Eds.). (1975). *Syntax and semantics: (Vol. 3) Speech Acts*. New York: Academic Press.
Coulthard, M. (1977). *Introduction to discourse analysis*. London: Longman.
Dittmar, N. (1976). P. Sand, P. A. M. Seuren, & K. Whiteley, (Trans.). *Sociolinguistics*. London: Edward Arnold.
Ervin-Tripp, S. M. (1972). Sociolinguistic rules of address. In J. Pride & J. Holmes (Eds.), *Sociolinguistics* (Chap. 14). Harmondsworth: Penguin.
Fillmore, C. J. (1968). The case for case. In E. Bach & R. Harms (Eds.), *Universals in linguistic theory* (Chap. 1). New York: Holt, Rinehart and Winston.
Fowler, R. (1977). *Linguistics and the novel*. London: Methuen.
Fowler, R. (1981). *Literature as social discourse*. London: Batsford.

Fowler, R., Hodge, R., Kress, G. R., & Trew, T. (1979). *Language and control*. London: Routledge & Kegan Paul.
Fowler, R., & Kress, G. (1979). Rules and regulations. In Fowler et al., *Language and control* (Chap. 2). London: Routledge & Kegan Paul.
Giglioli, P. P. (Ed.). (1972). *Language and social context*. Harmondsworth: Penguin.
Grice, H. P. (1975). Logic and conversation. In P. Cole & J. Morgan (Eds.), *Syntax and semantics* (Vol. 3) (pp. 41–58). New York: Academic Press.
Gumperz, J. J., & Hymes, D. (Eds.). (1972). *Directions in sociolinguistics*. New York: Holt, Rinehart and Winston.
Halliday, M. A. K. (1970). Language structure and language function. In J. Lyons (Ed.), *New horizons in linguistics*. (Chap. 7). Harmondsworth: Penguin.
Halliday, M. A. K. (1971). Linguistic function and literary style: An inquiry into the language of William Golding's *The Inheritors*. In S. Chatman (Ed.), *Literary style: A symposium* (pp. 330–368). New York and London: Oxford University Press.
Halliday, M. A. K. (1978). *Language as social semiotic*. London: Edward Arnold.
Halliday, M. A. K., & Hasan, R. (1976). *Cohesion in English*. London: Longman.
Hudson, R. A. (1980). *Sociolinguistics*. Cambridge: Cambridge University Press.
Hymes, D. (Ed.). (1964). *Language in culture and society*. New York: Harper and Row.
Kress, G. R. (Ed.). (1976). *Halliday: System and function in language*. London: Oxford University Press.
Labov, W. (1972a). *Language in the inner city*. Philadelphia: University of Pennsylvania Press.
Labov, W. (1972b). *Sociolinguistic patterns*. Philadelphia: University of Pennsylvania Press.
Labov, W., & Fanshel, D. (1977). *Therapeutic discourse*. New York: Academic Press.
Lakoff, R. (1975). *Language and woman's place*. New York: Harper and Row.
Leach, E. (1964). Animal categories and verbal abuse. In E. Lenneberg (Ed.), *New directions in the study of language* (pp. 23–64). Cambridge, MA: Massachusetts Institute of Technology Press.
Leech, G. N., & Short, M. H. (1981). *Style in fiction*. London: Longman.
Orwell, G. (1959) *1984*. Harmondsworth: Penguin. (Original work published 1949)
Orwell, G. (1960). Politics and the English language. In *Selected Essays*. Harmondsworth: Penguin. (Original work published 1946)
Pride, J. B., & Holmes, J. (Eds.). (1972). *Sociolinguistics*. Harmondsworth: Penguin.
Sapir, E. (1949). *Language, culture and personality*. Berkeley: University of California Press.
Saussure, Ferdinand de. (1974). (Wade Baskin, Trans.). *Course in general linguistics*. London: Fontana.
Searle, J. R. (1969). *Speech Acts*. London: Cambridge University Press.
Searle, J. R. (1975). Indirect speech acts. In J. Cole & J. Morgan (Eds.), *Syntax and Semantics: (Vol. 3) Speech Acts* (pp. 59–82). New York: Academic Press.
Sinclair, J., & Coulthard, M. (1975). *Towards an analysis of discourse: The English used by teachers and pupils*. London: Oxford University Press.
Trew, T. (1979a). Theory and ideology at work. In Fowler et al., *Language and control* (Chap. 6). London: Routledge & Kegan Paul.
Trew, T. (1979b). Linguistic variation and ideological difference. In Fowler et al., *Language and control* (Chap. 7). London: Routledge & Kegan Paul.
Trudgill, P. (1974). *The social differentiation of English in Norwich*. Cambridge: Cambridge University Press.
Whorf, B. L. (1956). *Language, thought, and reality*. Cambridge, MA: Massachusetts Institute of Technology Press.
Williamson, J. (1978). *Decoding advertisements*. London: Marion Boyars.

CHAPTER **6**

Discrimination in Discourse

Mary Sykes

INTRODUCTION

To discriminate is to "set up, or observe, a difference between, distinguish *from* another; make a distinction (-ate against, distinguish unfavourably) observe distinctions carefully" (Concise English Dictionary). The process of discrimination is therefore fundamental to human and social life, since all acts involving selection or choice involve discrimination on the part of the actor. The terms "racial discrimination" or "sex discrimination" as popularly or officially used, draw on the more limited and specific sense of the term discrimination; that is, discrimination against, the act of making a distinction that is less favorable to one party or another. The Race Relations Act of 1968 in Britain, for example, stated that a person discriminates against another if "he treats that other . . . less favourably than he treats or would treat other persons." It is clear also that this specific use of the term "discrimination" is used only to refer to acts rather than to mental processes, and to acts that have demonstrably unfavorable consequences for one party as against another, the objects of the act also being human rather than other animate or inanimate objects.

In order to demonstrate that an act of discrimination against a racial or ethnic group has occurred, three things need to be shown: (1) that differential treatment of two or more parties has occurred; (2) that this is less favorable to one of the parties; and (3) that the grounds for the differential treatment were racial or ethnic ones (rather than some other characteristic of the party that is relevant to the social act in question). It is by no means a straightforward task to establish that all three conditions exist in a case of suspected discrimination, be it discrimination in the recruitment practices of employers or discrimination in discourse. There are two major problems in demonstrating that racial or ethnic discrimination has occurred in a particular instance. The first is the difficulty of locating an appropriate 'control' against which the treatment of a particular party can be compared. The kind of control needed to demonstrate the third condition above, for example, would be so stringent in some cases that it could only be met under experimental conditions. In fact, the only valid estimates of the incidence of discrimination in Britain have been achieved through specially constructed situation tests approximating experiments (Daniel, 1968; Smith, 1977.). The difficulty of inferring the existence of the third condition in naturally occurring social acts has been a major stumbling block in the administration of Britain's antidiscrimination legislation. The difficulties are no less in examining discrimination in discourse. To some extent they are made greater by the relative absence in discourse of analogous events to the institutionalized and regularized practices of job recruitment or the letting and selling of accommodation, each of which may provide opportunities for comparing the treatments given to a number of different parties by the same potential discriminator.

The second problem is of a different kind and relates specifically to the second condition; that is, that the differential treatment be less favorable to one party. In most discussions of racial discrimination, be they academic, legal, or popular, the question of what constitutes favorable or unfavorable treatment is taken to be fairly unproblematic: It is the denial or hindering of access to various legitimate and (presumed to be) universal goals. This assumption of value consensus is occasionally challenged, as when, for example, Muslim parents in Britain began to demand separate single-sex schools for their daughters, which was contrary to the sex-egalitarian tendencies of state education policies. The state's attempt to provide equal educational treatment for all school children of every sex, race, or national origin was regarded by Muslims as less favorable treatment of their minority group, since it impeded the realization of their legitimate religious goals. Similarly, in the analysis of discrimination in discourse, though there are plenty of instances where treatment would be universally recognized as unfavorable (e.g., the use of certain derogatory racial labels), there are also cases where different audiences would fail to agree on whether the treatment of a group was favorable or unfavorable. Their judgment would depend on their view of the world, their ideology, and the evaluative criteria embedded in it. We shall say more about this later and about the problem of control mentioned above. For the moment let us simply note that these two difficulties impose limits on the degree of confidence with which we can bring a verdict of racial or ethnic discrimination in many cases. The tools of linguistic analysis allow us only to identify at most the differential treatment of parties in language, (i.e., the first condition): The rest of the burden of proof (i.e., the establishment of the second and third conditions) must often rely on reasoned argument only.

Before we go on to examine some examples of actual discourse, let us explain what we mean by discrimination in discourse and clear up one possible source of misunderstanding about what the expression refers to. When we speak of discrimination in language, we are not referring to the explicit informational content of utterances—for example, to utterances that have an explicitly hostile, stereotyped, or prejudiced propositional content. What we are referring to is the grammatical form in which the content is expressed and the patterns of lexical choices made by the speaker. Let us use some constructed examples to make the distinction clear:

(1)   *Whites are naturally more intelligent than blacks.*

This statement is simply the expression of a prejudiced attitude. There is nothing in the language used to express this view that is discriminatory between whites and blacks. In contrast,

(2)   *Whites are naturally more intelligent than niggers*

involves differential treatment in the choice of lexical items to denote black and whites. Clearly the utterance satisfies all three conditions of racial discrimination. Consider this example:

(3)   *Black females have the same natural intelligence as white women.*

Here the prejudiced propositional content of the earlier examples is absent, but lexical choice again has resulted in differential treatment of black and white women (assuming the reference is to adults in both cases). We would probably also agree that the use of the term *female* in this case is demeaning, and that this is therefore another case of racial discrimination in discourse. From these examples it can be anticipated that, on occasions, information content may favor a party while the treatment of them in lexical choice or syntax (see below) may be unfavorable (and vice versa). An example of this process with which we are all familiar is when someone is paying lip service to certain attitudes and makes a "Freudian slip," thereby betraying what we then presume (rightly or wrongly) to be their real attitudes.

Discrimination in discourse is not only a matter of lexical choice, though this probably is its most widely recognized form. Here is an example of a 'transformation' that involves differential treatment.

(4)   *Black youths stoned the police.*
        The police were stoned by white youths.

Both sentences provide the same information (except that the stoners are white in one sentence and black in the other). In the second sentence, however, the verb has become passive. This results in two things: First, it removes youths from the prime location in the sentence and thereby switches the emphasis away from them and onto the police, who now take the prime location, defining the topic of the sentence. Second, it distances the youths slightly from their action (stoning) by the insertion of the particle *by*. The importance of the youths as participants in the second sentence, as well as the closeness of their association with their own physical acts, has thereby been slightly diminished compared with the first sentence. This is a case of differential treatment. We might say it is also a case of less favorable treatment of the black youths if we regard stoning police as undesirable behavior. If as a description of an event in which black and white youths were stoning the police, we read,

(5)   *Black youths stoned the police. White youths were also involved in the trouble,*

we would be aware of a very considerable restructuring of the form in which the information about the white youths is presented when compared with that about the black youths. The first sentence contains a transactive verb,[1] of which the blacks are the agents. Causality is unambiguous—the verb denotes a specific action carried out by the agent that affects a second participant, the police. In the second sentence, in contrast, we have a one-participant structure in which white youths are the subjects of a nontransactive verb that denotes no specific actions on their part; we are not told whether they were actors, experiencers, or patients in the "trouble," nor what the processes were making up the trouble. In other words, the second sentence above mystifies the role of white youths in the event by the use of the nonspecific words *involved* and *trouble,* and at the same time their presentation as subjects of a one-participant verb has the effect of removing agency from them. The white youths, then, have been very considerably distanced by the speaker from the process of stoning, unlike the black youths, whom we might therefore claim have been discriminated against in the discourse.[2]

---

[1] A discussion of transactive–nontransactive models and their implications for the presentation of causality can be found in Kress and Hodge (1979, especially Chapter 3).
[2] For a systematic method of identifying the distribution of agency in a piece of discourse, see Trew (1979b).

THE QUESTION OF WHAT CONSTITUTES UNFAVORABLE TREATMENT

Unless a society is characterized by complete value consensus, different hearers of an utterance may disagree as to whether a particular treatment is favorable or unfavorable. The white youths in the example above might feel they had been unfavorably treated if they were members of a peer-group culture in which overt and active opposition to coercive forms of adult authority were highly valued. They might feel their status had been diminished by their assignment to a vague and secondary role in the events. Almost all modern societies, apart from the few remaining small, simple societies, are characterized by varying degrees of value conflict; that is, their value systems comprise a number of competing ideologies with roots and affiliations in different social groups defined on the basis of class, religion, national origin, occupation, sex, age, and so on. Ideologies are sets of ideas or theories about the nature of the world and how it works. They provide explanations for why things are as they are by defining the participants and processes in the social world and the relationships between them, as well as the criteria by which the latter may be evaluated and the means by which they may be changed. Ideologies therefore provide explanatory theories and guides to action: They enable us to make sense of the world, to evaluate it, and to act meaningfully in it. In most societies it is possible to identify a dominant ideology. This is usually reflected in the structure and operation of major state institutions and is often held by a large section of the members of the society. In opposition to this ideology, there frequently emerge very clearly defined, consciously held counter-ideologies, often the property of relatively small groups of politically conscious members seeking substantial change of some kind in the organization of the society.

We are aware of the different ideological affiliations of speakers when they use different words to refer to the same thing; for example, *chairman* versus *chairperson, freedom fighter* versus *terrorist, blacks* versus *niggers, riot* versus *demonstration.* We are also aware that the same word has different meanings, connotations, or referents in different ideologies; for example, *black militant* may be a term of praise or condemnation. Ideological variation, then, in any society means that there will be no agreed upon criterion of favorability or unfavorability in the description of a wide variety of social statuses, social actions, or social processes.

Let us give a couple of examples of the problems that this raises. One of the pieces of discourse we analyze in some detail describes the situation of homeless young blacks in British cities. It is produced by a statutory body set up to promote racial integration, and the aim of the article is clearly to evoke sympathy for the young people concerned and to stimulate appropriate voluntary and state aid. Syntactically the young blacks are presented as having no agency in their own misfortunes or in their petty crimes that bring them into constant conflict with the police. They are portrayed as hapless victims of forces beyond their control. The text would appear to be an example of favorable treatment of a disadvantaged minority and was undoubtedly well intentioned. However, some young blacks, particularly those involved in growing separatist or left-wing movements, would find this kind of presentation demeaning, since it presents them as basically passive, unable to reflect on or control their reactions to circumstance, and lacking independent will. This they might feel is unfavorable treatment, since they claim that their crimes are meaningful and consciously directed political acts against an oppressive white society. Such young blacks might find the generally very pejorative treatment of them (in terms of information content) by some British newspapers less offensive, since, while various undesirable characteristics and behavior traits are attributed to them, syntactically they are at least awarded the status of human actors capable of initiating action and affecting the course of social events. To return to an earlier point, then, the fact of ideological variation means that, strictly, discourse analysis can demonstrate only that a particular type of treatment has occurred, and the question of whether it is discriminatory or not may need to be debated.

EXAMPLE: SYNTACTIC ANALYSIS

We start with a fairly long text in order to show the significance of recurrent patterns of treatment of the various participants in a piece of discourse, and hence the importance of basing conclusions about treatment on whole utterances rather than individual sentences taken out of context. The following is an extract from a monthly magazine cum newsletter produced by the Community Relations Commission (now part of the Commission for Racial Equality), a statutory body set up to promote racial harmony and to advise the government on matters of health, education, and welfare of racial and ethnic minorities in Britain. The article is short and describes the conversion of a house by volunteers to provide temporary homes for black teenagers who are homeless. The extract comes from the first half of the article, where the problem of homelessness is set out.

> The Commons Select Committee on Police and Race Relations concluded that there were approximately three hundred young blacks roaming the streets of

> Birmingham. Homelessness among black youngsters is a growing problem and daily more and more young people, both sexes, become homeless.
>
> Case histories tell the same sad story—young black people find themselves overwhelmed by the problems of individual and ethnic identity. They get into trouble at school and then at work. Finally they find themselves at odds with their parents, and are asked to leave home. They feel rejected on all fronts. They begin to drift from place to place finding consolation only in unfortunate victims like themselves. These youngsters are usually between the ages of fourteen and nineteen and are often the products of broken homes. They are turned out into a complex world where slowly they begin to experience its hostilities. They become embittered and alone; unemployed and therefore become more and more alienated from society. They begin to sleep rough; in daytime they hang around arcades and amusement centres of Soho Road or drift into town in groups to their favourite haunt—the Bull-Ring Centre.
>
> Many of these youngsters drift into petty crime as a means of survival and are sent to remand homes for 'training'. On returning to the community social problems remain unchanged, homelessness is probably even greater, and prospects of employment greatly reduced. (Community Relations Commission, 1974, p. 3)

We focus on just one feature of the discourse, which we feel is particularly important: the attribution of responsibility or blame for the problem of homelessness. This means we must study the patterns of transitivity in the text. Transitivity indicates the relationships between participants and processes and is hence of prime importance in representing causality.[3] We try to show how the syntactic features of this text may have a paradoxical and unintended effect—that of allowing unsympathetic readers to "blame the victim."

Let us begin by listing the human participants identified in the discourse and the frequency of their appearance (in parentheses).

1. Commons Select Committee (1)
2. young blacks (14, plus 4 deleted pronouns in complementary clauses and 3 antecedents of present participles)
3. parents (1)

Young blacks are clearly the focus of this discourse, almost to the exclusion of other human participants. We now examine the nature of their relationship with the various verbs associated with them. In all references to them they are the subjects of verbs—as agents (8), as experiencers (e.g., *feel rejected*) (3), as patients (e.g., *become homeless, are sent to remand homes*) (8), and as the subjects of equatives (2). Blacks are portrayed in active roles, then, in somewhat less than half of their ap-

---

[3] Halliday's (1971) analysis of the patterns of transitivity employed by William Golding in his novel *The Inheritors* provides an illustration of the saliency of transitivity for the creation of a particular "reality."

pearances in the text. On closer inspection we can see that the actions they perform are of a limited kind: They are all nontransactive, involving no other participant than the actor (*roaming the streets* has the appearance of a two participant structure, but *streets* here is a locative rather than an object or affected participant). Their agency in social processes, then, is very circumscribed by these constructions, and hence the opportunity for attributing to them responsibility for events is reduced. Their agency is further minimized by lexicalization: At the level of meaning, many of these active verbs are hardly active at all; for example, *drift* (3), *hang around, sleep rough*. The constructions *get into trouble* and *drift into crime,* as opposed to the possible alternatives of causing or creating trouble and committing crimes, also avoid reference to intentionality in their actions, and this absence of conscious intent is further reinforced by the fact that no mental process verbs (such as thinking, deciding, concluding) are attached to them as actors. They do experience emotional states in their roles as patients and experiencers, but they do not perform mental acts.

The causal role of young blacks in their own misfortunes has been minimized by denying them any significant agency in the processes leading to homelessness and crime. At the same time, however, other possible causal agents or processes have been deleted, obscured, or mystified by a series of transformations and substitutions, which we now consider. As noted earlier, the text identifies only three human participants: Commons Select Committee, young blacks, and their parents. *Case histories* acts as a substitute for social workers (who write case histories), who are thereby excluded from the account. The Commons Select Committee and the *case histories* are in any case confined to the role of observers rather than agents in the processes, so we turn our attention to other human participants who may have played a causal role. There are three two-participant transactive verbs in the text that must take human agents. In all three cases, young blacks are the patients, but in all three cases the agents have been deleted through the use of the passive construction.

(6) (young blacks) *are asked to leave home*
(7) (young blacks) *are turned out*
(8) (young blacks) *are sent to remand homes*

In the first example we can readily retrieve parents as the agents (but note how the parents have been distanced from their actions by the construction of the sentence). In the second example we are hard put to identify conclusively the agent(s), or even what it is the young blacks are turned out of. The previous sentence, however, mentions broken homes (referring presumably to the separation of parents), and so we might infer that it is homes they are being turned out of again and that parents are the most likely agents of this process. *Turned out* is a much stronger expression than *asked to leave home,* and it may be significant that the speaker has used this expression only at a very considerable distance from the implied agents, parents. It would seem that though forced to acknowledge the causal role of parents in the process of homelessness, the speaker has a strong desire to protect them from attributions of blame.[4] If we look at the third example of the two-participant verbs listed above, we find that the agents cannot be retrieved by reference to any antecedents. Instead we have to rely on our knowledge of who has the legal power to send young people to remand homes (though, as the procedures have changed periodically, this is somewhat esoteric knowledge). The agents are a magistrate and a social worker, but their decision is the outcome of a long investigative and consultative process involving many participants such as police, complainants, witnesses, social workers, teachers or employers, parents or guardians, and so on. None of these agents appears in the text.

Some other features of the text that serve to obscure participants other then young blacks are the following mystifications: *get into trouble **at school** and then **at work*** and *feel rejected **on all fronts***; Here, instead of participants we are provided with locatives. Another substitution for human participants is *a complex world . . . its hostilities.* This is extremely vague and verges on the ungrammatical. As well as asking whose hostilities, we might also ask what sort of hostilities—physical aggression, social rejection, racial discrimination? The phrase *become . . . unemployed* does not tell us whether they are sacked by their employer, left voluntarily, or simply failed to find work after leaving school. (The adjective *unemployed* is interesting in its syntactic derivation; it is the result of a number of transformations, which students might like to trace for themselves.)

There is only one example of a two-participant transactive verb in the text for which the agent has not been deleted. Again, young blacks are the patients and the agent is nonhuman and abstract:

(9)   (young blacks are) *overwhelmed by the problems of individual and ethnic identity.*

Since this is the only case in the text of a specified agent affecting any other participant, then syntactically *problems of individual and ethnic identity* has been accorded considerable causal significance. Its position, close to the start of the account, enhances its causal power, since in the

---

[4] Trew (1979a) provides a powerful analysis of how agent deletions may be used by newspaper reporters to aid them in "dealing with awkward facts."

absence of explicit references to causal connections between events in the text the sequencing of information becomes important in suggesting causality. In a chronological sequence, as this seems to be for the most part, consequences follow causes, hence *getting into trouble at school and at work, finding themselves at odds with their parents,* and so on may be understood by the reader as consequences of the identity problems, given that there is a marked scarcity of other participants on whom to pin the blame. The phrase *individual and ethnic identity problems* is rather vague in its denotation. We might want to ask questions about the origins of the identity problems (e.g., are they the result of racial discrimination and rejection?), but the speaker assumes no explanation is necessary. Perhaps he or she assumes we will "read in" the role of racial discrimination. But it does not appear in the text, and therefore as it stands young blacks are overwhelmed by a characteristic of themselves, that is, their identity problems, and this seems sufficient to start off the whole sequence of "trouble," homelessness, and crime. Given the fact that other agents have been ignored or obscured, young blacks, as the primary focus of the text, may be blamed by default. The speaker has, however, avoided attributing any active part in the process to them, and so the problem may come to be seen as one that results not from what young blacks do but from what they are; that is, young blacks equal identity problems plus broken homes, which leads to social problems. This account of homelessness allows or even encourages the reader to blame the victim, though this was clearly not the intention of the producer of the account.

It might be argued at this stage by the unconvinced that this emphasis on syntactic relations is being overplayed and that readers of the article on homelessness would not be left with the message that young blacks are primarily to blame for the problem (with a little help from their parents), and that in any case any intelligent reader can retrieve most of the deleted or obscured agents in the text. While this is true, the impact of this text would nonetheless be very different if all the implied participants had been identified on the page. We would have had social workers, teachers and pupils, employers and workmates, police, magistrates, and possibly many others (*on all fronts*). At the very least, the mere presence of these named actors would dilute the concentration of references to young blacks, thus interrupting the clear flow of the sequence: young blacks → identity problems → homelessness → crime. More important, though, if agents were specified, readers might be more likely to ask questions about their role in the process. For example, if the second paragraph began "social workers tell the same sad story," then readers might be prompted to ask why social workers were not doing something about the problem rather than just telling stories; or if young blacks got into trouble "with teachers," then questions might be asked about teachers' competence in accepting or handling cultural differences in the classroom. One might ask about the well-documented discrimination by employers and police if the latter two had appeared in the text. We suggest that most readers do only a limited amount of extra work in reading beyond what is printed (unless they are linguists or the discourse has some referent that is of personal concern). In this text much of that work may be absorbed by retrieving agents, leaving little time as the eye passes over the words to raise questions about their roles and whether they may in one way or another have exacerbated or failed to intervene in the generation of the problem.[5]

The text constitutes an example of what we have decided to call the "welfarization" of a social issue, that is, the conversion of an issue that might be couched in terms of the denial of equal rights into a welfare problem—one that focuses on the existence of special needs among some people and the necessity for action directed at them rather than at the causes of their disadvantaged position. We call this process "welfarization" since its outcome strongly resembles the modes of conceptualization and description common to established welfare institutions in which the emphasis tends to be on clients' "needs" rather than their rights. A major criticism leveled at the Community Relations Commission by some black leaders is that the Commission spends too much of its time and resources on welfare work with blacks and not enough time combating the prejudice and discrimination of whites. What we are suggesting in addition is that the Commission also tends to convert issues of basic rights and the denial of equal opportunity into issues of welfare needs. The transformation of the issue is achieved subtly, simply by a change of emphasis away from the agents and processes producing disadvantage or inequality to the manifestations of that disadvantage in the form of "special needs" and to appropriate ways of meeting the needs. We have seen in the preceding analysis how this process operates syntactically. As to whether this discourse constitutes racial discrimination, two points may be made: one concerning the possible long-run consequences of the discourse and the other concerning what we count as racial discrimination.

---

[5] This point concerning the effect of agent deletions on readers' perceptions must remain speculative, since to my knowledge there has been no experimental work done on this specifically. However, much experimental work has been done by psycholinguists and others on readers' and hearers' speed of comprehension and recall of information when other grammatical variables in discourse are manipulated. A summary of some of this work can be found in Clark and Clark (1977, Chaps. 2–4), and an example of such work is Bates, MacWhinney, McNew, and Devescor (1982).

In terms of the consequences of welfarization, this kind of approach to race-relations issues may be damaging to the interests of ethnic minorities in the long run. Given progressive government cutbacks in welfare expenditure along with growing unemployment and antagonism toward blacks among the white working class, then constant demands by the Commission for extra resources to be diverted towards ethnic minorities for their "special needs" is unlikely to be met with sympathy by the general public. In fact, it is likely to further bolster the myth that ethnic minorities are a drain on the country's resources and so add strength to the arguments of neofascist groups such as the National Front and British Movement. Demands for special treatment can easily be interpreted as demands for preferential treatment, and further hostility may be the result.

Whether or not the treatment of young blacks in this discourse constitutes racial discrimination is problematic. The speakers desire to absolve young blacks from all direct responsibility for their plight resulted in an image of them as aimless and incapable of self-determination, thereby degrading their status as conscious human actors. But this (unfavorable) image is not restricted to blacks: It is a common feature of the welfare paradigm and it is just as frequently applied to white juvenile delinquents, the homeless, the unemployed, battered wives, and others by the various welfare agencies concerned. Blacks are therefore not being treated more or less favorably than would be whites in this situation. They have simply been assimilated into a preexisting mode of description that is commonly employed to describe welfare clients. (Whether or not they have been discriminated against in terms of their selection for this treatment would be very difficult to answer.

EXAMPLE: SEMANTIC ANALYSIS

In the next text the question of discrimination is much less problematic. The treatment is clearly unfavorable and is of a kind most unlikely to be applied to white people in a similar situation (today at any rate) and therefore may be fairly confidently identified as racial discrimination. To provide a contrast to the preceding analysis, we focus mainly on lexicalization, even though there is much in the syntax of the discourse that is interesting.

The discourse is a 1968 speech by the English politician Enoch Powell, and the subject is immigration to Britain from the New Commonwealth countries (mainly India, Pakistan, the West Indies, and parts of Africa). Powell is well known for his outspoken antiimmigration stance and is an advocate of repatriation of black immigrants on the grounds that integration is impossible, the "British way of life" is threatened, and racial strife will be the outcome of continued immigration. His speeches in 1968 earned him a large popular following as well as exclusion from the shadow cabinet of the Conservative Party. The effectiveness of his speeches in rousing popular feeling against black minorities lies not so much in any overtly hostile, accusing, or defamatory propositional content (this is relatively rare in his speeches and usually takes the form of supposed letters from his constituents that he reads out). Rather it lies in his representation of immigrants as an invincibly growing alien wedge gradually taking over large parts of British cities and in some unspecified way recreating " 'in England's green and pleasant land' the haunting tragedy of the United States." The achievement of this image of black immigration constituting a generalized threat for the future is aided by a lexicon and syntax that powerfully dehumanize their referents, representing them as an undifferentiated and faceless collectivity involved in mechanical and inevitable processes such as immigration, growth, and concentration.

We concentrate on two features of the lexicalization that dehumanize people from the New Commonwealth: the overwhelming dominance of the term *immigrant* (and its derivations) in the discourse, which homogenizes its referents, and the use of terms with nonhuman associations to refer to both people and the processes in which they are involved.

The Term *Immigrant*

The people who form the subject of the speech are very diverse in terms of their national origins and cultures (they come from India, Pakistan, the West Indies, Hong Kong, Singapore, Kenya, Uganda, and others): Each national group is often also sharply internally differentiated on the basis of class, regional, and political affiliations, and frequently religion and even language. The different groups have had different reasons for emigrating, different intentions with regard to their stay in Britain, and different degrees of familiarity with British culture on arrival. There is no recognition of this diversity in Powell's lexicon. If we count the nouns used to refer to people from the New Commonwealth living in Britain, we find the following frequencies: *immigrants* (14), *immigrant population* (8), *Afro-Asians* (3), *the immigrant* (3), *strangers* (2). There are only two occasions in the speech where Powell uses nationality labels; that is, terms that denote the human and social characteristic of having a nationality rather than merely having participated in a physical activity—immigration. One occasion is in reference to the repatriation policies of other countries, Ceylon and Guyana, where *Indians* and *West Indians* are both mentioned once. (In a sense, this is not a breach of Powell's style, since the homogenizing rule seems to apply only when people enter Britain and not when they emigrate to other countries.) The other occasion in which some diversity is recognized in appellation is in one of Powell's most famous lines, at the end of his speech: "The West Indian or Asian does not, by being born in England, become an Englishman. In law he becomes a United Kingdom citizen by birth; in fact he is a West Indian or an Asian still." The rationale for this breach of the rule is clear.

Apart from these two exceptions, the overwhelming term of reference is *immigrant*. The use of this term is in fact euphemistic; so cohesive is the association in Britain today between race and immigration that *immigrant* in common usage means black or colored immigrant and frequently means just black regardless of whether immigrant or not. That Powell is using the term in this way is indicated by his frequent use of the term *immigrant population* to include black children born in this country (i.e., who have not immigrated), and by his references to the immigrant birthrate, which is only meaningful (given very different rates of the nationalities involved) if the primary concern is with the rate at which the black population as a whole is growing. The term *Afro-Asians* is used in a very revealing way. This kind of hyphenated construction in noun form typically denotes the country of origin and country of settlement of a person, for example, Anglo-Indian (an English person who has lived a long time in India) or Afro-Carribean (a West Indian of African origins). As an adjective it refers to some relationship between two separate parties, for example, Sino–Soviet relations, Franco–Prussian war. When Powell speaks of "one-and-a-quarter million Afro–Asians," he is clearly not using the construction in either of these ways but is using it as a synonym for New Commonwealth people, that is, Asians and people of African descent. The use is deeply insulting, suggesting a kind of mixture; its absurdity as well as its discriminatory nature can be illustrated by imagining the speaker referring to his own parliamentary constituents of Wolverhampton at that time as Anglo-Africans or Afro-English. The absurdity culminates in the use of the term *individual Afro-Asians* later in the speech.

Words with Nonhuman Associations

We use the following extract from Enoch Powell's speech to illustrate some further features of the lexicalization and to analyze his syntax:

> Let us take as our starting point the calculation of the General Register Office that by 1985 there would be in this country 3½ million coloured immigrants and their offspring—in other words that the present number would have increased

between two and three-fold in the next seventeen years—on two assumptions, current rate of intake and current birthrate.

The first assumption is that the rate of net inflow continues at present. It has not indeed diminished since the estimate was made, but I am willing to suppose that, especially with the substantially greater limitations which a Conservative government has undertaken to apply, the rate would be markedly reduced during the period in question. For the purposes of argument I will suppose that it falls at a steady rate from 60,000 in 1968 to nil by 1985. In that case the total in the latter year would be reduced by about half-a-million, that is to 3 million.

I now turn to the second and more crucial assumption, the birthrate.... There are grounds for arguing that the immigrant birthrate is likely to rise during the next two or three decades; for instance the proportion of females must increase as dependents join male workers, so that a given total of immigrant population will yield more family units. (Reproduced in Stacey, 1970, pp. 105–107)

In examining discrimination in lexical choice it is not always the best strategy to focus on those individual items that appear derogatory, since particular usages can often be justified in particular instances. For example, the terms *offspring* and *females* in the passage above might be immediate targets for our analysis because their typical referent is nonhuman, animate. In the case of *offspring,* the speaker's justification might be that the alternative "children" would be inaccurate since some of the children of early immigrants are now adult (in fact a very tiny number in 1967) and that another alternative, "families," would result in confusion over the unit of enumeration. *Females* might be justified on the grounds that it is a nonderogatory term in the context of a discussion of demographic features and one that conveniently denotes both adults and children. Arguments over the discriminatory nature of individual terms in specific contexts, then, can be inconclusive and fairly fruitless. What is often more revealing is to study the range of lexical items actually used in relation to the range of items that the speaker could have used. In this way, any systematic preferences and avoidances in lexical choice can be identified and their significance more readily inferred and convincingly argued. If we carry out this exercise for Powell's speech as a whole, we find that his lexicon for family relationships and generations is a limited one and seems selected on the basis of certain rules. These are the terms and their frequency of use in the speech: *immigrants and their offspring* (2), *the offspring of immigrants* (1), *immigrant offspring* (1), *immigrant and immigrant descended population* (2), *immigrant children* (1), *children born to immigrants* (1), *children who have immigrated* (1), *Asian and West Indian children of school age* (1), *females* (who, as dependents, must be the wives, daughters, or fiancees of the "male workers") (1), *dependents* (2), *male workers* (who must be the husbands, fathers, or fiancees of their dependents) (1), *family units* (2). Terms that are not used are *husbands, wives, mothers, fathers, parents, sons, daughters, families*. The rule governing inclusion or exclusion of items in the speaker's lexicon would appear to be that terms that denote solely the formal, legal, or, as in most of the cases, biological relationships between family members are acceptable, while those which carry, in addition, connotations of individual and affective bonds between family members are avoided. Husband–wife and parent–child bonds carry high value and emotional loading as essentially human and desirable. The speaker's lexicon avoids the attribution of these bonds and relationships to the people he describes and therefore distances the reader both socially and emotionally from them. The speaker's use of the relatively sympathetic term *children* is interesting in this connection. Its use is to some extent a breach of the rule, but one that the speaker finds it hard to avoid since he wishes to discuss the racial composition of urban schools (the word appears four times in the space of two sentences, and these are the sole occasions of its use). The breach is made somewhat less serious, however, by the use of constructions in which the valued social relationship of parent–child denoted by the possessive is absent. We do not see the constructions *immigrants and their children* or *the children of immigrants*, which become "permissible" constructions when combined with the less sympathetic term *offspring*.

Another feature of lexicalization observable in the extract is the tendency of the speaker to use terminology more usually reserved for inanimate objects in describing people from the New Commonwealth and the processes in which they are involved, for example, *current rate of intake, the rate of net inflow, the total, a given total of immigrant population, yield, family units*. It is almost the language of industrial or agricultural production processes. This image is enhanced by the reference elsewhere to the "reservoir" of dependents who have not yet entered the country, suggesting the act of immigration is determined by the natural law of gravity rather than being the product of human will. Another way in which human intentionality on the part of immigrants is minimized is through the use of constructions that, while they describe the processes in which immigrants are involved, allow the elimination of these human participants from quite lengthy passages, as, for example, in the second paragraph of the extract. This is achieved mainly by two means, sometimes in combination: the frequent use of the terms *number(s), total(s), proportion(s), rate(s)* as the subjects of sentences without restatement of their referents for lengthy periods; and the use of nominalizations with agent deletions (e.g., *inflow*) in preference to presentations of immigrants as the subjects of active verbs. Here is an example of some of these syntactic processes from a later point in the speech: *The very growth in numbers would increase the already striking fact of dense geographical concentration.* Growth in numbers and *geographical concentration* as nominalizations also represent the outcome of many mental and physical acts on the part of immigrants and other participants. The phenomenon of geographical concentration, for example, is the result of an interplay between employers' demands for certain types of labor, the discriminatory practices of landlords, estate agents, local authority housing departments, building societies, the preferences of individuals to work with and or live near their kin and compatriots, and so on, all of which were (at the time of Powell's speech) and still are changing in various directions. The frequent use of nominalizations such as *immigration, inflow, growth,* and *concentration,* therefore (with their associated agent deletions), have the effect of both minimizing the role of New Commonwealth people as active conscious human agents and obscuring the complex and changing processes behind the outcomes they describe. This tends to misrepresent the essential contingency of these outcomes, and to suggest a certain mechanical inevitability about the association between people from the New Commonwealth and the processes of immigration, growth, and concentration. The behavior of these people then appears to be governed by natural laws, so that we find *areas where the immigrant population is spreading and taking root* as opposed to the human equivalent of "putting down roots" (this, we feel, is another example of an expression that would not be used by the speaker with reference to white immigrants, and hence is racially discriminatory). The apparently invincible nature of this natural process both maximizes the element of threat and at the same time justifies mechanical interventions such as stopping the "inflow" and reducing the size of the population by repatriation, policies that in reality frequently have tragic consequences for the individuals and families caught up in them.

CONCLUSION

We have examined two pieces of discourse very different in their intent and effect, and we have noted how discourse produced with sympathetic intent may be regarded as unfavorable in effect, as in the Community Relations Commission discourse. The second example, Enoch Powell's speech, we feel was racially discriminatory in the sense that it contained lexical items that would not be used by the speaker to refer to members of his own racial group. Many of the lexical items had strong nonhuman associations reminiscent of earlier colonial beliefs in which blacks were regarded as a subhuman species. To the extent that one is seeking to identify any specific language of racial discrimination with its own special grammar or lexicon, this might constitute an example of it. Examples of this type of discourse are, however, relatively rare in Europe today except in the literature of neofascist groups. For the most part, racial minorities are simply vulnerable to the same range of unfavorable linguistic treatments accorded to other social minorities or out-groups such as women, welfare clients, and strikers. They may be presented as irrational, unreasonable, passive, overdependent, vicious without provocation, depending on the circumstance and the ideology of the speaker, and like all out-groups they are vulnerable to stereotyping and homogenizing treatment.

We noted earlier how the fact of ideological variation makes the determination of the favorability or unfavorability of the treatment problematic in some cases. However, we offer here one minimum criterion for the evaluation of treatment: Any lexical or syntactic patterns that fairly systematically deny their human subjects the normal range of specifically human attributes should be regarded as degrading, regardless of the intent of the speaker. By human attributes we mean those characteristics that are presumed to elevate human beings above the rest of the animal world—consciousness and the capacity for meaningful social action, plus the infinite variety of social statuses and social relations that stem from these. We suggest that treatment in discourse that systematically implies mechanistic behavior, inability to reason or to act meaningfully, and that therefore denies the mediation of consciousness in behavior or affective states dehumanizes its subjects and should be regarded as unfavorable treatment, as should any discourse that treats large numbers of people as though they were homogeneous and hence denies normal human social variety. Both of the speakers whose discourse we have analyzed dehumanize their subjects in different ways and to different degrees, in the one case in order to render them harmless and in the other to evoke threat.

REFERENCES

Bates, E., MacWhinney, B., NcNew, S., & Devescor, A. (1982). Functional constraints on sentence processing: A cross linguistic study. *Cognition, 11,* 245–299.

Clark, H. H., & Clark, E. V. (1977). *Psychology and language.* New York: Harcourt Brace Jovanovich.

Community Relations Commission (1974). Harambee. *Community Relations Journal* February/March, p. 3.

Daniel, W. W. (1968). *Racial discrimination in England.* Harmondsworth: Penguin.

Halliday, M. A. K. (1971). Linguistic function and literary style. In S. Chatman (Ed.), *Literary style: A symposium* (pp. 330–368). New York and London: Oxford University Press.

Kress, G., & Hodge, R. (1979). *Language as ideology*. London: Routledge & Kegan Paul.
Smith, D. J. (1977). *Racial disadvantage in Britain*. Harmondsworth: Penguin.
Stacey, T. (1970). *Immigration and Enoch Powell*. Bungay, Suffolk: Chaucer Press.
Trew, T. (1979a). Theory and ideology at work. In R. Fowler, R. Hodge, G. Kress, & T. Trew, *Language and control* (pp. 94–116). London: Routledge & Kegan Paul.
Trew, T. (1979b). 'What the papers say': Linguistic variation and ideological difference. In R. Fowler, R. Hodge, G. Kress, & T. Trew, *Language and control* (pp. 117–156). London: Routledge & Kegan Paul.

CHAPTER **7**

Gender, Language, and Discourse

Candace West and Don H. Zimmerman

INTRODUCTION

> It is notable that until the impetus of the contemporary women's movement, linguists and sociolinguists who were alert to other sources of difference did not attend to sex-based language variation. As Kuhn (1962) has observed in studying the development of scientific paradigms, knowledge is strongly affected by external forces. Social movements—in this case the feminist movement—have often pushed disciplines into interests they long avoided. (Thorne, Kramarae, & Henley, 1983, p. 8)

Although interest in the relationship between discourse and gender can be traced as far back as 1664 (Jespersen, 1922 cited in Thorne & Henley, 1975, p. 5), it is only since the 1970s that it has emerged as part of a full-fledged field of inquiry. Initial accounts of connections between speech and gender were largely restricted to anthropological purview, perhaps because "It has been easier to see the differences of language between the sexes in other cultures than our own" (Kramer, 1975, p. 44). Early ethnographic reports tended to focus on the use of isolated elements of speech (e.g., pronunciation, noun affixes, or personal pronouns) in "strange and exotic" tribes rather than on discourse of the sexes in researchers' own cultures.

Bodine (1975) advances two possible explanations for our previous neglect of the topic: First, she notes that ethnographic attention to "men's" and "women's" languages was generally directed toward those characteristics of speech that were the exclusive domain of one sex or the other. Since European languages are commonly marked less by "sex-exclusive differentiation" than by "sex-preferential differentiation" (i.e., fewer absolute differences than differences in frequency of occurrence), European researchers may have found the relationship between discourse and gender in their native tongues less noticeable than in others'.

Second, Bodine hypothesizes that research on gender's relationship to the languages of Europe was impeded by researchers' tendencies to take for granted the "special" character of "women's speech" in relation to men's: In general, everyone knew that "even our own (English/French/Spanish/German . . .) women speak in their own (modest/peculiar/illogical . . .) way, using trivial vocabulary, avoiding harsh and unseemly words, speaking a conservative form of the language, talking too much . . ." (1975, p. 131). Thus, if the peculiar nature of "women's discourse" was assumed to be obvious, there was little incentive to study it.

This situation has changed in a variety of respects. For example, the first comprehensive bibliography on the relationships between language, speech, and gender was published in 1975 (Thorne & Henley, 1975, pp. 204–305). It contained 20 items written in the first half of this century, 12 items from 1951 to 1960, 34 items from 1961 to 1970 (during the emergence of the field of sociolinguistics), and a total of 81 items written between 1971 and 1974. An updating of this bibliography (Thorne et al., 1983) lists approximately 800 items, the majority of which have been written since the publication of the original.

The scope, as well as the size, of the field has increased dramatically. No longer confined to anthropological ken, interest in discourse and gender crosses a variety of disciplinary boundaries (including those between linguistics, psychology, sociology, philosophy, English, literature, women's studies, and speech communication). Ethnographers' reports have been supplemented by laboratory experiments, survey questionnaires, philosophical argumentation, literary analysis, and naturalistic observations of cultures much closer to home.

Our aim in this chapter is to provide a broad but selective overview of issues and problems confronting scholars in this exciting new area of research. Do women and men speak differently? How does gender affect their being talked to or talked about? What is the relationship between the structure of a language and the use of that language by the sexes who speak it? These are among the questions that will concern us. Obviously, an exhaustive review of answers to these questions is beyond the scope of this chapter, and readers are encouraged to consult the bibliography we append at the end of our review. Here, we attempt to illustrate the variety of ways in which analyses of discourse contribute to our understanding of the relations between women and men in social life.

LANGUAGE AND SPEECH OF WOMEN AND MEN

Traditionally, linguists have found it useful to distinguish between language structure (and content), on the one hand, and language use, on the other. This distinction has been expressed in numerous ways (e.g., language versus speech, *langue* versus *parole*, etc.), all of which highlight the separation between language as an abstract system and the context of its use (Spender, 1980, p. 13). Since discourse analysis has conventionally been regarded as the analysis of language in use, a conceptual distinction has often been made to separate studies of gender and discourse from investigations of sexist language.

However, segregation of the two spheres of interest in research on women is increasingly called into question (Spender, 1980; Thorne *et al.*, 1983). To be sure, numerous structural analyses (of sexist language) demonstrate the ways in which women are ignored, trivialized, and deprecated by the words and terms of address that define them. For example, women are not granted an autonomous existence by languages that name them in relation to men. Titles are used to distinguish married women from single ones (e.g., *Mrs.* vs. *Miss; Señora* vs. *Señorita; Frau* vs. *Fräulein*); surnames tie women to husbands and fathers (Lakoff, 1975; Stannard, 1977); and women are conceptualized as part of man, through purportedly generic masculine terms (*he, man, mankind*—see Huber, 1976; Martyna, 1978, 1980a, 1980b; Schneider & Hacker, 1973). Words used for females (e.g., *woman*) tend to acquire pejorative connotations (e.g., "mistress or paramour" in the 1800s; see Schulz, 1975; Stanley, 1977), leading to their replacement by euphemistic referents (e.g., the colloquial use of *lady* today; see Lakoff, 1975; Mencken, 1963). Even occupations and organizational titles have segregated the sexes into distinct categories of existence (e.g., actor and actress, waiter and waitress, policeman and policewoman, Congressman and Congresswoman), with modifying markers tagged to exceptions to the rule (e.g., woman doctor, male nurse, woman lawyer, male secretary, see Miller & Swift, 1977, pp. 43–48).

While such findings of sexism in language structure are seemingly far removed from the concerns of discourse analysis (with language in use), Spender (1980) offers a powerful argument for viewing these areas as inextricably linked. She begins with a deceptively simple observation: Man made language. To support this observation, she draws on Ardener's critique of the neglect of women informants in anthropological investigations and Smith's (1978) analysis of the exclusion of women in formulations of cultural meanings:

> Women have been largely excluded from the work of producing the forms of thought and the images and symbols in which thought is expressed and ordered. . . . The circle of men whose writing and talk was significant to each other extends backwards in time as far as our records reach. (Smith, 1978, p. 281)

Discourse involves the use of particular linguistic systems, which regulate the symbols we use to express our thoughts and the means whereby they are ordered. To the extent that women are excluded from the creation of a linguistic system, they are "obliged to use a language which is not of their own making" (Spender, 1980, p. 12). Hence, studies of women's discourse investigate the use of language that has been externally imposed on those who use it.

To enable us to fully appreciate the implications of this fact, Spender invites us to recall the origins of earlier controversies over analyses of Black English and working-class speech:

> It is worth noting that approximately ten years ago there was widespread belief that there was something *wrong* with the language of Blacks and of the working class, but that within those ten years the explanations have shifted so that there is now general consensus that the "deficiency" lies not in Blacks or the working class but in society. We can now appreciate that what has been termed "correct" English is nothing other than the blatant legitimation of the white middle-class code. (1980, p. 13)

In reviewing research on the speech of women and men, we are well advised to keep in mind the moral of Spender's analyses: Difference and deficit are two separate matters.

Difference and Deficit: In Retrospect

In the early 1970s the surge of interest in relationships between speech and gender stimulated innumerable hypotheses regarding sex differences in communication. Virtually every source of linguistic variation (e.g., pronunciation, vocabulary, grammar, syntax) was regarded as a possible harbinger of distinctions between the sexes. For example, women were thought to use intensifiers (*so, such, quite*) more often than men (Key, 1972); to employ more fillers (*uhm, you know*) than their male counterparts (Hirschman, 1973); and to make more liberal use of particular terms of endearment (*dear, honey, sweetie*) in a broader range of settings (Eble, 1972). The style of women's speech was also seen to be distinctive—avoiding strong or forceful statements and relying on expressions that convey hesitation and uncertainty (Lakoff, 1975). Even topics of talk were thought to be sex typed, with women's discourse focused on people and their personal lives while men's concentrated on more instrumental matters (Harding, 1975).

The accumulated impact of such descriptions led some to advance notions of co-occurring "genderlects" (systems of sex-linked linguistic signals) for women and men (Haas, 1979; Kramer, 1975; McConnell-Ginet, 1980) and others to posit the existence of a separate "women's language" (Lakoff, 1975). In general, such characterizations tend to stress differences (rather than similarities) between the sexes (Thorne *et al.*, 1983)—often, to the detriment of women:

> The overall effect of "women's language"—meaning both language restricted in use to women and language descriptive of women alone—is this: it submerges a woman's personal identity, by denying her the means of expressing herself strongly, on the one hand, and encouraging expressions that suggest triviality in subject matter and uncertainty about it; and, when a woman is being discussed, by treating her as an object—sexual or otherwise—but never a serious person with individual views. (Lakoff, 1975, p. 7)

However, empirical studies of actual speech find only two areas of consistent sex differences (Thorne et al., 1983, pp. 12–13). The first is in phonetics: Women employ standard or "correct" pronunciations more than men do in a variety of different languages, for example, voicing full /ing/ verb endings in English language communities (see Anshen, 1969; Fasold, 1968; Fischer, 1958; Labov, 1966, 1972; Milroy, 1976; Shuy, Wolfram, & Riley, 1967; Trudgill, 1975); pronouncing the liquid /l/ in articles and pronouns in French Canadian cultures (see Sankoff & Cedergren, 1971); or retaining the consonants /n/ and /t/ when they appear between vowels in Chukchi, a Siberian language (see Bogoras, cited in Bodine, 1975). The second area in which sex difference is a recurring finding is nonsegmental: Woman show more pitch variability and more variable intonation than men do (Coleman, 1971; Crystal, 1969; Herbst, 1969; McConnell-Ginet, 1978; Sachs, 1975; Takefuta, Jancosek, & Brunt, 1972).

Other hypothesized distinctions between men's and women's speech have not been substantiated by empirical research. For example:

> No consistent sex differences have been found in amount of vocabulary or choice of adjectives or adverbs, although in different social groups the sexes may use somewhat different lexicons. . . . Finally, no consistent sex differences have been found in the use of various syntactic forms, such as patterns of question-asking. (Thorne et al., 1983, p. 13)

In fact, Thorne et al. suggest that such notions as separate genderlects or languages for the sexes connote more same-sex similarity and cross-sex difference than exists. Theories predicted on gender differences are ill equipped to explain findings of considerable overlap in the speech characteristics of women and men.[1]

In short, the surge of interest in speech and gender led to many frag-

---

[1] To be sure, many such studies were generated out of previously existing stereotypes:
> When the women's movement of the late 1960's spurred unprecedented interest in relationships of women, men and language, feminists turned to earlier sources like Jespersen [1922], pursuing their leads, but also questioning their sexist pronouncements. In the process, we often ended up addressing questions we ourselves had not posed. (Thorne et al., 1983, p. 8)

Thus, not only was language "man made" (in Spender's 1980 meaning of this description), but questions that stimulated research on gender and language were also generated by presumed deviations from the male norm.

mented investigations of isolated variables that overreported differences between the sexes. Where gender was employed merely as an additional factor in sociolinguistic surveys, findings lacked consensus and were frequently in contradiction with one another. Reviewing the first decade of research in this area, Smith (1979, pp. 115–117) makes several points that are pertinent to the cautionary flavor of our discussion here. First, he observes that the mere association of sex with a feature of speech is insufficient to link the two directly. Unless the correlation is perfect, the association may be due to the relationship between sex and some other variable (e.g., age or socioeconomic status). And, as Brown and Fraser (1979, pp. 53–55) note, sex-stereotyped speech may be less a reflection of sex than the fact that speech is associated with activities that tend to be segregated by sex (e.g., occupational domains of action). Speech registers are linked to activity types, which are in turn subject to the exigencies of the sexual division of labor.

Thus, Smith (1979) urges renewed attention to Bodine's (1975) distinction between sex-preferential tendencies and those that are sex exclusive. In the absence of sex-exclusive forms (all-or-none differences), we cannot conclude that differences in the speech of men and women are directly related to sex differences (and thus, primarily markers of sex as opposed to other identities). Smith further notes that some sex-exclusive forms (e.g., the high-pitched "baby talk" of women) may be employed only by some members (e.g., mothers tending to small children). In this case, the association is not directly sex to speech, but activity type to speech (which in turn is differentially distributed with regard to sex.)

The perceived necessity for such caveats might imply that research on the relationship between discourse and gender has not changed all that much since the accounts of early anthropologists (who, as Bodine, notes, focused on isolated elements of speech and took for granted the special character of "women's speech" as a unique entity). However, "The most fruitful research on gender and speech has conceptualized language not in terms of isolated variables, nor as an abstracted code, but within contexts of actual use" (Thorne *et al.*, 1983, p. 14).

GENDER AND DISCOURSE IN CONTEXT

The notion of context implies a variety of social dimensions that might contribute to our understanding of gender differentiation in the use of language. For example, the various genres of discourse addressed in Volume 3 of this handbook (e.g., interviews, conversations, or debates) constitute one dimension of context (in the case of these examples, we can observe contextual variation with regard to how turns at talk are allocated). Another dimension consists of situational elements:

> Is the speaker talking to same or opposite sex, subordinate or superordinate, one listener or many, someone right there or on the phone; is he reading a script or talking simultaneously; is the occasion formal or informal, routine or emergency? Note that it is not the attributes of social structure that are here considered, such as age and sex, but rather the value placed on these attributes as they are acknowledged in the situation current and at hand. (Goffman, 1964, p. 134)

Still other variables are included in Hymes' (1964, p. 10) description of the components of communicative events (e.g., the settings in which discourse ensues or the range of codes available to participants).

For those interested in the relationship between discourse analysis and social issues, the social context is of additional importance. But this sort of inquiry necessitates "analysis which extends beyond the immediate structure of communicative events" (Thorne & Henley, 1975, p. 13). Whereas linguists may view their primary aim as searching for possible sex differences in speech, analysts of discourse are further interested in how and why they occur. For example, what is the social significance of women's tendency to use more "correct" phonetic variants? And, if anatomy does not fully account for differences in pitch between the sexes (Mattingly, 1966; McConnell-Ginet, 1978), why do women use a wider range of pitch than men?

In order to address questions such as these, we must move from language to society as our theoretical starting point, incorporating findings in the sociology, anthropology, and psychology of gender:

> With this shift in perspective, gender becomes not just a variable which correlates with various linguistic details, but rather a complicated social and cultural phenomenon. At the same time, speech is seen in broader focus—as a kind of action, as an intimate part of the fabric of social life. (Thorne & Henley, 1975, p. 14)

Thus, Thorne and Henley explain the sexual differentiation of language in terms of the social differentiation of women and men (through the social elaboration of gender, the sexual division of labor, and the structure of male dominance in society).

A final contextual concern is the local vicinity of discourse in which particular events take place. Attention to variation in this dimension may well resolve questions of conflicting findings in existing research. For example, consider the growing body of inconsistent observations on the use of tag questions by women and men (for an excellent review of this research, see Thorne *et al.*, 1983, p. 13). Lakoff stimulated much of the debate in her 1973 and 1975 works, suggesting that the tag-question formation is used more often by women than by men in conversational situations. To be sure, she did not submit statistical evidence for her claim, but she was careful to distinguish the particular conversational circumstances that constitute "legitimate" contexts for the use of tags (a point often missed by her critics). Where the facts of an assertion are suspected rather than known (*I had my glasses off. He was out at third, wasn't he?*) or where small talk is the aim (*Sure is hot in here, isn't it?*), Lakoff argued that tag questions were legitimately employed to elicit a response from one's co-conversationalists (1975, p. 16). However, she specified another context for tag questions: "[one] in which it is the speaker's opinions, rather than perceptions, for which corroboration is sought. . . . this sort of tag question is much more apt to be used by women than by men (1975, p. 16). Hence, Lakoff suggested that a particular type of tag question (not tag questions in general) was characteristic of "women's language" in a particular context (conversational situations).

Subsequent empirical studies have yielded inconsistent support for Lakoff's suggestion, but few have attended to the careful discriminations of her original (1973, 1975) formulations. For example, whereas Lakoff hypothesized that women would use more tag questions in conversational situations, several researchers have found "contradictory" evidence using findings obtained in nonconversational environments (e.g., Dubois & Crouch, 1977, researched the use of tags at a formal professional conference; Baumann, 1976, looked at the distribution of tag questions in a classroom setting; and Johnson, 1980, examined their incidence at task-oriented meetings of corporation engineers and designers). Moreover, while Lakoff distinguished various functions of tag questions on the basis of their contexts, subsequent studies have often neglected these distinctions (e.g., Crosby & Nyquist, 1977, p. 314, who offer a small-talk tag question to illustrate their operational definition) or substituted new ones that are extraneous to Lakoff's original hypothesis (e.g., Dubois & Crouch, 1977, p. 293, who differentiate "formal" tags—*weren't you?*—from "informal" ones—*right?*). Thus, the empirical status of Lakoff's suggestion remains to be assessed by works that do not confound coding and context.

The more important point for analysts of discourse is that the local context of any particular object of inquiry may well determine its status as an object of inquiry. For analysts of relationships between discourse and gender, this point is best illustrated by a series of studies that examine discourse within contexts of actual use.

Women's Work in Discourse between the Sexes

At the forefront of research on discourse between women and men are a succession of reports by Fishman (1977, 1978a, 1978b, 1980, 1983) on the sexual division of labor in casual conversation. Fishman's point

7 Gender, Language, and Discourse

of departure in these analyses is her contention that interaction not only takes work (in order to be successful) but is work in and of itself:

> Interaction requires at least two people. Conversation is produced not simply by their presence, but also by their display of their continuing agreement to pay attention to one another. That is, all interactions are potentially problematic and occur only through the continual, turn-by-turn efforts of the participants. (1978a, p. 398)

Among the various chores involved are such things as beginning or ending a conversation (Sacks, Schegloff, & Jefferson, 1974; Schegloff, 1972; Schegloff & Sacks, 1974) and sustaining a focus on a topic of talk.

Fishman's analyses of casual conversations between heterosexual intimates relaxing at home suggest that women do far more work to maintain a flow of conversational topics than their male partners. For example, one report indicates that women use more attention-getting beginnings and questions to ensure men's responses to their topics of talk:[2]

(1) (Fishman, 1978a, p. 403)
((The woman is reading a book in her academic specialty and the man is making a salad))
F: I didn't know that.
(#)
M: Hmmm?
(#)
F: Um you know that ((garbage disposal on)) that organizational stuff about Frederic Taylor and Bishopgate and all that stuff?
(#)
M: UhHmm ((yes))=
F: =In the early 1900's people were trying to fight favoritism to the schools
(4.0)
M: That's what we needed. (18.0) I never did get my smoked oysters.

And, subsequently in this same dialogue:

(2) (Fishman, 1978a, p. 403)
F: Hmm. That's very interesting. Did you know that teachers used to be men until about the 1840s when it became a female occupation?
(2.0)

---

[2] Transcribing conventions employed in this chapter are presented in the Appendix. For purposes of consistency and internal cohesion, Fishman's (1978a, 1978b) transcribing conventions have been converted to those used elsewhere in this chapter. Otherwise, fragments of transcript are preserved as they appear in her published works.

M: Nhhmm ((no))
(#)
F: Because they needed more teachers because of the increased enrollment.
(5.0)
M: And then the salaries started going down probably.
(#)
F: Yeah relatively and the status
(7.0)
M: Um, it's weird. We're out of oil again.

Despite these prefaces to their remarks (*D'ya know what?*, *That's very interesting*), women's attempts to launch conversational topics met with limited success. In both the above excerpts, we see men's rejoinders consisting of single turns and minimal responses (*UhHmm, Nhhmm*) before alternative topics are introduced (*I never did get my smoked oysters, We're out of oil again*).

In contrast, Fishman observes that women engage in a good deal of active support work to sustain men's conversational topics (1978b). Through precisely timed monitoring and displays of appreciation, women's work in conversation carries men's topical development through considerably longer streams of discourse:

(3) (Fishman, 1978b, p. 16A)
M: I saw in the paper where Olga Korbut
 Korbut=
F: =Yeah=
M: =went to see Dickie.
(#)
F: You're kidding! What for?
(#)
M: I don't know.
(2.0)
F: I can just imagine what she would go see Dick Dick Nixon for. I don't get it.
(7.0)
M: I think she's on a tour of the United States
(3.0)
F: Has he sat down and talked to her?
(#)
M: Shows the picture in the paper
(1.0)
F: Today's paper? (2.0) You're kidding me.

Fishman's interpretations of these data point to the skill with which women's monitoring responses (= *Yeah* =) and displays of appreciation (*You're kidding!*) are placed virtually between breaths in men's topical development.

Fishman's analyses illuminate the ways in which particular characteristics of "women's speech" may in fact constitute solutions to problems women face in conversations with men. By virtue of their lesser likelihood of securing men's attention when they speak, women may employ more questions to ensure getting listened to. Conversely, men's greater reliance on statements to open up topics of talk (Fishman, 1978a, p. 402) may derive from their own greater likelihood of being listened to—regardless of what they have to say. And, like women's work in the home, their interactional labors are made to seem invisible: "Since interactional work is related to what constitutes being a woman, with what a woman *is*, the idea that it *is* work is obscured. The work is not seen as what women do, but as part of what they are" (Fishman, 1978a, p. 405).

Competition, Cooperation, and Context in Children's Discourse

Whereas Fishman's analyses focus on cross-sex conversations between white middle-class adults, an elegant study by Goodwin (1980) illustrates the ways in which language can be used differently by black working-class boys and girls (ages 8 through 13). Goodwin's objects of inquiry are the directives (speech acts that try to get another to do something) used by children in coordinating the various tasks involved in playing together (e.g., making slingshots in the boys' groups and making bottle rims into rings in the girls'].

As her point of departure, Goodwin notes that the particular activities boys and girls engage in might be coordinated in any number of ways. For example:

> The sling shot is an individual instrument, and, in theory, play with it could be construed as an individual activity in which all participants fend for themselves, the only preparation being that each have a sling shot and an adequate supply of "slings" to shoot. (Goodwin, 1980, p. 158)

However, the children she observed did not organize their play in diverse ways; instead, their play activities displayed distinctive modes of social organization depending on the gender of participants.

The boys engaged in the making of slingshots in competitive fashion, with two hierarchically arranged teams vying for control over the process. Virtually every stage of construction became the occasion for negotiations over status, "such as where the preparation would occur, who would provide the materials, who had rights to materials, the allocation of necessary tools, the spatial organization of participants, when the activity was to move from stage to stage and so on" (Goodwin, 1980, p. 158).

Drawing on Labov and Fanshel's (1977) distinction between "aggravated" and "mitigated" forms, Goodwin analyzes the ways in which children used directives to effect competitive play among boys and cooperative play among girls. For example, boys established and displayed their positions vis-à-vis others in their group by issuing directives in the form of explicit commands:

(4) (Goodwin, 1980, p. 158)
1 Michael: Gimme the pliers!
  Poochie: ((gives pliers to Michael))
2 Michael: All right. Gimme some rubber bands.
  Chopper: ((giving rubber bands to Michael)) Oh.
3 Michael: All right. Give me your hanger Tokay.
  Tokay: ((Gives hanger to Michael))

In this slingshot session, Goodwin observes that Michael's imperatives take an aggravated form (with references to the rights of the speaker or obligations of the recipient, p. 159).

In contrast, the directives of girls making rings from bottle rims took a mitigated form, often suggesting or proposing joint actions:

(5) (Goodwin, 1980, p. 165)
        ((Girls are looking for bottles.))
30 Sharon: Let's go around Subs and Suds.
   Pam: Let's ask her "Do you have any bottles".
        ((Girls are looking for bottles.))
31 Terry: Let's go. There may be some more on Sixty Ninth Street.
   Sharon: Come on. Let's turn back y'all so we can safe keep em. Come on. Let's go find some.

Here, for example, Goodwin notes that *Let's* operates as a proposal, which "shows neither special deference toward the other party (as a request does) nor claims about special rights over the other (as a command does)" (1980, p. 166).

These differences in the discourse of young boys and girls might be taken as further evidence of the existence of separate genderlects. However, Goodwin demonstrates that the cooperative organization of girls' play groups is not a function of girls' differential abilities. When girls bossed younger siblings around, acted the part of a mother or teacher, or argued with boys, they displayed considerable skill in the use of explicit commands:

(6) (Goodwin, 1980, p. 170)
    61 Sharon: Run to Mommy.
                            ((Delin pulls down the hood of her jacket))
    62 Terry: Don't put that down. Put that back up! It's supposed to be that way.
    64 Sharon: Now go over there and get your paper, .h And I want every body over here, to act like grow:n men and grown women.
                            ((Nettie is sitting on top of Johnny))
    66 Johnny: Get off! Get off or//I'll hit you with my thing!
          Nettie: Cindy smack him. You'se a mother.

Thus, the preference for the use of mitigated directives in girls' play groups does not arise as a result of girls' lack of competence with aggravated forms. Instead, Goodwin concludes: "Different approaches of girls and boys to talk in similar activities are not only indicative but also constitutive of characteristically different social organizations" (1980, p. 173).

Conversational Dominance in Cross-Sex Discourse

Despite the popularity of conventional wisdom (which holds that women talk too much), a growing body of research indicates that men talk more (and for longer) than women in discourse between the sexes (e.g., Hilpert, Kramer, & Clark, 1975; Kenkel, 1963; Strodtbeck, 1951; Strodtbeck, James, & Hawkins, 1957; Strodtbeck & Mann, 1956). One factor that figures centrally in this phenomenon is the tendency of males to interrupt females much more often than the reverse (Argyle, Lalljee, & Cook, 1968; Eakins & Eakins, 1976; McMillan, Clifton, McGrath, & Gale, 1977; Natale, Entin, & Jaffe, 1979; Octigan & Niederman, 1979; Willis & Williams, 1976).

Yet even within this area, the local context of particular conversational events is crucial to determining their analytical status. For example, Shaw and Sadler's (1965) experimental study of cross-sex dyadic interaction found females were more dominant than males when frequency of interruption was used as the index of dominance. But males were found to be more dominant than females when dominance was defined by the number of times talk was initiated. Shaw and Sadler advance a possible explanation for this inconsistency in a methodological caveat: interruptions were tallied by a voice-actuated chronograph that did not distinguish among different types of simultaneous speech. So, "when the male was actively contributing ideas and task-oriented suggestions, the female might have been 'interrupting' with agreeing, reinforcing comments" (1965, p. 350). Given Fishman's (1978b) findings indicating women's tendencies to insert monitoring responses and displays of appreciation virtually between breaths in men's utterances, it would not be surprising if Shaw and Sadler's tally of interruptions included a great many instances of females' support work.

The critical conceptual issue is how to determine which identity (among a number of identities that could be correctly imputed to participants) actually animates a spate of talk. As a preliminary to addressing this question, we suggest that three types of participant identity need to be explicitly distinguished: master identities, for example, sex, race, and age, which crosscut all occasions of discourse; situated identities, for example, student, salesperson, busdriver, which inhabit particular settings and may be associated with special registers; and discourse identities, for example, questioner and answerer (in an interview), or teller and audience (in a storytelling sequence). It is quite clear that social interaction, including discourse, is managed with an eye to the identities of participants; that is, behavior, including speech, is adjusted according to whom one is speaking to (as well as to the setting and occasion of the encounter). It is therefore important to know which identity or identities are implicated in a given segment of discourse. For example, Schegloff (1978) reports an instance in which an ambiguous utterance was taken by its recipient to be a question (of clarification) to which a clarifying reply was addressed. The other party apparently intended the utterance as a display of agreement for which acknowledgment was the proper response. The respective unaligned discourse identities were thus questioner–answerer and affiliator–acknowledger. The intended affiliator, upon noting the mishearing, interrupted to invite the recipient to reanalyze the previously misheard utterance and try again. The point here is that the interruption is motivated by the mishearing, and as a repair-initiation, is directed to that error under the influence of a particular discourse identity. Thus, if interruption is the discourse feature of concern, care must be taken to determine the active identity under whose auspices it was initiated (see West & Zimmerman, 1983). It may be, as Fishman's work suggests, that the constituent tasks of conversing with another are divided on a sexual basis, with women assuming certain identities more frequently than men, and viceversa.

Our own studies of conversations between women and men (West,

1979, 1982; West & Zimmerman, 1977, 1983; Zimmerman & West, 1975) employ work in conversational analysis (Jefferson, 1973; Jefferson & Schegloff, 1975; Sacks *et al.*, 1974) to distinguish interruptions from other instances of simultaneous speech. For example, the Sacks *et al.* (1974) model for turn taking in conversation suggests that the proper place for transition between speaker turns is the terminal boundary of a possibly complete utterance (i.e., word, phrase, clause or sentence, depending on its context). The model also suggests that speakers will be oriented to minimizing silences and simultaneous speech. However, speakers' efforts to minimize silences encourage them to achieve turn transition as close as possible to the actual completion points of others' possibly complete utterances. Hence, Sacks *et al.* (1974) note the routine occurrence of brief simultaneities in the near vicinity of possible completion points:

(7) (West & Zimmerman, 1977, p. 523)
    Female 1:   I don't like it at all ⌈ but- ⌉
    Female 2:   ⌊ You d ⌋ on't

In this excerpt, the second speaker initiates a next utterance just at what would ordinarily be the end of the first speaker's utterance. However, the addition of a conjunction by the first speaker (*but-*) produces a collision between them. We call this type of simultaneity an '*overlap*' and view it as largely produced by constraints of the turn-taking system.

Interruptions, in contrast, involve deeper intrusions into the internal structure of speakers' utterances, that is, more than a syllable away from the terminal boundaries of possibly complete utterances. Seen strictly in terms of the turn-taking model, deep incursions into the turn space of current speakers constitute violations of turn-taking rules.[3] The following excerpts illuminate the potential effects of interruptions on the organization of turn and topic development:

---

[3] The turn-by-turn organization of talk means that both the relevance and coherence of talk are locally managed by participants at any particular point in conversation (e.g., given a subsequent occurrence, what may have begun as topic X may be transformed into topic Y). Clearly, not all instances of simultaneity are disruptive, and our distinctions among various types of simultaneous speech involve much more than the differentiation between overlaps and interruptions (see West, 1978, pp. 242–250). Jefferson (1973), for example, comments on the precision placement of a characteristic class of events that overlap a present speaker's utterance in such a way as to indicate both active listenership and independent knowledge of what the overlapped utterance is saying. Our point here is that beginning to speak prior to a possible turn transition place (i.e., prior to completion of a possibly complete unit type) can be a communicative act with sequential consequences for conversation (see Jefferson & Schegloff, 1975; West & Zimmerman, 1983).

(8) (West & Zimmerman, 1977, p. 527)
  Female: Both really (#) it just strikes me as too 1984ish y'know to sow your seed or whatever (#) an' then have it develop miles away not caring if
  Male: ⌊Now::⌋it may be something uh quite different (#) you can't make judgments like that without all the facts being at your disposal

And:

(9)
  Female: So uh you really can't bitch when you've got all those on the same day (4.2) but I uh asked my physics professor if I couldn't chan⌈ge that⌉
  Male: ⌊Don't ⌋touch that
  (1.2)
  Female: What?
  (#)
  Male: I've got everything jus' how I want it in that notebook (#) you'll screw it up leafin' through it like that.

In these fragments, we see males using interruptions as sanctioning devices to cut off both the females' turns at talk and the topics they were attempting to develop.

Our initial study of same-sex and cross-sex exchanges recorded in natural settings (i.e., drug stores, coffee shops, and other public places in a university community) found that interruptions were initiated very infrequently in same-sex conversations, where they appeared in symmetrical distributions between speakers (Zimmerman & West, 1975). However, in cross-sex exchanges, the pattern was grossly asymmetrical: males initiated 96% of the total interruptions we observed, and they interrupted more in every conversation in our collection. Subsequent comparison of our cross-sex exchanges with a set of parent–child interactions recorded in a physician's office (West & Zimmerman, 1977) found that females and young children apparently receive similar treatment in conversations with males and with adults (e.g., parents initiated 86% of interruptions in exchanges with children). Even exchanges recorded in a laboratory setting between previously unacquainted persons display a much higher incidence of male-initiated than female-initiated interruption (West, 1979, 1982; West & Zimmerman, 1983).[4]

---

[4] Conversationalists in these studies were white and apparently middle class. Adult speakers included in our samples range in age from 18 to 35; children in the parent–child exchanges ranged from 4 to 8 years of age.

We are impelled to the conclusion that, at least in those contexts we have examined, men deny equal status to women as conversational partners with respect to rights to the full utilization of their turns and support for the development of topics. Thus we surmise that just as male dominance is exhibited through male control of macroinstitutions in society (e.g., the occupational structure, the family division of labor, and other institutional contexts where life chances are determined), it is also exhibited through control of at least a part of one microinstitution.

CONCLUSIONS

In this chapter, we have attempted to provide an overview of the issues and problems confronting analysts of discourse between the sexes. As should be evident, this is a rapidly expanding area of study and a relatively youthful one. The growth and changing scope of the field testify to the wealth of new insights that have emerged in its first decade of existence. On taking stock, we have learned that rigid separation of interests in language structure and language use is not always appropriate where women are concerned; just as the speech of blacks and members of the working class was seen to be deficient because it differed from that of whites, so too women's speech has been devalued when it deviated from the male standard. However, sex differences in language use turn out to be far fewer than was previously supposed. And even these would more accurately be described as sex-preferential tendencies than as sex-exclusive uses.

The most promising avenues of inquiry have been opened by studies of discourse in its actual context. Where researchers have turned their attentions from gender as an isolated variable in sociolinguistic surveys to speech as a kind of action between humans of varying situational identities, we have developed a much richer understanding of the ways in which discourse helps construct the fabric of social life.

APPENDIX: TRANSCRIPTION CONVENTIONS

The transcript techniques and symbols were devised by Gail Jefferson in the course of research undertaken with Harvey Sacks. Techniques are revised, symbols added or dropped as they seem useful to work. There is no guarantee or suggestion that the symbols or transcripts alone would permit the doing of any unspecified research tasks: They are properly used as an adjunct to the tape-recorded materials.

I don' ⎡know⎤ don't 　　　⎣you ⎦	Brackets indicate that the portions of utterances so encased are simultaneous. The left-hand bracket (or, double oblique) marks the onset of simultaneity, the right-hand bracket indicates its resolution.
I don'//know	
We:::ll now	Colons indiate that the immediately prior syllable is prolonged.
But-	A hyphen represents a cutting off short of the immediately prior syllable.
CAPS or underscoring	Both of these are used to represent heavier emphasis (in speakers' pitch) on words so marked.
'Swat I said = 　　　= But you didn't	Equal signs are used to indicate that no time elapsed between the objects "latched" by the marks. Often used as a transcribing convenience, it can also mean that a next speaker starts at precisely the end of a current speaker's utterance.
(1.3)	Numbers encased in parentheses indicate the seconds and tenths of seconds ensuing between speaker turns. They may also be used to indicate the duration of pauses internal to a speaker's turn.
(#)	Score sign indicates a pause of about a second that it wasn't possible to discriminate precisely.
(word)	Single parentheses with words in them indicate that something was heard, but the transcriber is not sure what it was. These can serve as a warning that the transcript may be unreliable.
((softly))	Double parentheses enclose descriptions not transcribed utterances.
I (x) I did	Parentheses encasing an *x* indicate a hitch or stutter on the part of the speaker.
Oh Yeah?	Punctuation marks are used for intonation, not grammar.
( )	Empty parentheses signify untimed pauses.
°So you did.	The degree symbol represents softness, or decreased amplitude.
.hh hh hunh-heh, eh-heh	These are breathing and laughter indicators. A period followed by *hh*'s marks an inhalation. The *hh*'s alone stand for exhalation. The *hunh*'s, *eh*'s, and *heh*'s are laughter particles.
(.)	The period encased in parentheses denotes a pause of one tenth of a second.

BIBLIOGRAPHY

Anshen, F. (1969). Speech variation among American Negroes in a small Southern community. Unpublished Ph.D. dissertation, New York University.

Argyle, M., Lalljee, M., & Cook, M. (1968). The effects of visibility on interaction in a dyad. *Human Relations, 21,* 3–17.

Baumann, M. (1976). Two features of 'women's speech'. In B. L. Dubois & I. Crouch

(Eds.), *The sociology of the languages of American women* (pp. 33–40). San Antonio, TX: Trinity University Press.

Bodine, A. (1975). Sex differentiation in language. In B. Thorne & N. Henley (Eds.), *Language and sex: Difference and dominance* (pp. 130–151). Rowley, MA: Newbury House.

Bosmajian, H. (1974). The language of sexism. In *The language of oppression* (pp. 90–121). Washington, DC: Public Affairs Press.

Brown, P., & Fraser, C. (1979). Speech as a marker of situation. In K. R. Scherer & H. Giles (Eds.), *Social Markers in speech* (pp. 33–61). London: Cambridge University Press.

Butturff, D., & Epstein, E. (1978). *Women's language and style*. Akron, OH: L & S Books.

Coleman, R. O. (1971). Male and female voice quality and its relationship to vowel formant frequencies. *Journal of Speech and Hearing Research, 14,* 565–577.

Crosby, F., & Nyquist, L. (1977). The female register: An empirical study of Lakoff's hypotheses. *Language and Society, 6,* 313–322.

Crystal, D. (1969). *Prosadic systems and intonation in English*. Cambridge: Cambridge University Press.

Dubois, B. L., & Crouch, I. (Eds.). (1976). *The sociology of the languages of American women*. San Antonio, TX: Trinity University Press.

Dubois, B. L., & Crouch, I. (1977). The question of tag questions in women's speech: They don't really use more of them, do they? *Language in Society, 4,* 289–294.

Eakins, B. W., & Eakins, R. G. (1976). Verbal turn-taking and exchanges in faculty dialogue. In B. L. Dubois & I. Crouch (Eds.), *The sociology of the languages of American women* (pp. 53–62). San Antonio, TX: Trinity University Press.

Eakins, B. W., & Eakins, R. G. (1978). *Sex differences in human communication*. Boston: Houghton Mifflin.

Elbe, C. C. (1972). How the speech of some is more equal than others. Papers presented at the Southeastern Conference on Linguistics, Washington, DC: Georgetown University.

Fasold, R. W. (1968). A sociolinguistic study of the pronunciation of three vowels in Detroit speech. Washington, DC: Center for Applied Linguistics.

Fischer, J. L. (1958). Social influences on the choice of a linguistic variant. *Word, 14,* 47–56.

Fishman, P. (1977). Interactional shitwork. *Heresies, 1,* 99–101.

Fishman, P. (1978a). Interaction: The work women do. *Social Problems, 25,* 397–406.

Fishman, P. (1978b). What do couples talk about when they're alone? In D. Butturff & E. L. Epstein (Eds.), *Women's language and style* (pp. 11–22). Akron, OH: L & S Books.

Fishman, P. (1980). Conversational insecurity. In H. Giles, W. P. Robinson, & P. M. Smith (Eds.), *Language: Social psychological perspectives* (pp. 127–132). New York: Pergamon Press.

Fishman, P. (1983). Interaction: The work women do. In B. Thorne, C. Kramerae, & N. Henley (Eds.), *Language, gender and society* (pp. 89–101). Rowley, MA: Newbury House.

Goffman, E. (1964). The neglected situation. *American Anthropologist, 66,* 133–136.

Goodwin, M. H. (1980). Directive-response speech sequences in girls' and boys' task activities. In S. McConnell-Ginet, R. Borker, & N. Furman (Eds.), *Women and language in literature and society* (pp. 157–173). New York: Praeger.

Haas, A. (1979). The acquisition of genderlect. *Annals of the New York Academy of Sciences, 327,* 101–113.

Harding, S. (1975). Women and words in a Spanish village. In R. Reiter (Ed.), *Towards an anthropology of women* (pp. 283–308). New York: Monthly Review Press.
Henley, N. (1977). Tinkling symbols: Language. In *Body politics: Power, sex and nonverbal communication* (pp. 67–81). Englewood Cliffs, NJ: Prentice-Hall.
Herbst, L. (1969). Die Umfänge der physiologischen Hauptsprechtonbereiche von Frauen and Männern. *Zeitschrift für Phonetik, 22*, 426–438.
Hilpert, F., Kramer, C., & Clark, R. A. (1975). Participants' perceptions of self and partner in mixed sex dyads. *Central States Speech Journal, 26*, 52–56.
Hirschman, L. (1973). Female differences in conversational interaction. Paper presented at the meeting of the Linguistic Society of America, December, 1973, San Diego, CA.
Huber, J. (1976). On the generic use of male pronouns. *The American Sociologist, 11*, 89.
Hymes, D. (1964). *Language and culture in society*. New York: Harper and Row.
Jefferson, G. (1973). A case of precision timing in ordinary conversation: Overlapped tag positioned address terms in closing sequences. *Semiotica, 9*, 47–96.
Jefferson, G., & Schegloff, E. (1975). Sketch: Some orderly aspects of overlap in natural conversation. Unpublished manuscript, Department of Sociology, University of California, Los Angeles.
Johnson, J. L. (1980). Questions and role responsibility in four professional meetings. *Anthropological Linguistics, 22*, 66–76.
Kenkel, W. F. (1963). Observational studies of husband–wife interaction in family decision-making. In M. Sussman (Ed.), *Sourcebook in marriage and the family* (pp. 144–156). Boston: Houghton Mifflin.
Key, M. R. (1972). Linguistic behavior of male and female. *Linguistics, 88*, 15–31.
Key, M. R. (1975). *Male/female language, with a comprehensive bibliography*. Metuchen, NJ: The Scarecrow Press.
Kramer, C. (1975). Women's speech: Separate but unequal? In B. Thorne & N. Henley (Eds.), *Language and sex: Difference and dominance* (pp. 43–56). Rowley, MA: Newbury House.
Kramarae, C. (Ed.). (1980). *Voices and words of women and men*. Oxford and New York: Pergamon Press. (First published as a special issue of *Women's Studies International Quarterly, 3*, 135–323.)
Kramarae, C. (1981). *Women and men speaking*. Rowley, MA: Newbury House.
Kramarae, C., & Treichler, P. (Eds.) (1982). *Women and Language News*. Newsletter, University of Illinois at Urbana-Champaign, 244 Lincoln Hall, 702 South Wright Street, Urbana, IL: 61801
Labov, W. (1966). *The social stratification of English in New York City*. Washington, DC: Center for Applied Linguistics.
Labov, W. (1972). *Sociolinguistic patterns*. Philadelphia: University of Pennsylvania Press.
Labov, W., & Fanshel, D. (1977). *Therapeutic discourse: Psychotherapy as conversation*. New York and London: Academic Press.
Lakoff, R. (1973). Language and woman's place. *Language in Society, 2*, 45–79.
Lakoff, R. (1975). *Language and woman's place*. New York: Harper & Row.
McConnell-Ginet, S. (1978). Intonation in a man's world. *Signs: Journal of Women in Culture and Society, 3*, 541–559.
McConnell-Ginet, S. (1980). Linguistics and the feminist challenge. In S. McConnell-Ginet, R. Borker, & N. Furman (Eds.), *Women and language in literature and society* (pp. 3–25). New York: Praeger.
McMillan, J. R., Clifton, A. K., McGrath, D., & Gale, W. (1977). Women's language: Uncertainty or interpersonal sensitivity and emotionality? *Sex Roles, 3*, 545–559.
Mattingly, I. M. (1966). Speaker variation and vocal tract size. *Journal of the Acoustical Society of America, 39*, 1219 (abstract).

Mencken, H. L. (1963). *The American language.* (Fourth edition, and the two supplements). R. I. McDavid, Jr. (Ed.). New York: Knopf.

Miller, C., & Swift, K. (1977). *Words and women: New language in new times.* Garden City, NY: Anchor Press/Doubleday. (First published by Anchor Press/Doubleday in 1976.)

Milroy, L. (1976). *Belfast Working Papers on Language and Linguistics, 3,* 1–58.

Natale, M., Entin, E., & Jaffe, J. (1979). Vocal interruptions in dyadic communication as a function of speech and social anxiety. *Journal of Personality and Social Psychology, 37,* 865–878.

Nilsen, A. P., Bosmajian, H., Gershuny, H. L., & Stanley, J. P. (Eds.). (1979). *Sexism and language* Urbana, IL: National Council of Teachers of English.

Octigan, M., & Niederman, S. (1979). Male dominance in conversation. *Frontiers, 4,* 50–54.

Orasanu, J., Slater, M. K., & Adler, L. L. (1979). Language, sex and gender: Does 'la différence' make a difference? Special issue of *The Annals of the New York Academy of Sciences, 327,* 3–121.

Sachs, J. (1975). Clues to the identification of sex in children's speech. In B. Thorne & N. Henley (Eds.), *Language and sex: Difference and dominance* (pp. 152–171). Rowley, MA: Newbury House.

Sacks, H., Schegloff, E., & Jefferson, G. (1974). A simplest systematics for the organization of turn-taking for conversation. *Language, 50,* 696–735.

Sankoff, G., & Cedergren, H. (1971). Some results of a sociolinguistic study of Montreal French. In R. Darnell (Ed.), *Linguistic diversity in Canadian Society* (pp. 61–87). Edmonton, Alberta and Champaign, IL: Linguistic Research.

Schegloff, E. (1972). Sequencing in conversational openings. In J. Gumperz & D. Hymes (Eds.), *Directions in sociolinguistics* (pp. 346–380). New York: Holt, Rinehart and Winston.

Schegloff, E. (1978). On some questions and ambiguities in conversation. In W. Dressler (Ed.), *Current trends in textlinguistics* (pp. 81–102). Berlin: De Gruyter.

Schegloff, E., & Sacks, H. (1974). Opening up closings. In R. Turner (Ed.), *Ethnomethodology* (pp. 197–215). Middlesex: Penguin Education. (Originally published in *Semiotica, 8,* 1973.)

Schneider, J., & Hacker, S. (1973). Sex role imagery and use of the generic 'Man' in introductory texts: A case in sociology of sociology. *The American Sociologist, 8,* 12–18.

Schulz, M. (1975). The semantic derogation of women. In B. Thorne & N. Henley (Eds.), *Language and sex: Difference and dominance* (pp. 64–75). Rowley, MA: Newbury House.

Shaw, M. E., & Sadler, O. W. (1965). Interaction patterns in heterosexual dyads varying in degrees of intimacy. *The Journal of Social Psychology, 66,* 345–351.

Shuy, R. W., Wolfram, W. A., & Riley, W. K. (1967). Linguistic correlates of social stratification in Detroit speech. Final Reports, Project 6-1347. Washington, DC: US Office of Education.

Smith, D. (1979). A peculiar eclipsing: Women's exclusion from man's culture. *Women's Studies International Quarterly, 1,* 281–296.

Smith, P. M. (1979). Sex markers in speech. In K. R. Sherer & H. Giles (Eds.), *Social markers in speech* (pp. 109–149). Cambridge: Cambridge University Press.

Spender, D. (1980). *Man made language.* London: Routledge & Kegan Paul.

Stanley, J. P. (1977). Paradigmatic woman: The prostitute. In D. L. Shores (Ed.), *Papers in language variation* (pp. 303–321). Birmingham: University of Alabama Press.

Stannard, U. (1977). *Mrs. Man.* San Francisco: Germain Books.

Strodtbeck, F. L. (1951). Husband and wife interaction over revealed differences. *American Sociological Review, 16,* 468–473.
Strodtbeck, F. L., James, R. M., & Hawkins, C. (1957). Social status in jury deliberations. *American Sociological Review, 22,* 713–719.
Strodtbeck, F. L., & Mann, R. D. (1956). Sex role differentiation in jury deliberations. *Sociometry, 19,* 3–11.
Takefuta, Y., Jancosek, E. G., & Brunt, M. (1972). A statistical analysis of melody curves in the intonation of American-English. In A. Rigualt & R. Charbonneau (Eds.), *Proceedings of the 7th International Congress of Phonetic Sciences, 1971* (pp. 1035–1039). The Hague: Mouton.
Thorne, B., & Henley, N. (Eds.). (1975). *Language and sex: Difference and dominance.* Rowley, MA: Newbury House.
Thorne, B., Kramerae, C., & Henley, N. (Eds.). (1983). *Language, gender and society.* Rowley, MA: Newbury House.
Trömel-Plötz, S. (1979). *Frauensprache in unserer Welt der Männer.* Frankfurt/Main: Fischer Taschenbuch Verlag.
Trudgill, P. (1975). Sex, covert prestige, and linguistic change in the urban British English of Norwich. In B. Thorne & N. Henley (Eds.), *Language and sex: Difference and dominance* (pp. 88–104). Rowley, MA: Newbury House.
Vetterling-Braggin, M. (Ed.). (1981). *Sexist language: A modern philosophical analysis.* Totowa, NJ: Littlefield, Adams & Co.
West, C. (1978). Communicating gender: A study of dominance and control in conversation. Unpublished Ph.D. dissertation, University of California, Santa Barbara.
West, C. (1979). Against our will: Male interruptions of females in cross-sex conversation. *Annals of the New York Academy of Sciences, 327,* 81–97.
West, C. (1982). Why can't a woman be more like a man? An interactional note on organizational game playing for managerial women. *Work and Occupations, 9,* 5–29.
West, C., & Zimmerman, D. H. (1977). Women's place in everyday talk: Reflections on parent–child interaction. *Social Problems, 24,* 521–529.
West, C., & Zimmerman, D. H. (1983). Small insults: A study of interruptions in cross-sex conversations between unaquainted persons. In B. Thorne, C. Kramarae, & N. Henley (Eds.), *Language, gender and society* (pp. 102–117). Rowley, MA: Newbury House.
Willis, F. N., & Williams, S. J. (1976). Simultaneous talking in conversation and sex of speakers. *Perceptual and Motor Skills, 43,* 1067–1070.
Zimmerman, D. H., & West, C. (1975). Sex roles, interruptions and silences in conversations. In B. Thorne & N. Henley (Eds.), *Language and sex: Difference and dominance* (pp. 105–129). Rowley, MA: Newbury House.

CHAPTER **8**

On the Discourse of Immigrant Workers: Interethnic Communication and Communication Strategies

Norbert Dittmar and Christiane von Stutterheim

INTERETHNIC COMMUNICATION: PROBLEM SPACE

Everybody knows that Central Europeans move their heads from left to right whereas Greeks move their heads up and down when saying yes. There are a lot of verbal and nonverbal differences involved in interethnic communication that can cause misunderstanding, failure, and distrust in communication. The meanings of verbal and nonverbal signs have to be matched according to social, cultural, and situational background. Interactants may have different presuppositions, intuitions, and goals in communication, at least, if they come from different national, social, and ethnic milieus. Relaxed, unmarked, routinized conversation runs well when interactants share the same background in culture and knowledge. Anthropologists and sociolinguists have pointed out that symmetrical, congruent, informal, and successful communication presupposes shared knowledge of social and cultural values. The inappropriate word in a given situation may rather heavily affect the "well-being" in interaction and produce differences in behavioral strategies.

In interethnic communication (immigrant–native and foreigner–foreigner communication), interactants must do much more conversational work in order to accommodate each other in discourse than in "normal" everyday conversation. This accommodation takes place in all kinds of interactions. The social–psychological theory of accommodation (Giles & Smith, 1979; Thakerar, Giles, & Cheshire, 1982) tries to explain some of the motivations underlying certain shifts on people's speech styles during social encounters, and some of the social consequences arising from them. The social–psychological adaptation of ego to other and vice versa has mainly two functions: the establishment or signaling of sympathy and positive, emotional proximity (convergence), or the expression of distance through the establishment of symbolic distance between two social territories (divergence) (Thakerar, Giles, & Cheshire, 1982).

Although communicative convergence or divergence plays a central role in interethnic communication, much greater focus lies on the transmission of referential and propositional meaning in conversation. Accommodation presupposes the acceptance of negotiated meaning under the conditions of different linguistic and cultural backgrounds and the tolerance of local meaning management as a precondition of understanding. From the point of view of communication, the immigrant (or migrant) is usually in the subordinate position and the native in the superior. According to the asymmetry in linguistic and cultural knowledge, both interactants have to decide whether each of them tolerates their role complements: the foreigner as a linguistically and culturally incompetent, helpless, socially subordinate petitioner (supplicant) and the native as the competent, knowing, advising helper who knows how things are done in his context. On both sides, there may be acceptance or refusal of these social and communicative roles. Ethnic and cultural prejudice and stereotype influence decisions and choices. Acceptance of the complementary roles facilitates convergence: The foreigner advances in learning and adjusts himself to the foreign norms; the native reduces the amount of prejudices and gets self-affirmation for helping. The refusal, of course, produces divergence: The foreigner refuses to learn and accommodate to foreign norms and values and fully maintains his own cultural and linguistic identity (very often produced through the feeling that the "ethnic other" does not like him, or considers him culturally and socially inferior, which leads to strong ethnic pride and separation); the native considers the foreigner to be unworthy of help and despises his social and ethnic background.[1] Positive efforts have to be undertaken by both parties if convergence is aimed for. With immigrants, very often the opposite takes place: Divergence is the result of (1) mutual prejudice or stereotypes, (2) arrogant refusal of migrants by socially superior native groups, and (3) refusal of social adaptation or integration in a given country on the part of a foreign group that tries to maintain its social, cultural, and

---

[1] In Western European countries, where foreign labor has reached a high percentage, job competition between natives and immigrants contributes considerably to the rise of stereotypes.

linguistic identity. There are only a few studies available that inform us about native–immigrant contacts in European industrialized societies (Apitzsch, 1982; HPD, 1975; Klein & Dittmar, 1979; Schumann, 1979; Stölting, 1980).

Encounters between natives and immigrants can take place in the following domains:

1. Administrative institutions; e.g., labor offices, boards of advisors, banks, post offices
2. Shops
3. Language training and other schooling institutions
4. Medical care institutions
5. Work situations
6. Public places, parks, and streets
7. Free-time activity environments; e.g., restaurants, bars, nightclubs, sports clubs
8. Private places: home, apartment, garden.

We briefly discuss these eight domains under the headings of interaction quality and frequency. Verbal interactions in (1), (2), and (6) take place from time to time more or less inevitably, but they are restricted on the average to referential communication, short verbal exchanges, and necessary regulations.

Communication in (4) necessarily demands more intensity on both parts, native and immigrant, in order to improve the effectivity of serious medical help. In contact situations, the verbal style on the part of the native may be "foreigner talk". To bridge the gap of mutual understanding in these domains, immigrants often rely on their children, who act as interpreters for them.

Domain (3) involves directed learning in classroom settings. During school hours, the teacher becomes the target model for the immigrants as far as language and cultural habits are concerned. Communication in the classroom is mostly formal and artificial; often, there is only very little progress, and one of the greatest problems is the fact that the teaching apparently has little or no effect on the defective routines of "broken language" in everyday natural situations.

At the working place (5), immigrants have some contacts with natives. But the communication is usually restricted to instrumental functions (see HPD, 1975, pp. 60–100). On the part of the native, foreigner talk (Ferguson, 1971) is not unusual. The working encounters lead only in rare exceptions to private contacts. Interactions in clubs (7) between natives and immigrants occur, particularly sports clubs, but they are generally motivated by instrumental and goal-oriented understanding.

They are more informal, compared to other contexts, and they favor the intake of the local vernacular on the part of the immigrant. Contacts in private places (8) between natives and immigrants are rare.

As can be seen from this short outline, social and cultural distance prevails in the interaction between natives and immigrants (Schumann, 1979; von Stutterheim, 1984). Only a very low percentage of the immigrants (below 5%) reach a level of good and acceptable competence in their second language (Klein & Dittmar, 1979). The restriction to formal and necessary interactions in order to resolve immediate needs gives rise to prejudices, fear of contact, and mutual mistrust (mostly on the part of the natives). This holds at least for adolescents (Apitzsch, 1982) and adults (HPD, 1975; Klein & Dittmar, 1979; Schumann, 1979).[2]

ASPECTS OF VERBAL INTERACTION BETWEEN NATIVES AND IMMIGRANTS

Natives and nonnatives have to cope with considerable meaning discrepancies in discourse due to contrasts in linguistic, social, and cultural background. In this section we give an overview of some typical features of native–nonnative interaction that occur in normal contact situations and where at least some effort of mutual cooperation can be taken for granted.

First, we mention some discourse strategies immigrants apply in order to survive in communicating in a second language. Second, we consider the verbal techniques natives rely on in such encounters. Third, we briefly summarize two categories of interethnic communication that deal with interactions of natives and those nonnatives who have a good knowledge of a second language, but due to other reasons fail in communication.

Communication Strategies of Immigrants

The following list of strategies gives an illustrative, selected overview.

Topic Abandonment   The nonnative does not dispose of the lexical units or grammatical–semantic devices in discourse. After attempts to give information or to tell a story, he gives up. Examples are given in Tarone, Fauenfelder, and Selinker (1976), Becker, Dittmar, and Klein (1979), Nemoianu (1980), HPD (1979), and Dittmar (1981).

---

[2] Once again, prejudices are considerably determined by economic factors, for example, job competition.

8 On the Discourse of Immigrant Workers

Appeal to Authority. The lack of words or grammatical meaning can be bridged by requests for information. This is illustrated by (1)[3]

(1)
    T–1: *Der (ein Franzose) geht zu essen, aber*—**wie die Dinger heißt, weiß ich nicht**
    G: *Speisekarte*
    T–1: 'This one (a Frenchman) goes to eat, but—I don't know how do you call it'
    G: 'menu'

Appeal to authority is a strategy to prevent miscommunication. Examples are presented and discussed in Tarone, Frauenfelder, and Selinker (1976).

Approximation and Paraphrase. The clauses of example (2) illustrate approximation of the correct first-language unit. The example is drawn from Dittmar (1981).

(2)   a. *eine Woche Schwimmbad*
           one week Swimmingpool
    b. *eine Woche Wasser*
           one week water
    c. *eine Woche Meer*
           one week sea

(Intended was the German equivalent of the Spanish sentence *una semana la pasaron a la playa*.)

In (2), the Spanish immigrants do not know the German word *Strand* (beach) for *playa*. They try to convey the meaning by approximating the intended word. We call approximation the substitution of a word or expression *within a certain word class* for the intended concept that cannot be expressed appropriately in the second language. Approximation follows the principle of *genus proximum*.

Paraphrase involves meaning equivalents beyond an expression within a word class. Examples can be found in Tarone, Frauenfelder, and Selinker (1976) and Dittmar (1981).

Self-Corrections. Self-corrections can have several communicative and social functions in the discourse of an immigrant learner—anticipation of misunderstandings, monitoring of speech in order to optimize the

---
[3] The following utterances are drawn from recordings with Turkish adolescents that were made by Norbert Dittmar, Gabriele Nöldner, and Aslihan Tokdemir in 1980 in Berlin.

learning process, insecurity of target or communication norms, indication of positive attitudes toward integration, and others. Typical self-corrections concern the lexical choice of words and, of course, the grammar of the second language. Typical findings in that area are

> (1) Semantically weak or empty categories, such as gender or case, are *more* often corrected than semantically important categories such as person, number, or tense. (2) Frequency highly correlates with susceptibility to monitoring. (3) Semanticity and frequency have to be completed by factors of on-line productions; thus, anticipating corrections are less successful than retrospective corrections. (Dietrich, 1982, p. 149).

The following example (3) illustrates self-correction.

(3)
       N: *Haben Sie auch schon mal Ärger gehabt?*
       M: *ja, ja, hab ich schon Ärger **gemacht***
       N: *nicht Ärger gemacht, sondern Ärger ...*
→ M: ***gehape, gehape, gehab***
       N: 'Did you get already into trouble?'
       M: 'yes, yes, I **caused** already a lot of trouble'
       N: 'not caused trouble, but you got ...'
       M: '**got, got, got**'

In the line marked by →, M corrects herself (self-correction).[4]

Signals of Requested Feedback and Stereotypes. Apparently, every learner of a second language has to fear that at each moment in the verbal interaction he will not be understood. We therefore find in the discourse of immigrants a high rate of feedback signals like "you understand?", "understood?". The immigrant seems to remind the hearer by this signal that he has a limited knowledge of the second language and that a permanent search for the intended meaning is necessary. The closing of a speech event can be marked by such expressions as (1) *alles fertig* (all ready), (2) *alles kaputt* (all broken), (3) *alles klar* (all ok), (4) *prima—danke—auf wiedersehen* (ok—thanks—bye bye). There are more complex expressions, too. Collections can be found in Hakuta (1974) and Dittmar (1982).

Strategies of Using and Relying on the First Language. The use of the first language to attempt to convey the intended meaning in the second language is shown here on three levels: transfer of lexical items, transfer of syntactic patterns, and entire code switching. That the phonetic output

---

[4] Data from HPD (1975); Klein and Dittmar (1979). N is a German, M a Spanish female immigrant.

in the second language considerably reflects the phonetics of the mother tongue need not be explained; numerous descriptions have shown this (e.g., Hager, 1982; Rieck, 1974; Tarone, 1978).

Lexical transfer is illustrated in the following example:[5]

(4)   *Zum Essen hat er in ein* **Lokanta** *gegangen and* **gesetzt**
      'He went to a restaurant in order to eat and sat down'

The Turkish adolescent who uttered this sentence in German transfers Turkish *lokanta* (*restaurant—lokant:* similar phonetic shape) and *oturmak* (the meaning difference in German of *sich setzen* and *sitzen* is covered by *oturmak*).

Syntactic transfer may be illustrated by word-order phenomena. The order of words in the second language is built upon the syntax of the first language. Example (5) illustrates this.

(5)   *Aber eine Kinder,* **egal** *Deutschland egal España, en España eine* **Kinder kleine,** *Vater Deutschland und Schule España, alle zusammen.*
      'But one child, either in Germany or in Spain, if there is a little child who goes to a Spanish school and whose father lives in Germany, the family should stay together'.

What is transferred from the source language, Spanish, are the constructions *egal...egal* (Spanish *igual...igual*), which in German have to be expressed by *entweder...oder,* and the postposition of the adjective in *Kinder kleine* where German prescribes the placement of the adjective before the noun.

The transfer from the first into the second langage can have sources from all linguistic levels. The errors involved can sometimes be easily repaired by natives—particularly if they know parts of the immigrants' first language—but often misunderstandings follow. Empirical findings are reported in Becker, Dittmar, and Klein (1978) and in Klein (1981).

Code switching occurs if (1) a second-language learner uses his first language to express his intention under the assumption that the addressee understands at least something of his mother tongue, or (2) bilingual immigrants not balanced in the two languages switch from one language to the other according to topic, person, situation, or social domain. An exhaustive analysis of the first type of code switching is presented in Poplack (1981). Gumperz (1982, pp. 59–99) considers code switching to be embedded in discourse and interaction. In a sociolinguistic perspective,

---

[5] The data from (4) are from a Turkish adolescent in Berlin who had a conversation in German with Gabriele Nöldner, Aslihan Tokdemir, and Norbert Dittmar.

it has a social function. Gumperz distinguishes between "conversational" and "metaphorical" code switching.

Summarizing the essential points that have been raised so far, we can say that the following aspects are relevant in interethnic communication that deviates from the normal and regular organization of native–native discourse.

1. Because of lack of linguistic knowledge (lexicon, syntax, semantics, speech acts), the second-language learner may be forced to avoid, abandon, reduce, or complicate a message he intends to perform at any point in discourse.
2. "Repairs" play a different role in interethnic discourse: The native construes the intention of the second-language speaker in adjusting syntactic, semantic, and pragmatic extensions and deviations of meaning; "repairs" are frequent if speakers cooperate; if they do not occur, this may indicate unwillingness to cooperate and could lead to mutual nonacceptance and stigmatization.
3. The need for securing semantic information produces a higher frequency of feedback signals and questions concerning understanding.
4. Several principles of accommodation in discourse can be found.

   a. The native either reduces his language by maintaining grammaticality or he applies a variety of ungrammatical simplified registers: foreigner talk (Ferguson & De Bose, 1977).
   b. Both parties can facilitate communication and understanding by switching to a shared common language (the first language of the foreigner or a shared third language); if the native understands parts of the foreigner's first language, switching on behalf of the foreigner will be frequent.
   c. Nonverbal behavior becomes an important function (gaze, posture, gesture, proxemics, etc.).
   d. Introduction of an interpreter bridges the lack of mutual understanding (children for their parents).
   e. The use of questions, procedures for getting and keeping the floor, the principles of topic cohesion, speech rate, and intonation (among other markers) have specific functions in interethnic communication that differ from normal everyday talk.

As we have seen in the last sections, accommodation takes place in discourse in different facets and functions. Wide attention has been paid in the literature to the simplified variety natives frequently apply in talking to foreigners, in particular immigrants (foreigner talk). In the next section, we give a short account of this simplified register.

Foreigner Talk

According to Ferguson, foreigner talk is used by speakers of a language to outsiders who are felt to have very limited command of the language, or no command at all (Ferguson, 1971). Foreigner talk belongs to the language varieties of 'simplified registers'. Examples are the way a mother talks to her child or the native to the foreigner. There are two hypotheses about the social function of foreigner talk:

1. The simplified register of the native serves to facilitate understanding by the foreigner (HPD, 1975; Hinnenkamp, 1982).
2. Foreigner talk "expresses disdain, and continuously re-affirms the degradation of the foreign worker" (Bodeman & Ostow, 1975).

We can conclude from several case studies that (1) is a prominent characteristic of foreigner talk, whereas (2) may but need not happen.

Based on the available empirical studies, Ferguson and De Bose consider foreigner talk as "the variety of language that is regarded by a speech community as primarily appropriate for addressing foreigners" (1977, p. 103). According to Ferguson and De Bose, widespread (universal?) foreigner talk features are

> slow, exaggerated enunciation; greater overall loudness; use of full forms instead of contractions; short sentences; parataxis (pure or with adverbial connectives such as *maybe; bye-and-bye*); repetition of words; analytic paraphrases of lexical items and certain constructions; reduction of inflections (often by the selection of one or two all-purpose forms, e.g., *me* for *I, my, mine, me* in English, infinitive for all non-past verb forms in Italian, *die* for all forms of the definite article in German); lack of function words (e.g., articles, prepositions, auxiliaries); use of feedback devices such as invariable tag questions; avoidance of strongly dialect or slang forms in favor of more standard forms; limited number of phonological simplifications . . . ; special lexicon of quantifiers, intensifiers, and modal particles used in constructions not matching 'normal' language; use of foreign or foreign-sounding words (1977, p. 104).

Illustrating some of the mentioned foreign talk features, we quote a natural conversation of an Italian immigrant and a German worker in a factory near Heidelberg (participant observation and tape recording by Norbert Dittmar, reported in HPD, 1975, pp. 60–100). We do not explain the underlying intentions of the two workers because this would demand too much space (see HPD, 1975). The situation simply is this: Luigi (L) apparently has defective glasses; Karl (the German, K) tries to find out what problem L has with his glasses and what the doctor perhaps intended when giving him advice.

Interaction in foreigner talk and "Pidgin-German"	Approximate English version
K: *das gut, Brille?*	this good, glasses?
L: *vielleicht momentan jetzt alles gut; vielleicht zehn Minuten, viel dolor*	perhaps at present now all good; perhaps ten minutes, much dolor
K: *ja, ja, Doktor sprechen schon?*	yes, yes, doctor speak already?
L: *ja, ich sprechen Doktore*	yes, I speak doctor
vielleicht ein Stück bissel kaputt	perhaps one piece little bit broken
K: *vielleicht Doktor denken, du momentan schreiben oder Zeitung verstehst, lesen; vielleicht zehn Minuten wieder weg, weiss net; vielleicht niks alles Tag, verstehst, nur momentan vielleicht schreiben oder so, verstehst?*	perhaps doctor thinks, you at present write or newspaper, understand, read; perhaps ten minutes already away, don't know; perhaps no all day, understand, only this moment perhaps write or so, understand?
L: *ah, bissele gut, ja vielleicht zehn Minuten viel dolor das*	yeah, little bit good, perhaps ten minutes much dolor, this
K: *ja, du muss doch mal zum Doktor gehen, nochmal Doktor, sagen, ich zehn Minuten viel Schmerzen, verstehst?*	yeah, you have to go to the doctor, once again doctor, say, me ten minutes much pain, understand?
L: *vielleicht andere Kollege . . .*	perhaps other colleague . . .
K: *ja, vielleicht bissel Dolmetscher, ja andre Kollege wo mehr Deutsch, ja . . . du brauchst ein Kollege wo bissel spricht, ja, ja, du musst noch einmal zum Doktor gehen, verstehst; noch einmal Doktor und sagen: viel Schmerz, zehn Minuten gucke normal und dann viel Schmerz, verstehst? keine Brille halbe, verstehst?*	yeah, perhaps little bit interpreter, yeah, other colleague that more German, yeah . . . you need a colleague that little bit speak, yeah, yeah, you should go once again to the doctor, understand; once again doctor and say: much pain, ten minutes normal, and then much pain, understand? no half glasses, understand?
L: *. . . sage andreKollege, niks gut, vielleicht halbe hier, halbe hier . . .*	say other colleague, no good, perhaps half here, half there
K: *vielleicht Schmerze Kopf, verstehst?*	perhaps pain head, understand?

Most features of the pidginized German of K fit the description given by Ferguson and De Bose. The most salient characteristics are

1. Simplification: dropping of morphology; omission of articles, prepositions, avoidance of subordinate clauses (parataxis); use of infi-

nitives; use of simple verbs (*sagen, sprechen, gucken, schreiben, gehen*) instead of more specific (composite) verbs;
2. Short sentences;
3. Hypercorrect use of the German standard (K normally speaks a Palatinate dialect);
4. The semantic concept of modality is frequently expressed by the adverb *vielleicht* instead of modal verbs or more complex grammatical constructions;
5. There is only one negator: *niks;*
6. We find only three quantifiers: *bissele, ein,* and *viel;*
7. The more K pidginizes his speech, the more he slows down his enunciation and marks parts of the words by strange pitch and intonation contours.
8. Salient frequency of feedback signals with the function of controlling understanding: *ja, verstehst?*
9. Wrong order: *Schmerze Kopf* instead of *Kopfschmerzen, Brille halbe* instead of *halbe Brille*.

In-depth explanations of the features of K's foreigner talk are given in HPD (1975, pp. 93–98). Further examples of the communication strategies and tactics of natives talking to foreigners via a simplified register can be found in Long (1982), who reports detailed results of an empirical study of foreigner talk.

Sociopsychological Perspectives on Interethnic Communication

The type of discourse between natives and immigrants is very much dependent on sociopsychological factors in interaction. Sentence length, semantic complexity, paraphrase and speech-act accommodation, communicative care, creative constructions in the second language, and willingness to detect approximative meaning in the foreigner's discourse promote different continua in convergence or divergence in conversational attempts at accommodation. From an interethnic or intercultural point of view, the outcome of convergence or divergence may be seen in the framework of Tajfel's theory of intergroup relations. Tajfel and Turner (1979) conceived an intergroup–interindividual continuum,

> where at one extreme [the interindividual pole] encounters would be found between two or more people. These encounters were fully determined by their interpersonal relationships and individual characteristics, and at the other extreme [the intergroup pole] there would be encounters which were fully determined by the participants'

> knowledge of their memberships in contrastive social categories. The more participants in an encounter view the situation as being towards the intergroup end of the continuum, the more they tend to treat members of the intergroup as undifferentiated items in an unified social category rather than in terms of their individual characters. . . . Tajfel's theory . . . enables us to predict that the more individuals define situations in intergroup terms and decide to maintain or to achieve a positive social identity, the more likely speech divergence is to occur. (Thakerar, Giles, & Cheshire, 1982, p. 214)

Tajfel's theory of intergroup relations is not the only one that contributes to a better understanding of interethnic communication and interaction. We have two further approaches. Let us call the first one the 'theory of communication codes' and the second one the 'theory of ethnic boundaries'.

The theory of communication codes has been outlined by J. J. Gumperz in numerous articles (Gumperz, 1978, 1982; Gumperz & Cook-Gumperz, 1981). Gumperz assumes that failures in interethnic communication are mainly due to ethnic differences in communicative style and only partly to differences in grammar. Verbal and nonverbal signs have to be synchronized in order to transmit the right social meaning in interaction. Both kinds of signs are associated not only with referential meaning, but also with social symbols.

Contextualization cues (Gumperz, 1982, pp. 130–139) can be performed by single phonetic, grammatical, lexical, paralinguistic, pragmatic, and nonverbal devices. They carry social meaning and they contribute, according to Gumperz, mainly to success or failure in interethnic communication. The performance of speech acts according to the right native norms and conventions is crucial in so-called gate-keeping situations (Erikson, 1976) such as job interviews, consultations, or school situations, in which the immigrant's discourse can lead to success or failure.

In the light of the theory of ethnic boundaries, failure in communication is functional (perhaps "useful") in order to establish, maintain, and even reinforce ethnic boundaries—there is apparently a social need for producing the mutual impression and perception that "other" is significantly different from self. In particular, ethnic boundaries play an important role in big cities where there is no "territorial" boundary. According to Barth (1969), ethnic boundaries guarantee the integrity and identity of group values. The essential assumption is that ethnic categories are produced by attributions of identity in interactions by the actors themselves. In this perspective, interethnic communication produces the social organization of ethnic boundaries. Case studies in this paradigm have been carried out by Frake (1968) and Moerman (1974). Language, in this approach, is seen as a tool that reflects and creates the validity of social relations between groups and their mutual experience with one another.

Gumperz, Frake, Moerman, Erikson, and others exemplify their theoretical approaches with case studies. Methodologically, we have to realize that we do not yet know the dependent and the independent variables. If we say that external features of ethnicity govern interethnic communication, we do not explain why, for example, Japanese people in Germany are less ethnically stigmatized than Turks or Pakistanis. This can be explained, of course, only if we take the sociopolitical and sociohistorical background of ethnic stigmatization into account. If we take language as a dependent, and ethnicity as an independent, variable, we overlook the fact that individuals in interethnic encounters decide for themselves whether ethnic boundaries are relevant or not. This decision depends on a number of factors. Some encounters rely on the identity of the participant's occupation (shopkeeper, footballer, or gardener), and in such cases different ethnic backgrounds are not important; some reinforce existing stereotypes and prejudices; others constitute ethnic boundaries.

The theories mentioned above account for some of the facets and "games" of interethnic communication. We have only dealt with some case studies and hypotheses. Substantial empirical work has still to be done, in particular because massive migration throughout the world has considerably changed our societies in the last 30 years.

DISCOURSE ORGANIZATION

Interlanguage as a Restricted Communication Mode

An approach that views second-language acquisition and use in the context of social interaction, where language is regarded in its function of meeting specific communicative needs on the part of the learner as well as a barrier that has strong impact on social relations between the members of the host-society and the foreigner (see Dittmar & Thielicke, 1979), implies a shift in perspective in the field of second-language research. What has been the main objective in the field over a long period, the learner's explicit knowledge of second-language forms and structures, now appears to be only one aspect of a much more complex phenomenon.

The notion of second-language competence should go beyond the mere description of the respective linguistic devices. In the introduction to a collection of articles written within this kind of framework, Hatch specifies what is meant by knowledge of appropriate communicative rules: "Researchers have overlooked the need for the learners to acquire knowledge of the rule-bound system that exists *at the discourse level* (Sacks, Schegloff & Jefferson, 1974). Furthermore, learners using a second language manifest a knowledge of the pragmatics of the language—the ability to use a language which is appropriate to a particular context" (Hatch, 1978, p. 6). These claims have led to a redefinition of the notion of 'competence', which now includes the acquisition of strategies of social interaction (Dittmar and Thielicke, 1979), conversational maxims, context-dependent speech act rules, discourse organization principles—besides the acquisition of the explicit linguistic means. In analyzing second-language acquisition in the context of its multifaceted functions, one is faced with the problem that the proven methodology in that field, that is, structural analysis of utterances on the sentence level, is no longer the appropriate tool to cope with the new aspects in question. A new methodology needs to be developed that allows for a systematic categorization of the factors at work and that therefore can be used as a basis for comparative studies across languages and across learner varieties within one language.

Fortunately, second-language research benefited from work that has been carried out in the field of sociolinguistics (e.g., Dittmar, 1976; Labov & Fanshel, 1977) and ethnolinguistics (Grimshaw, 1982; Gumperz, 1982). Discourse analysis and speech act theory have proved to be fruitful approaches for second-language research.

In the following, we want to look at one particular language variety—the pidginized interlanguage of foreign workers in Western industrial countries—and to give examples of discourse analysis in order to show not only what the explanatory values of that approach are but also where unsolved problems still remain.

The first problem is linked to the assumption of a single specific interlanguage, spoken by immigrant workers. This is certainly a generalization that has no correspondence in reality. Interlanguage has to be regarded as a continuum, which implies that the language is neither interpersonally nor intrapersonally a stable system of particular syntactic and lexical forms. In any group of foreign workers, there are speakers who have moved close to target-language norms, while others have fossilized on a level of highly simplified speech. The degree of competence achieved is closely related to what Schumann calls "social and psychological distance" of the individual learner. "Social and psychological distance are seen as the primary factors hindering second-language development. . . . The pidginization hypothesis predicts that where social and psychological distance prevail, we will find pidginization persisting in the speech of second-language learners" (Schumann, 1979, p. 115).

Looking at a large sample of "*Gastarbeiterdeutsch*" (immigrant workers' German), a picture arises that suggests that the majority of foreign workers who emigrated as adults have developed a linguistic system showing basically the same features across the group. The acquisition of the foreign language is determined and limited by the communicative function

8 On the Discourse of Immigrant Workers

it has to serve (Schumann 1978), which means that language proficiency is not regarded as a goal in itself but that the acquisitional process stops when the indispensable practical needs of everyday survival are considered to be covered sufficiently. The close relation between communicative tasks and language acquisition implies "that it is not permissible to separate the linguistic features of a learner language from its social status and function in interaction" (Dittmar, 1982, p. 13). Several studies have taken this approach, analyzing pidginized language varieties in the context of their role in interaction and communication. Before providing concrete examples of data analysis, we give a summary of what are considered to be the main features of pidginized language varieties. Although we are confronted with a rather heterogeneous terminology in the literature, the substance of the observations and explanations seems to converge in a few generally accepted principles:

1. Pidginized Varieties (PV) Make Use of the Pragmatic Mode. "The pidgin speech exhibits almost an extreme case of the pragmatic mode of communication" (Givón, 1979, p. 99). Givón explains the claim in the following way: "The most fascinating feature of pidgin speech is the fact that although it seems 'not to have any syntax' its pragmatics at the discourse level is virtually intact. Thus although identifying subject and predicate is a tantalizingly difficult task, identifying the message and in particular the topic-comment is much easier" (1979, p. 99). The following points can be regarded as an explanation of what is meant by 'pragmatic mode' as a general characteristic.

2. PV Are Highly Context Dependent. Mainly due to the lack of syntactic means, the PV cannot go beyond performing immediate labeling tasks. "The tasks or topics of communication in the pidgin-using society are immediate, obvious and non-remote. They are right there in both space and time" (Givón, 1979, p. 101). Given these communicative restrictions, the context becomes a factor in its own right. One can distinguish between different levels of contextual reference: the discourse context in a given conversation, the situational context, and the context of presupposed 'world knowledge'. In contrast to a fully competent speaker, who may also draw upon these sources according to a particular register he intends to apply, the speaker of PV has to rely on contextual information. The integration of the pragmatic background becomes a necessary condition for successful discourse, and its contribution to communication cannot be replaced by supplying the explicit information through linguistic devices.

3. PV Work on the Basis of Implicit Reference. Again, one can learn from results provided by studies on discourse analysis in general because the pidginized speaker makes use of properties of natural languages. The

difference lies in the function and in the extent of the application of a specific pragmatic device and the role it plays in a particular linguistic system.

As has been shown in the previous chapter, the possibilities of interactional negotiation are limited in the case of the pidginized second-language speaker. Large parts of the information given remain on the level of implication. The following example is taken from a study on temporal reference in the speech of Turkish foreign workers (von Stutterheim 1984). In the early fossilized varieties, no syntactic devices are used to establish temporal reference, and verbal morphology and temporal conjunctions have not been acquired. Instead, two forms of implicit reference are used, which can be called 'associative' and 'inherent' temporal reference. An example of the first category would be *Türkei grosse Haus, Deutschland alles kleine Wohnung* (Turkey big house, Germany all very small apartment). Only if the listener can associate the names given with the specific knowledge he has about these countries in relation to a specific life history is he able to make sense of a given utterance with respect to a particular temporal order. The information has to be deduced from external knowledge. Inherent temporal reference would be used in cases like (a) *Turkey vacation come back, my husband ill,* or (b) *Turkey vacation, my husband ill.* The temporal relation between the reported events—sequence in (a), simultaneity in (b)—can be inferred from the particular semantics of the verb or noun group, in the first part of the utterance, which implies the temporal property of 'perfectivity' for (a) and of 'state' for (b). The role the various forms of implicit reference play in PV has been shown on the sentence level, but it is an important principle in the structuring of whole stretches of discourse. In order to "instruct" the listener how and what to infer, the speaker applies a set of discourse organization principles.

4. PV Have Developed a Number of Discourse Organization Principles. The following discourse structuring devices are typically used in pidginized varieties:

a. Topic comment or theme–rheme structure: for example, *ich Kinder— vielleicht 100 Kinder alle Tag* (Me children—perhaps 100 children all day) (Dittmar, 1981, p. 19). The sentence contains two levels of informative importance. In terms of a functional view of language, the theme provides the known information, or background, in a sentence and the rheme the new information, or foreground, part of the utterance (Dittmar, 1981, p. 16).

b. The series of reported events correspond to the real-time order of events. This means that a temporal reference point is fixed first—

this can be in the form of a question from the interlocutor—and then the subsequent speech is organized such that the sequence of the reported events reflects their actual temporal order.

c. Two referential domains are contrasted. The pairs of contrast can be logical or temporal in nature and are typically marked by an adverb, *heute vier Schule neu mein Dorf,* or an explicit temporal frame, *ich kleine Kind—eine Schule vielleicht hundert Kinder* (I little child—one school perhaps 100 children) (Dittmar, 1981, p. 19), where a temporal opposition in the sense 'before . . . now' is expressed. Where logical contrasts are built up, for example, to introduce hypothetical meaning, the explicit lexical information is usually given. The interpretation demands drawing a conclusion from more than one formally unlinked utterance fragment, for example, *ich viel arbeite, viel Geld—wenig arbeite, wenig Geld.* (Me much work, much money—little work, little money). This general discourse organization principle is based on the distinction between the 'backgrounded' and 'foregrounded' parts of an utterance.

5. PV Demand Interpretative and Speculative Work on the Part of the Interlocutor. The impression of the second-language utterances mean that interpretation plays a critical role. The listener has to be active in guessing and associating on the basis of his contextual knowledge. The possibility of checking an interpretation is very limited, and so the message is partly constituted by the interlocutor. This implies that the course and the success of a conversation are highly dependent on the attitude and the subjective estimation of the interlocutor.

This characterization of a pidginized interlanguage has clearly demonstrated that social and (inter)personal factors play a crucial role in the communication between a native speaker and a second-language speaker. In looking at the organization, the content, and the communicative success or failure of a conversation, the method of discourse analysis can provide an adequate framework for integrating social factors into a study of second-language acquisition and usage.

There have only been a few analyses available based on empirical data from the group in question (i.e., immigrant workers). All of them still have exploratory character and have developed their own individual descriptive categories. The effort of putting them together in a general theory of conversational analysis has still to be undertaken.

In the following, we present an example that deals with an informal conversation between a foreign worker and a German interviewer at the home of the informant. The main discourse type in this context is 'narration'. This study has been carried out by Dittmar, Klein, and von

Stutterheim, who analyzed temporal reference in the speech of nine informants with different source languages (Italian, Spanish, Turkish) and different levels of proficiency.

Temporality in Learner Narratives

The aim of this study is to show how temporal reference is established by linguistic and pragmatic means and how temporal relations are used to structure events in larger stretches of discourse. In narratives where the speaker reports on concrete events and personal experiences, temporality plays a threefold role. (The following general remarks on temporality are taken from Klein, 1981.)

1. The event as a whole has to be embedded in the discourse context.
2. The event has a complex internal structure consisting of subevents and various temporal relations between them.
3. At any moment in his story, the speaker can insert items of information that are not temporally fixed by the event and its temporal structure itself.

The way in which this threefold structure is expressed is based on

1. the speaker's assumptions about what the listener knows or is able to infer on the base of his given knowledge. For example, the speaker can generally assume that the listener knows the time of utterance, and so "anchoring" can be carried out relative to the time of utterance without being explicitly introduced. He may also assume that the listener knows the calendar system and that he can anchor his story with the aid of this system;
2. the expressive devices the speaker has at his disposal, including tense markers, adverbials, and the linear arrangement of utterances.

The analysis of several narratives yielded the following picture of discourse organization principles that work on the basis of shared knowledge:

1. 'Framing'; that is, a time span is introduced, and this time span functions as a reference time for the following events that it includes.
2. 'Chaining'; that is, a time span is introduced, and subsequent events are anaphorically related to it, either explicitly (*und dann*) or via asyndetic serialization.
3. 'Repeated anchoring'; that is, a deferred time of utterance is introduced by a *verbum dicendi*. In more complex cases, this third technique may in turn involve framing and chaining, and perhaps even repeated anchoring again.

8 On the Discourse of Immigrant Workers

If the appropriate linguistic means are not available, the speaker has to follow one of the discourse organization principles in order to avoid misunderstanding. This implies that a higher level of second-language command allows for more freedom in organizing the order of reported events in ongoing discourse. The early pidginized speaker, however, with only a few adverbs at his disposal, is strictly tied to a number of pragmatic principles (e.g., implicit reference, principle of natural serialization).

Francisco C. in the Role of an Interpreter: The Example of a Narrative in a Pidginized Variety

In the following, we give an exploratory account of temporal reference in a narrative told by Francisco C. (SP-22).[6]

Informant and Data

This 40-year-old male Spanish informant comes from Royales de Hoyo (Castilia Vieja) and at the time of the conversation he had been in Germany for 6 years (date of immigration: 1968, date of tape-recorded conversation: 1974). In Spain he was an agricultural worker; in Germany he works as an unskilled laborer in a quarry (near Heidelberg). He is married, but lives alone in Germany. He has never participated in formal language training. At his place of work, he has contacts with Germans, but the work does not allow him to talk much. He has no contacts with Germans outside work (he lives in a dormitory not located in a residential area). After having earned enough money, he intends to go back to Spain. He prefers having work, but in Spain there is none. Therefore, he has no clear future plans: "but God knows what will happen." The narrative analyzed here is part of a two-hour conversation with the informant in 1974 in the dormitory where the informant was living. Apart from the informant, Bert-Olaf Rieck, Elisabeth Thielicke, and Norbert Dittmar participated in the conversation.

Some Characteristics of the Informant's Second-Language Variety

The informant's German is pidginized. There is no inflectional morphology. In his discourse, simple words are put together in a certain order. The predominant grammatical category are nouns. Only a few verbs are used, such as *to work, to sleep, to speak/say, to think, to do, to come, to go*. There is one demonstrative pro-form (*dies*); concepts like modality and causality are usually referred to by particular lexical items. Nearly all grammatical surface markers are missing. Temporal reference is established in the discourse of SP-22 by (1) natural order of events, (2) lexical expressions (calendar time, adverbs), (3) contrast of lexical items, and (4) combination of lexical items.

---

[6] SP-22 is an informant of the Heidelberg Project. More details about the project and the informant will be found in HPD (1975) and Klein and Dittmar (1979).

The analysis proceeds in three steps: (1) presentation of the narrative, (2) comments on the underlying structure of temporal order, and (3) a more abstract account of the temporal sequence.

Problems of Understanding Francisco C.'s Narrative

1. *In erste Jahr ich komme in Urlaub, in Madrid.*
   'In the first year I come to holidays in Madrid'
2. *Eine Frau—*
   'a woman (came to ask me something)'
3. *nja du grosse, bei mir, nicht bei dir*
   (not translatable. The approximate meaning is: 'You are (pointing to the interviewer) tall in comparison with her, but in comparison with me, she was not tall'. Apparently, the woman was as short as the informant.)
4. *Ich komme, ja*
   'I am coming'
5. *hier Frau* (points to a place)
   'here woman'
6.   *kollege nicht verstehen, Frau nicht verstehen*
   'colleague not understand, woman not understand' (the woman and another person could not understand each other)
7. *Und meine Frau sprechen, Name Paco, Paco, "esa mujer es alamana o francesa"?*
   'and my wife said: "Paco, Paco, es mujer es alamana o francesa?" '
8. *Ich spreche: "Guten Tag, buenas tardes"*
   'I speak: "Hello, buenas tardes" '
9. *y (= und) Kollege sprechen Frau: "Wieviel Uhr Zug Paris?"*
   'and woman speak(s) (to the) colleague: "What time train (to) Paris?" '
10. *Kollege spreche: "no te comprendo", nicht verstehen, "no te comprendo", nicht verstehen.*
    'Colleague speak: "no te comprendo", not understand, "no te comprendo", not understand.'
11. *Ich meine Koffer, meine Tochter, Frau, meine Familie, meine Tante in Madrid.*
    'I and my suitcase, my daughter, wife, my family, my aunt were in Madrid.'
12. *Ich viel kommen Madrid,*
    'I often come to Madrid,'
13. *meine Tante in Madrid.*
    'my aunt in Madrid.'

8 On the Discourse of Immigrant Workers

14. *Ich gucke*
    'I look'
15. *spreche: "Guten Tag"*
    'I speak: "Hello" '
16. (paralinguistic cues indicating turn taking)
    "Guten Tag"
    ' "Hello" '
17. (paralinguistic cues indicating turn taking)
    "Deutsch?"
    ' "German?" '
18. (paralinguistic cues indicating turn taking)
    "Ja, Hallo wieviel Uhr Zug Madrid Paris?"
    ' "Yes! Hello, what time train Madrid Paris?" '
19. *Ich spreche: "Hallo Kollege", spreche: "Amigo, quando sale el tren de Madrid para Paris?"*
    'I speak: "Hello colleague", speak: "My friend, at what time does the train leave from Madrid to Paris?" '
20. *Y me dijó: "A las siete horas"* [laughter]
    'and he told me: "Seven o'clock" '
21. *mhm, hä? normal spreche Deutschland "siebzehn Uhr"*
    'normally speak Germany: five o'clock p.m.'
22. *spreche: "Hallo, siebzehn Uhr, via Nummer neun"*
    'speak: "Hello, five o'clock, via number nine" '

Comments on the Narrative

In the first sentence, the past time reference point *in erste Jahr* (that means '5 years ago', because at the time of the interview the informant had been living for 6 years in Germany) and the locality (Madrid) are established. That (1) refers to the past can be inferred from (a) previous discourse (the informant is speaking about experiences during his stay in Germany), (b) *in erste Jahr,* (c) *Urlaub* (he is not on holiday now), (d) *Madrid* (the conversation takes place in Heidelberg). (a–d) indicate the past reference point. (2) introduces a woman, apparently an actor in the story. There is no deictic expression indicating that she was in Madrid, but we guess that this is the case, since generally nobody would say meaningless things in normal conversation. Note that no local specification is given. (3) seems to be a specification of the woman just mentioned. This can be inferred from the intonation and the context. Why this particular property (tallness) is selected is not clear at all.

(1) establishes the temporal frame and the reference point. (1–3) give the setting of the story. The events (in Labov's terminology, the "complication phase") begin with (4). (4) and (5) contain implicit local deixis.

Given that the woman has a certain position in the place establishing a local reference point (5), Francisco is moving toward her position. Note the interesting fact that his perspective (the movement of coming) is mentioned before the local reference point is given. (4) and (5), put together, establish the directionality of the action. (5) is some kind of orientation marker for the ongoing action. The present setting and time of speech (the deictic expression *here,* accompanied by a gesture) is used as a contrasting device in order to mark movement and 'time in progress'. An interesting strategy of the informant seems to be the recourse to the present using locative deixis. The implicit meaning of (5) is 'imagine that this distance I am showing you here in this room is the same as in the past event'. We could call this lack of a feature turn an 'analogy strategy'. (6) reestablishes the time reference point introduced by (1). It is temporally linked to (4) although there is no temporal connector at the verbal surface. It is the second link in a temporal sequence of contingent actions. Note that the colleague has not been introduced to the setting. He is mentioned here as if he were a person who has already been introduced. There is no clear relationship between *colleague not understand* and *woman not understand.* There could have been two temporally ordered events: X did not understand and then Y did not understand. Because of the lack of syntactic and semantic means, the informant has to describe the perspective of the two persons separately instead of showing simultaneous occurrence.

Account of the Temporal Sequence

There is a first interesting hypothesis here: Simultaneity with regard to time cannot be marked. (7) specifies the "action" (performing a speech act) of a fourth person who has not been introduced before—her participation in the happening is just taken for granted. Because *Frau* is specified by *meine,* and *esa mujer* is referred to by her speech act, we understand that *meine Frau* is another woman, probably the wife of the informant. (6) and (7) are linked by *und.* The temporal sequence is not established by temporal devices, but by 'order of mention' equals 'temporal sequence of events'. To be involved in the activity of speaking (announcement) and then actually saying something (two sentences in reported speech) is in real-time terms one action only. We therefore consider (7) to be one point in the temporal chain. Instead of answering (7), (8) specifies the speaking activity of the informant by mentioning a fourth event that is not explicitly temporally connected to (7). (8) displays nicely the informant's bilingual knowledge. As soon as we take (9) into account, we realize that *buenas tardes* in (8) is not directed to a specific person (the colleague or the woman). It has the function of signaling: "I am

8 On the Discourse of Immigrant Workers

able to remove your misunderstanding because I am bilingual." (9) specifies the occasion of the misunderstanding: *What time does the train leave for Paris?* (9) is temporally connected to (8) by 'order of mention' equals 'temporal order' (no explicit marking). (10) expresses the ongoing complication—the misunderstanding between the woman and the colleague. Once again, there is no explicit temporal marker. But the change of turn (Y replies to X) is some kind of pragmatic temporal marker.

(11) goes back to the time reference of (1), interrupting or removing the temporal sequence from (4) to (10). At the most dramatic point in the narrative (10), Francisco suspends the ongoing action by giving more background information about the setting: He had a suitcase, and he was apparently accompanied by his daughter, his wife, and his aunt. The probable place of the interaction, the station, is not mentioned anywhere. But "suitcase" and the question in (9) indicate that the interaction took place in the station. (12) leaves ("fades out") the whole past time frame and makes a general statement located in the time of speech. (13) gives the reason for (12). Both propositions are timeless, general statements. They refer back to the time of speech.

(14–20) is once again a temporal sequence. What is the point in the temporal chain from which (13) departs? It could be (8), but in fact it is (10). (14) presupposes that complication introduced by (10). The *Guten Tag* in (8) could not have happened before (9) and (10), because there had to be a legitimate reason for entering the interaction. (15) and (16) are ritual greetings with the pragmatic function of "we both agree on the fact that the intervention of a third person in the present communication conflict can be useful." In (16–18) the transition from one turn to the other by the speaker is not marked explicitly. But it is very clearly indicated by intonation. Thus, there is no explicit marking of temporal chaining, but nevertheless the temporal sequence is established by pragmatic devices. (17) means: "Are you a German?" The "yes" in (18) is the clear response. (19) is the initial attempt to resolve the complications formulated in (9) and (10). In (18), the German woman repeats her question given in (9). This question is translated by the informant in (19) and the Spanish answer by the colleague is given in (20). (21) refers back to the 'neutral' time of speech (general statement). Once again, the informant leaves the temporal chaining. At the same time, he shows that he is "really bilingual." (22) is the definite resolution of the complication in (9) and (10). The translation is completed, the informant showed his bilingual knowledge. From (14–22) no explicit temporal marking has been established. But the fact that some pragmatic principles have been applied successfully is reason enough to state that we should appreciate what one can do with very limited linguistic means.

CONSEQUENCES FOR SOCIAL RELATIONS

When talking about the social implications of language behavior, one characteristic feature of the role of language has to be born in mind: Language command itself does not essentially determine people's reactions toward foreigners. It is the correlation between this command and the particular socioeconomic and cultural status of a person or group that forms the conditions for social evaluation. Grimshaw developed a typology of 'varieties of communicative non-success' where he stresses that communicative success is "affected by the participants' assessment of conversational goals and their interpersonal relationships of power and affect." (Grimshaw, 1982, p. 30).

In the case of the foreign workers, linguistic incompetence has become a permanent state. Germans do not regard them as learners, but as pidgin speakers without any chance of, or desire for, language improvement. This, too, has consequences for mutual judgments. Thus the following conclusions are not claimed to hold true for any second-language learner, but only for a specific group of foreign workers.

1. The distortion of initial intention and message abandonment leads to misunderstanding or unintelligibility. Realizing this defect in communication, the interlocutors will react differently. From the point of view of the foreign workers, this may cause insecurity and resignation, leading them to drop whatever particular communicative goal they may have had in mind. The German interlocutor will give up trying to achieve clear understanding. The continuation of the conversation—if there is any—becomes a matter of politeness rather than an exchange of information, opinions, and so on. Moreover, uncertainty about the precise meaning of an utterance may create mutual suspicion. When it comes to the communication of unfamiliar ideas or facts, negotiation may be completely impossible.

2. The imprecision of second-language utterances involves the message being partly constituted by the interlocutor and may therefore turn out to be remote from the speaker's intention. The extensive role of inference and speculation introduces all kinds of prejudice and personal evaluation on the part of the listener, thus possibly confirming the stereotype he may already have.

In this context, cultural difference becomes an important factor. Social habits and moral conceptions function as major constituents of the interpretational background. In order to bridge a cultural gap such as exists between Turks and Germans, for example, extensive exchange of information and ideas would be necessary. As this does not take place, the different behavior patterns remain fundamentally strange in most cases. Furthermore, they are often taken as a reason for contempt or rejection. Differing norms of politeness ad hospitality constitute such examples. Germans often feel Turkish customs to be annoying and troublesome, and even worse, they can take them as a sign of stupidity and simplemindedness.

Especially in situations where the interlocutor is not a willing friend, but rather somebody who is not interested in making efforts to achieve correct understanding (authorities, colleagues at work, etc.), the main result of a conversation will be the creation of further grounds for mutual rejection. So language might in fact become an independent factor in avoidance of contact and in the mutually negative evaluation of Germans and the foreign workers.

3. The fact that foreign workers are often unable to argue or to explain a particular statement has an impact on their social standing. As the articulation of their needs is the necessary condition for achieving anything in a society, the foreign workers have little chance of changing their situation.

ACKNOWLEDGMENT

We are grateful for critical and helpful comments by Gisela Apitzsch and Eric Kellerman on the first version of this essay.

REFERENCES

Apitzsch, G. (1981). *MBSE - Ein Schritt zur sozialen Integration ausländischer Jugendlicher? Eine kritische Analyse vor dem Hintergrund der Entstehungsbedingungen und unter besonderer Berücksichtigung der Maßnahmen beim Bildungswerk der hessischen Wirtschaft.* Unpublished M.A. thesis, Freie Universität Berlin.

Apitzsch, G., & Dittmar, N. (1985). On the contact between German and Turkish adolescents: A case study. In K. Knapp, H. Emminger, & A. Knapp-Potthof (Eds.), *Intercultural Communication.* Berlin: de Gruyter. (to appear)

Barth, F. (1969). Pathan identity and its maintenance. In F. Barth (Ed.), *Ethnic groups and boundaries* (pp. 117–134). Boston: Little, Brown & Co.

Becker, A., Dittmar, N., & Klein, W. (1979). Sprachliche und soziale Determinanten im kommunikativen Verhalten ausländischer Arbeiter. In U. Quasthoff (Ed.), *Sprachstruktur—Sozialstruktur* (pp. 158–192). Königstein/Ts: Scriptor-Verlag.

Becker, A., & Perdue, C. (1982). Ein einziges Mißverständnis. Wie die Kommunikation schieflaufen kann und weshalb. *Osnabrücker Beiträge zur Sprachtheorie, 22,* 96–121.

Bodemann, Y. M., & Ostow, R. (1975). Lingua Franca und Pseudo-Pidgin in der Bundesrepublik: Fremdarbeiter und Einheimische im Sprachzusammenhang. *Zeitschrift für Literaturwissenschaft und Linguistik, 18,* 122–146.

Borris, M. (1973). *Ausländische Arbeiter in einer Großstadt.* Eine empirische Untersuchung am Beispiel Frankfurt. Frankfurt: Europäische Verlagsanstalt.

Dietrich, R. (1982). Selbstkorrekturen. Fallstudien zum mündlichen Gebrauch des Deutschen als Fremdsprache durch Erwachsene. *Zeitschrift für Literaturwissenschaft und Linguistik, 45* (12), 120–149.

Dittmar, N. (1976). *Sociolinguistics: A critical survey of theory and application.* London: Edward Arnold.

Dittmar, N. (1980). Ordering adult learners according to language abilities. In S. Felix (Ed.), *Second language acquisition* (pp. 205–232). Tübingen: Gunter Narr.

Dittmar, N. (1981). On the verbal organization of L_2 tense marking in an elicited translation task by Spanish immigrants in Germany. *Studies in Second Language Acquisition 3* (2), 136–164.

Dittmar, N. (1982). Semantische Eigenschaften pidginisierter Lernervarietäten des Deutschen. *Zeitschrift für Literaturwissenschaft und Linguistik, 45,* 9–34.

Dittmar, N., Klein, W., & von Stutterheim, C. v. (1982). *On the acquisition of temporality in German by adult migrant workers. A Case Study of Spanish, Italian and Turkish Learners.* Working paper., Max-Planck-Institute Nijmegen, Freie Universität Berlin.

Dittmar, N., & Thielicke, E. (1979). Der Niederschlag von Erfahrungen ausländischer Arbeiter mit dem institutionellen Kontext des Arbeitsplatzes in Erzählungen. In H. G. Soeffner (Ed.), *Interpretative Verfahren in den Text- und Sozialwissenschaften* (pp. 85–103). Stuttgart: J. B. Metzlersche.

Edmondson, W. J. (1982). On the determination of meaning in discourse. *Linguistische Berichte, 78,* 33–42.

Erickson, F. (1976). Gate-keeping encounters: The social selection process. In P. R. Sanday (Ed.), *Anthropology and public interest* (pp. 11–145). New York: Academic Press.

Ferguson, C. A. (1971). Absence of copula and notion of simplicity: A study of normal speech, baby talk, foreigner talk and pidgins. In D. Hymes, *Pidginization and creolization of languages,* (pp. 141–156). Cambridge: Cambridge University Press.

Ferguson, C. A. (1982). Simplified registers and linguistic theory. In L. Obler, & L. Menn (Eds.), *Exceptional Language and Linguistics.* New York: Academic Press.

Ferguson, C. A., & De Bose, C. E. (1977). Simplified registers, broken language, and pidginization. In A. Valdman (Ed.), *Pidgin and creole linguistics* (pp. 99–123). Bloomington and London: Indiana University Press.

Frake, C. O. (1968). The ethnographic study of cognitive systems. In J. A. Fishman (Ed.), *Readings in the sociology of language* (pp. 434–466). The Hague and Paris: Mouton.

Giles, H., & Smith, P. M. (1979). Accommodation theory: Optimal levels of convergence. In H. Giles & St. Clair (Eds.), *Language and social psychology.* London: Basil Blackwell.

Givón, T. (1979). From discourse to syntax. Grammar as a processing strategy. In T. Givón (Ed.), *Syntax and semantics* (Vol. 12), *Discourse and syntax* (pp. 81–112). New York: Academic Press.

Grimshaw, D. A. (1982). Comprehensive discourse analysis: An instance of professional peer interaction. *Language in Society, 11* (1), 15–47.

Gumperz, J. J. (1978). Dialect and conversational inference in urban communication. *Language in Society, 7,* 393–409.

Gumperz, J. J. (1982). *Discourse strategies.* Cambridge: Cambridge University Press.

Gumperz, J. J., & Cook-Gumperz, J. (1981). Ethnic differences in communicative style. In C. A. Ferguson & S. B. Heath (Eds.), *Language in the USA* (pp. 430–445). Cambridge: Cambridge University Press.

Hager, M. (1982). Terminal devoicing in German by Americans. *Linguistische Berichte, 79,* 63–71.

Hakuta, H. (1974). Prefabricated patterns and the emergence of structure in second language acquisition. *Language Learning, 24* (2), 287–298.

Hatch, E. M. (1978). Discourse analysis and second language acquisition. In E. M. Hatch (Ed.), *Second language acquisition* (pp. 401-474). Rowley, MA: Newbury House.

Hatch, E. M., & Long, M. H. (1980). Discourse analysis, what's that? In Larsen-Freeman (Ed.) *Discourse analysis in second language research* (pp. 1-40). Rowley, MA: Newbury House.

Heidelberger Forschungsprojekt 'Pidgin-Deutsch' (HPD) (1975). *Sprache und Kommunikation ausländischer Arbeiter.* Analysen, Berichte, Materialien, Kronberg/Ts: Scriptor-Verlag.

Heidelberger Forschungsprojekt 'Pidgin-Deutsch' (HPD) (1978). The acquisition of German syntax by foreign migrant workers. In D. Sankoff (Ed.), *Linguistic variation* (pp. 1-22). New York: Academic Press.

Heidelberger Forschungsprojekt 'Pidgin-Deutsch' (HPD) (1979). *Studies in the second language acquisition of foreign workers.* Unpublished Working Report 5, University of Heidelberg.

Hinnenkamp, V. (1982). *Foreigner talk und Tarzanische.* Eine vergleichende studie über die Sprechweise gegenüber Ausländern am Beispiel des Deutschen und des Türkischen. Hamburg: Buske.

Hübner, T. (1982). *The analysis of an interlanguage.* Papers given at the Second German–North American Workshop on Second Language Acquisition. Göhrde.

Klein, W. (1981). Knowing a language and knowing how to communicate. In A. R. Vermeer (Ed.), *Language problems of minority groups* (pp. 75-95). Tilburg.

Klein, W., & Dittmar, N. (1979). *Developing grammars: The acquisition of German by foreign workers.* Heidelberg and New York: Springer Verlag.

Labov, W., & Fanshel, D. (1977). *Therapeutic discourse: Psychotherapy as Conversation.* New York: Academic Press.

Larsen-Freeman, D. (Ed.). (1980). *Discourse analysis in second language research.* Rowley, MA: Newbury House.

Levinson, S. C. (1980). Speech act theory: The state of the art. *Language Teaching and Linguistic Abstracts, 13* (1), 5-24.

Long, M. H. (1982). Adaption an den Lerner. Die Aushandlung verstehbarer Eingabe in Gesprächen zwischen muttersprachlichen Sprechern und Lernern. *Zeitschrift für Literaturwissenschaft und Linguistik, 45* (2), 100-118.

Moerman, M. (1974). Accomplishing ethnicity. In R. Turner (Ed.), *Ethnomethodology,* (pp. 54-68). Harmondsworth: Penguin Books.

Nemoianu, A. M. (1980). *The boat's gonna leave: A study of children learning a second language from conversation with other children.* Pragmatics & Beyond 1, Amsterdam: John Benjamins.

Poplack, S. (1981). "Sometimes I'll start a sentence in English Y TERMINO EN ESPAÑOL": Toward a typology of code-switching. *Linguistics, 18* (7/8), 581-618.

Rieck, B.-O. (1974). *Die Interlingua spanischer Arbeitsimmigranten.* Eine empirische Untersuchung. M. A. Thesis, Germanistisches Seminar der Universität Heidelberg.

Sacks, H., Schegloff, P., & Jefferson, G. (1978). The simplest systematics for the organization of turn taking for conversation. In J. Schenkein (Ed.), *Studies in the organization of conversational interaction* (pp. 7-56). New York: Academic Press.

Schumann, J. (1978). *The pidginization process: A model for second language acquisition.* Rowley, MA: Newbury House.

Schumann, J. (1979). The genesis of a second language. In K. C. Hill (Ed.), *The genesis of language* (pp. 48-61). The first Michigan Colloquium, Ann Arbor.

Schumann, J. (1982). Discussion Paper Given at the Second European-North-American Workshop on Cross-Linguistic Second Language Acquisition Research. Göhrde.

Schmidt, R. W., & Richards, J. C. (1979). Speech acts and second language learning. *Applied Linguistics, 1* (2), 129-157.

Stölting, W. (1980). *Die Zweisprachigkeit jugoslawischer Schüler in der Bundesrepublik.* Serie Balkanologische Veröffentlichungen, Band 3. Wiesbaden.
Streeck, J. (1982). Kulturelle Kodes und ethnische Grenzen: Ursachen und Funktionen interethnischer Fehlkommunikation. In J. Rehbein (Ed.), *Interkulturelle Kommunikation.* Tübingen. (to appear)
Stutterheim, C. v. (1984). The expression of temporality in learner varieties. *Linguistische Berichte, 92,* 31–45.
Tajfel, E. (1978). *Differentiation between social groups: Studies in the social psychology of intergoup relations.* London: Academic Press.
Tajfel, H., & Turner, J. C. (1979). An integrative theory of intergroup conflict. In W. G. Austin & H. Wordel (Eds.), *The social psychology of intergroup relations.* Oxford: Pergamon Press.
Tarone, E. U. (1978). The phonology of interlanguage. In J. C. Richards (Ed.), *Understanding second and foreign language learning* (pp. 15–33). Rowley, MA: Newbury House.
Tarone, E. U., Frauenfelder, U., & Selinker, L. (1976). Systematicity/variability and stability/instability in interlanguage systems. In H. D. Brown, (Ed.), *Papers in second language acquisition.* Special Issue No. 4.
Taylor, D. M. (1980). Ethnicity and language: A social psychological perspective. In H. Giles, W. P. Robinson, & P. M. Smith (Eds.), *Language: Social psychological perspectives* (pp. 133–145). Oxford and New York: Pergamon Press.
Thakerer, J. N., Giles, H., & Cheshire, J. (1982). Psychological and linguistic parameters of speech accommodation theory. In C. Fraser & K. R. Scherer (Eds.), *Advances in the social psychology of language* (pp. 205–255). Cambridge: Cambridge University Press.

CHAPTER **9**

The Problem of Justice in the Courts Approached by the Analysis of Plea Bargaining Discourse*

Douglas W. Maynard

INTRODUCTION

A perennial concern in American studies of the court process is the issue of justice, and nowhere is the concern more evident than in research on the sentencing of criminal offenders. Basically, the question has been whether all persons who are arrested receive "equal treatment before the law" or whether they are discriminated against on the basis of their age, race, socioeconomic status, sex, or other extralegal attributes (Hagan, 1975b).

Almost universally, the approach to this question has been to examine the influence of various legal and extralegal[1] factors on the decisions made, rather than to investigate the actual discourse, especially plea bargaining, by which various outcomes are negotiated and produced. This chapter investigates tape-recorded plea bargaining talk, wherein defendants and their offense-related statuses are discussed, to explore

---

[1] There is some debate over whether the distinction between legal and extralegal factors is a proper one (Bernstein, Kelley, & Doyle, 1977, p. 750). In the discussion below, I use "offense-related" and "offender-related" as terms to make the distinction; this does not necessarily skirt the issues raised by Bernstein, Kelley, and Doyle (1977a) and Farrell and Swigert (1978), but it is a convenience that is grounded in the way such factors are utilized or treated by the legal practitioners in this study. See "Sentencing Decisions" below.

* Segments of this chapter have been previously published in *Semiotica*, *Social Problems*, and *Sociological Quarterly*.

just how defendant attributes in that discourse are related to dispositions. One aim of the research is to critique the predominant mode of variable analysis (Blumer, 1956) in sentencing research, which ignores the interactive, interpretative process by which decisions are made. The critique explores methodological problems that are basic to sentencing research, demonstrating the potential complexity of interactions among variables describing defendants. Where previous discussions emphasize the need for more sophisticated research techniques through which more variables could be controlled, this inquiry suggests that the problem of justice may not be adequately explored by statistical modeling of the decision process. A second aim of this chapter is to demonstrate how sentencing decisions are accomplished by certain discourse procedures. An appreciation of these procedures suggests a "gestalt" modeling of the process and points toward the investigation of practitioners' commonsense knowledge. This provides an understanding of cultural patterns, including conceptions of justice, displayed in the actual institutional discourse through which the fates of criminal defendants are decided.

THEORY AND RESEARCH

Studies of sentencing speak to four prominent sociological traditions in the study of deviance. First, there is labeling theory. Depending on whether one takes a weak or strong position with respect to this perspective, factors associated with the values and activities of those responding to a deviant will account for some or most of the variance in decisions made regarding defendants (Bernstein, Kick, Leung, & Schulz, 1977). Second, conflict theory is often the starting point for these investigations, suggesting that race and class are important determinants of sentences in the courts. The hypotheses generated by conflict and labeling theory often appear indistinguishable,[2] but the difference seems to be that labeling theory simply posits the existence of bias in the criminal justice process, while conflict theory attributes that bias to power relations inherent in a class society (Chiricos & Waldo, 1975). A third theory, often counterposed to conflict or labeling approaches, is the functionalist or "legal consensus" perspective that emphasizes offense-related factors, hypothesizing that items such as prior record and offense charged will be more influential

---

[2] A related tradition does not derive from any explicit theoretical perspective other than a concern with "equality before the law" (see Hagan, 1975a, p. 536, fn. 4), a focus that fits with that of labeling and conflict theorists. But here, researchers speak to policy makers and others interested in the extent to which the official ideal of equality is being implemented in the courts (e.g., Swigert & Farrell, 1977).

than other factors. Finally, an organizational perspective focuses on such things as bail decisions, charging decisions, and the relationship between various subsystems in the criminal justice process, such as prosecution and probation (e.g., Hagan, Hewitt, & Alwin, 1979).

Prior to the 1970s, much of the research on disposition patterns was methodologically unsophisticated, either not using statistical procedures or employing tests of significance sensitive to distortion because of the large sample sizes. Thus, while a range of offender-related variables were examined, including race, age, occupation, income, and sex, Hagan (1974) argues that statistically significant relationships between these variables and sentences emerge as substantively unimportant when measures of association are computed. For noncapital cases, knowledge of these independent variables increases accuracy in predicting the dependent variable by less than 1%. In summary, Hagan (1974, p. 375) remarks, "the central finding of this review of past research is that there is generally a small relationship between extra-legal attributes and sentencing decisions."

Since this time, research on sentencing and other court decision stages has become methodologically more sophisticated, utilizing multiple regression, path, and log–linear types of analyses. The major contribution of this research seems to be an appreciation of the complexities of the process by which a defendant is routed through the court. And it seems that offender-related variables, such as race, socioeconomic status, sex, and so on, have differing and even contradictory effects on criminal justice decision making, depending on the stage of the process examined and the kinds of variables that can be controlled (Bernstein, Kelley, & Doyle, 1977; Eisenstein & Jacob, 1977; Hagan, 1975b, 1977; Hagan et. al., 1979; Myers, 1979; Myers & Hagan, 1979; Swigert & Farrell, 1977; Thomson & Zingraff, 1981).[3]

Still, when research finds that variables have a significant effect, it does not explain a large proportion of the variance in sentencing outcomes. "The single finding that *is* consistent throughout this literature," Hagan et al. (1979, p. 508) note, "is that whether legal-consensus [offense-related] or class conflict [offender-related] factors are the focus of the

---

[3] With respect to class, for example, some studies find no substantial effect on sentencing (e.g., Bernstein, Kelley, & Doyle, 1977; Chiricos & Waldo, 1975; Eisenstein & Jacob, 1977), while others argue that there is (e.g., Lizotte, 1978; Swigert & Farrell, 1977). With offense-related factors, some investigations turn up significant effects of the "nature of the offense" (e.g., Eisenstein & Jacob, 1977; Chaps. 9, 10), others find "prior record" to have an effect (e.g., Feeley, 1979, pp. 132, 142), and some document the influence of both factors (e.g., Bernstein, Kelley, & Doyle, 1977; Chiricos & Waldo, 1975; Clarke & Koch, 1976).

analysis, the unexplained variance looms large." The sources of the unexplained variance are thought to derive from a variety of shortcomings in the research. One view cites the overrepresentation of lower-class defendants (Greenberg, 1977; Hopkins, 1977; Reasons, 1977; Hagan, Nagel, & Albonetti, 1980), the paucity of longitudinal data (Greenberg, 1977; Hagan, 1974; Thomson & Zingraff, 1981), and the lack of control over significant variables such as criminal stereotypes (Swigert & Farrell, 1977) and evidence (Myers & Hagan, 1979). In brief, the problem seems to be lack of adequate data sets (see Hagan *et al.,* 1979), and the implication is that if we had wider variation among independent variables, we would be able to account for more variance in the dependent variables.[4]

This may be true, but another view emphasizes what is termed the "subtlety," "complexity," and "intricacy" of the process (e.g., Chiricos, Jackson, & Waldo, 1972; Eisenstein & Jacob, 1977; Feeley, 1979; Myers & Hagan, 1979) and calls for "new kinds of data on sentencing" (Hagan, 1974, p. 380), including more intensive observations and descriptions of the actual decision making (Abel, 1980; Bernstein, Kelley, & Doyle, 1977; Feeley, 1979). This is the thrust of the research here. We will see that attention to decision making as a naturally occurring discourse process reveals an endogenous organization, the description of which makes sense of some of the contradictory findings and lack of explanatory power in models that, it is argued, distort the process by exogenously imposing a structure on it. Part of the distortion results from a standard of justice implicit in research that is different from that actually employed as part of plea bargaining discourse.

SENTENCING DECISIONS

The plea bargaining conversations that are the data for the following discussion were recorded in a California municipal court during Pretrial and Settlement conferences that took place once a week. Negotiations on 52 cases of petty theft, drunken driving, fighting in public, loitering, and other misdemeanor offenses were recorded over a 3-month period, with the cooperation of two judges, six public defenders, three private defense attorneys, and six district attorneys. Tape recordings were made either in an unused jury room off of the courtroom, where attorneys talked without the judge's presence, or, when a district attorney and

---

[4] The state of research on criminal courts is duplicated in studies of juvenile courts (e.g., see the discussion and review in Horitz & Wasserman, 1980). Although this paper does not explicitly address this literature, many of the points made throughout are relevant to decision making in juvenile courts.

public defender could not settle a case, recordings were made in the judge's chambers with his participation. Although he does contribute something to the discussion of a few cases in this jurisdiction, as in many others (e.g., see Feeley, 1979; Neubauer, 1974; Nimmer, 1974), the judge essentially "rubber stamps" the decisions that prosecuting and defense attorneys make.

We are concerned here with "person-descriptions" that appear in the plea bargaining discourse. A person-description is an utterance in which reference to some individual is accompanied by a biographical formulation concerning the person. Some examples follow.[5]

Reference Form + Descriptive Item
(1) She + is advanced middle aged (39.010)
(2) He's + sixty one (25.166)
(3) She's + a very hysterical person (3.038)
(4) This + is a rather bizarre fellow (17.022)

As can be seen, any of a wide variety of biographical items are incorporated in person-descriptions. In this data, however, there does appear to be a distinction between offense-related and offender-related descriptions, which is exhibited in the ways legal practitioners use them. We first investigate offense-related factors and then probe the use of offender-related descriptions.

Offense-Related Factors: Beginning the Negotiations

When a particular prosecutor and defense lawyer meet, they negotiate a series of cases. Discussion of any particular one is regularly started by citing the name of the defendant, the offense charged, and any prior conviction of the defendant. When the offense charge is mentioned, it is often done by stating the title of the charge:

(5) (10.001)
    PD2:   Okay Jeffrey Walker's a petty theft

However, the penal code section number, rather than the title of the offense, may be cited. (In the following, the title of the offense is put in square brackets but is not part of the utterance.)

---

[5] These and the examples that follow are excerpted from the more extensive and more detailed transcripts of the plea bargainings. The exact source is noted: Thus, in (1), (39.010) refers to case 39, line 10 of the transcript. Words in parentheses were not clear on the recordings, and are "candidate hearings."

(6) (41.001)
    PD2:   Uh well what about Fridley
    DA3:   What about Fridley. That's a four fifteen [disturbing the peace]

(7) (24.001)
    J1:   And now that brings us to Frank Bryan. Is he the poor chap sitting out there all by himself?
    PD2:   Yeah he's the sweet man with the nice smile. And this is a six forty seven "f" [disorderly conduct] and a one forty eight [resisting public officers]

These examples show that the name or number of the offense is utilized to identify the case. Prior offenses, however, are employed as descriptions of the defendant; that is, they appear in person-descriptions. (Square brackets below denote simultaneous speech.)

(3) (8.001)
    J2:   Uh Rodriquez
    PD2:   Now this man has at least two priors that I know of. Is it three priors or two priors
    J2:   [Three priors
    DA: [Three priors

In this example, no reference is made to the offense charged, which is drunken driving. Thus, not every discussion begins with the naming of the charge; nor is the defendant's record said each time. This may be because, unlike other information about the case and the defendant, the charge and prior record are listed on the docket sheet for the pretrial conference, and knowledge of them is simply assumed as the negotiation starts.

When the offense is named or prior record is cited, then, it is an expressed acknowledgment of what is known about the defendant and the offense and sets the context for further discussion. Operating within the courtroom subculture, judges and lawyers determine what will happen to a defendant in part on the basis of his or her prior offenses.[6] Thus, in the last example, after answering the PD's question as to whether there were two or three priors, the DA continued as follows:

---

[6] The courtroom subculture is discussed by Rosett and Cressy (1976), Eisenstein and Jacob (1977), Heumann (1977), and Buckle and Buckle (1977). As used here, it refers to the practice, among legal personnel, of establishing "going rates" (within legislatively established limits) for common misdemeanors such as drunk driving and petty theft.

9 The Analysis of Plea Bargaining Discourse 159

(9) (8.006)
```
DA:    In all cases where there at least two convictions
PD2:   Okay
DA2:   We would argue that they may be referred for a probation
       and sentencing report
```

In this jurisdiction, then, action on a case is "officially" (i.e., in the courtroom subculture) related to a defendant's prior record, a function that is not accorded other possible attributes of a defendant.

Offender-Related Factors

There is a pattern to the use of offender-related factors that is here highlighted by discussion and analysis of person-descriptions in negotiations over two separate defendants and offenses. It is argued that offender-related descriptions are not employed in a mechanical checklist fashion but are artfully selected and contextually employed to justify a position on the appropriateness of a particular sanction.

Example 1

This is a petty theft case involving a woman who was charged with taking several small items, including needles and thread, from a supermarket.

(10) (43.001)
```
1  PD1:  This lady lives in Sea City, she had her house burned,
2        and she uh apparently she's staying with relatives. But
3        at any rate she came up here, she has three small children,
4        two and a half month old baby, the youngest. Seems to
5        me that some disposition other than twenty four hours in
6        jail is-, would be appropriate in this case rather than the
7        standard
```

As is evident in lines 4–6, the standard penalty for a person who shoplifts in this jurisdiction is 24 hours in the county jail. The public defender is arguing, then, that some disposition other than the standard one "would be appropriate in this case" because of the biographical items he mentions in lines 1–4, a phenomenon that becomes more apparent in the following example. This segment of the conversation occurred after (10) above and after the PD and DA had proceeded to discuss the articles the defendant allegedly took from the supermarket:

(11) (43.070)
```
1  PD1:  The thing of it is, you know, this lady has come- she did
2        come up here from Sea City, you know, to face the
3        punishment. She knows that she's facing twenty four
4        hours. No question about that, she knows that. Um, but
5        it just seems to me that uh twenty four hours in jail for
6        something like that is just-
7  DA3:  Okay, I understand that, I've- I don't see that I can make
8        an exception on this
```

Here, PD1 reminds the DA that the defendant did show up in court, possibly attempting to depict her as someone who, even while fulfilling her parental responsibilities, meets her public obligations, and who is thus deserving of leniency.[7]

After DA3 suggests he cannot make an exception (lines 7–8), there follows some discussion regarding what to do, and how to manage the plea, and then PD1 makes another pitch for his defendant.

(12) (43.101)
```
1  PD1:  I don't feel that strongly about it except that I just feel
2        like that, you know, she was arraigned, she went back
3        to Sea City, she came up here knowing that she's facing
4        this, she's got a two and a half month old baby, she's
5        been trying to support herself and two kids or three kids
6        and this- and uh, I bet you she's probably gone through
7        enough hell as it is, you know, and I don't think twenty
8        four hours is gonna-
9  DA3:  I- uh, the judge may be responsive to that
```

Subsequently, PD1 talked to the defendant and she agreed to plead guilty as charged and accept the standard penalty. No appeal was made to the judge and she was sentenced to the 24-hour jail term. In summary, the PD here employed a series of offender-related factors or person-descriptions in the negotiations, including his client's house having burned, her having children to support, and her traveling back and forth to make court appointments, all of which were tailored to the argument, in paraphrase, that she had suffered enough and need not be punished more.

---

[7] As Feeley (1979, p. 187) has observed, the question for defendants, at least in misdemeanor criminal cases, "is not whether to go to trial, but whether to show up in court at all." Thus, someone who does appear can be assessed in a morally positive way.

Example 2

This is a case of petty theft in which the defendant had taken a permit worth some $40 that provided parking access to the local college. As in the last example, there is no argument over the guilt or innocence of the defendant, but over what would be the proper disposition in the case. We see that the negotiations in this can instantiate how, as Rosett and Cressey (1976, p. 102) have argued, criminal justice personnel often first decide how an offender should be treated and then find an offense to fit the punishment.

The PD began the conversation by telling the DA:

(13) (29.006)
 PD2: John, y'know I've scratched my brains trying to think of an alternative to theft . . . uh, having to do with failing to pay for his parking

Over the course of the conversation, PD2 attempts to establish the propriety of a alternative to theft, and in a manner similar to the last example, person-descriptions are employed as part of that work. Two person-descriptions occur in the first line of the following segment.

(14) (26.031)
 1 PD2: He's a young guy, a student out there and the court's file
 2   would have a letter from the dean of students asking for
 3   a, uh any possible courtesy in this case I think that the
 4   dean of student's position is that uh the guy should not
 5   have a criminal record

The issue of the defendant being a young guy (line 1) is, we will see, repeatedly brought up. For now, the description of him being a student out there is of focal interest because of its intimate relation with the immediate conversational context. It has already been established that the misappropriation of the parking sticker occurred at the college, so identifying the defendant through his occupation (*student*) and specifying that occupation with a locational formulation (*out there*) links the description to the preceding reference to the college. That is, the location formulation is a prototypical example of an indexical expression (Garfinkel & Sacks, 1970), the sense of which is provided by the reference to the college provided earlier.

Furthermore, the identification of the defendant as a student at the college where the offense was committed constitutes him as a "course-of-action" type who rightly belongs at the college and whose offense appears as something done within a round of activities typically motivated and executed by virtue of that identity. That is, Sacks (1972) has suggested that police see isolated behaviors of a person on the street in terms of the "course of action" he or she is inferentially engaged in (Zimmerman, 1974, p. 142). Here, the PD displays a similar sense-making effort: Taking a parking sticker is not viewed as a solitary activity, but one done by the defendant as part of a meaningful course of involvements that could be glossed as "attending the local college." In addition, the description of the defendant as a student reflexively links with the formulation of the letter writer (line 2) as *dean of students*. The earlier reference to *college* and *student* permit that formulation to be heard as discussing not just any dean who has written the letter *asking for a possible courtesy* (lines 2–3), but an administrative official at the locale where the theft occurred and where the defendant is a student. In sum, the description of the defendant as a *student out there* is retrospectively and prospectively related to other items relevant to the PD's topical talk.

That this topical talk is justifying a lesser charge becomes more apparent in subsequent conversation. After the above segment, there was discussion regarding a vehicle code violation that would be an alternative to the theft charge, wherein PD2 suggests that a fine would not be unreasonable were the defendant to plead to the vehicle code charge. The DA, however, asks the PD why the logic of the PD's argument would not apply to everyone of the misuse of parking sticker cases.

(15) (26.084)
```
1   PD2:   My logic is that uhm I don't think that the young man
2          considered himself a thief and that one of the things we
3          punish is y- somebody that takes something out of a store
4          bloody well knows it's stealing, and bloody well knows
5          who he is and what he's done
```

Following this segment is some talk in which the DA attempts to retain a classification of the offense as theft. However, the PO returns to a focus on the defendant rather than the offense.

(16) (26.127)
```
1   PD2:   Its a very serious thing to lay a theft charge on somebody
2          like that
```

The indexical term *somebody like that* retrieves the descriptions of the defendant so far proferred. These include that he is (1) a young guy, (2) a student at the college where the theft occurred, and (3) one who did not consider himself a thief.

Then, after some talk regarding the dean's letter, and further argument over whether the theft or vehicle code charge is more appropriate, PD2 makes explicit what he considers to be the consequences of laying larceny on the defendant.

(17)

1	PD1:	Uh you take a young student, I think he's eighteen or
2		nineteen years old, he's uh just starting out, trying to get—
3		you know, in college, uh and you lay larceny on him. Uh
4		true he can come back in a year and get it taken off his
5		record, but for many other purposes uh its going to be
6		known, for example if he ever tries to get security clearance
7		uh whether or not the court seals his records uh they will
8		know about the conviction

Those consequences, formulated in lines 5–8 are related to expansions of the earlier descriptions (1) and (2) above: The *young student* is *eighteen or nineteen years old,* is *just starting out,* and *in college* (lines 1–3).

In subsequent talk, PD2 reminds the DA of the dean's letter, and another public defender joins the argument by also suggesting that the act of the defendant is "not something you want to give them theft on," and restating the argument of PD2 that the defendant did not think of it as theft. Then, PD2 tells a series of stories regarding other persons, including himself, who as students broke rules with impunity. The DA finally relents:

(18) (26.255)
    DA3:   Well uh maybe I can make an exception in this case

It is agreed that the theft charge will be dismissed and the defendant will plead guilty to a vehicle code infraction (a noncriminal offense) and pay a $65 fine.

To sum up: Much from this negotiation has been omitted or glossed, except for the person-descriptions appearing in the segments above. The way in which the PD eventually achieved a desired outcome involved a number of strategems, including the reference to the dean's letter, the telling of stories, the help of a fellow public defender, and so on. Thus, with respect to the descriptions of the defendant, the point is not that they unilaterally affect the eventual outcome. What has been shown rather is that they are part of a context in which the attempt to obtain a lesser charge for the defendant is being enacted. The descriptions of the defendant as a young man, a student at the college, as one who did not think of himself as a thief, are matters which are specifically fitted with the disposition requested by the PD, a noncriminal charge.

Discussion

In actual decision making, descriptions of defendants are partially constitutive of the activity of warranting or justifying proposed dispositions (Maynard, 1982). Defendant attributes provide matters to invoke regarding an argument for disposition and are utilized in conversation to the extent that they can justify a defense or prosecution position regarding the disposition.[8] That they are used does not mean they necessarily affect the final decision, as that is measured by whether the agreed-to disposition is the one proposed in relation to the person-descriptions.

This seems straightforward enough, but it is something neglected when research employs models of the sentencing process that, in a manner parallel to that suggested by Garfinkel (1967), posit an actor who is a "judgmental dope." With this term, Garfinkel (1967, pp. 66–75) pointed to the technique in sociology of depicting structures of social action as the outcome of "hierarchies of need dispositions," "common culture," "common understandings," or the like (see Giddens, 1979; Wilson, 1970). In the sentencing literature, the attempt is to explain patterned decisions by reference to an abstract set of factors or attributes fitting with the preestablished categories of the investigator's research scheme. Presumably, decision makers determine the value of these categories in checklist fashion. If the right factor or combination of factors is present, they assign the case an appropriate outcome. The researchers' task is to find out which categories are regularly used.

Where sentencing decisions are an outcome of negotiations such as those examined here, decision makers may approach a defendant's prior record in somewhat of a checklist fashion (see "Offense-Related Factors" above). But offender-related factors are selectively and contextually employed in arguments for and against specific dispositions; this is pursued in the next section.

METHODOLOGICAL PROBLEMS

This study points to features of the decision-making process that have been precluded from investigation in most research that attempts to

---

[8] Note that in both examples, the person doing argument was the public defender. This reflects an asymmetry in the negotiation process, as discussed by Feeley (1979, p. 177). At least in misdemeanor plea bargainings, prosecutors are relatively passive. They seem to assume that standard penalties are appropriate for most cases and leave it to defense attorneys to convince them otherwise in particular instances or to make an argument that a given case is not an instance of a "normal crime" (Sudnow, 1965). Thus, it is the public defenders in this study who produce most of the person-descriptions. District attorneys, however, do the same sort of justifying work with person-descriptions when the occasion calls for it (see Maynard, 1982).

The Selectional Problem

Atkinson and Drew (1979, p. 117) have observed that "any empirical description is in principle a selection from alternative ways of describing the 'same' person." Put differently, there is an indefinitely large array of potential "mentionables"[9] regarding any given person. These mentionables provide matters to utilize in argument for or against a given disposition. Thus, a negotiator may bring out any defendant attribute that would justify some disposition (see Mather, 1974, p. 201), provided that it is regarded as a relevant and reasonable matter to invoke.[10]

Two issues are raised by the selectivity exhibited in the use of person-descriptions in negotiation. First, and most obvious, is that while a few theoretically interesting factors have been considered in sentencing research (e.g., age, race, socioeconomic status, sex), other possibly important variables are left out. In Example 1, the woman shoplifting defendant was described in terms of her home town and her status as a mother of three chidren. While some studies may include parental status, it is rare that they include number of dependents, and rarer still for them to examine the effect of a person's home town. In Example 2, the defendant was categorized as a young guy, a student, and one who did not consider himself a thief. While researchers often test the effects of age and occupation, it is not the practice to incorporate a variable such as the attributed self-concept of a defendant. The point here is not that future studies should include these specific categories, but that they represent an array of factors that are potentially usable in any particular negotiated decision.

A second issue is that by examining factors of theoretical interest, but which are not relevant in specific cases, prior research may be including variables unrelated to disposition outcomes. For instance, in neither Example 1 or 2 is reference made to the race or socioeconomic status of the defendants, perhaps the two variables of most interest in the research tradition being discussed.[11]

---

[9] The term is taken from Schegloff and Sacks (1974).

[10] The point here is that while there is this indefinite array of mentionables regarding a defendant, not just any of them will be deemed acceptable in the courtroom subculture. District attorneys, public defenders, and others are expected to be "reasonable" in what they say. See Maynard (1982).

[11] It could be argued, of course, that actors who do the negotiation know about other relevant variables "in their mind," even if they do not discuss them, and that they act

The conclusion is that to the extent that disregarded factors may be systematically related to dispositions and that researchers include variables that remain unconsidered by practitioners, the models employed in sentencing research are misspecified (Myers & Hagan, 1979), biasing coefficients of significant variables or exaggerating estimator variances as the case may be (Hanushek & Jackson, 1977).

The Contextual Problem

Defendant descriptions in negotiations do not just constitute categorical, "demographic" identities, which are the ones that models investigating decision making usually examine. In Example 1, the defendant was described as someone who had her house burned. She was also depicted as having been arraigned, then going home, and returning to the court. Those descriptions worked with other traditional sorts of attributes (e.g., woman, parent) to provide the warrant for characterizing the defendant as someone who "had gone through enough hell as it is," and as a responsible person deserving of a lesser penalty. While a coding process would pick up the traditional categorical descriptions, it would clearly miss these details of biography.

But it is not just that research schemas would eliminate such details, a problem inherent in any generalizing practice. There is a deeper trouble, which is that neither categories nor details stand alone, but are contextually interrelated. In Example 2, one description of the defendant was that he was a student "out there," at the college where the alleged crime occurred. Whether the defendant might be coded as "employed" in a dichotomous classification scheme (employed–not employed), or even if the category "student" is utilized in a research study, what was crucial was not just that he was a student, but that being a student at the college was partially constitutive of what the act was made out to be and was related, among other things, to the report of the dean of the college writing a letter in the defendant's behalf. These items, it was argued, constituted him as

---

on what they know irrespective of what gets exhibited in talk. Thus, what is required is research on attitudes, along the lines developed by Hogarth (1971) in his study of judicial decision making. There are two problems here, however. One is that plea-bargaining decisions are mutually determined, which sets constraints on the degree to which a prosecutor's or defense attorney's knowledge or beliefs can affect sentencing outcomes. Second, and more important, it is clear that the intersubjective reality of defendant attributes, as displayed in conversation, is considerably complex in terms of the selectivity (discussed here) and contextualness (discussed below) exhibited in their use. It cannot be presupposed that the subjective processes by which the attributes are related to desired outcomes are any less complex than the public (conversational) displays of that relationship.

a course-of-action type compatible with other character descriptions (young, did not conceive of himself as a thief) that, according to the PD, compelled a lesser charge. The description "student out there," in other words, fit with other aspects of the context of talk and action in which it was employed; and it was critical that the description in its detail be utilized. If he was a student at some other college, for example, his act would have been very differently constituted.

The general implication of this is that temporal, locational, and biographical contexts of categorical descriptions can define the relationship of those attributes to dispositions administered. As Feeley (1979, p. 163) has observed, the "facts" of a defendant's background "can cut two ways,"[12] and one of the clearest examples of this is the research on race effects by Gibson (1978). He shows that, in the aggregate, sentences in a sample of 1219 felony cases did not show any influence of the race of the offenders. At the individual level, however, some judges did discriminate against blacks, while others were more lenient. The result was that the antiblack and problack judges balanced each other to give the appearance, at the institutional level, of no regular effects of race on sentencing.

While Gibson (1978) relies on attitudinal data for his analysis, the argument here is that attitudes are just one kind of contingency that regularly determines the way that defendant attributes affect disposition decisions. The actual effects of those attributes will be obscured when they are examined independent of various contingencies or contextual details. Recognition of this problem is clear in the earlier noted efforts to control the influence of various factors, such as evidentiary strength, criminal stereotypes, and so forth. The trouble is that when explicit consideration is given to contextual variables, they are still conceived as having an external, exogenous influence on the decision process rather than being an endogenous part of the discourse. This is a subtle but crucial distinction and highlights why the introduction of "new" variables is only a partial solution. From the former (exogenous) standpoint, the implication is that contextual factors can be prespecified and controlled.[13] From the latter (endogenous) standpoint, all one can predict is that they

---

[12] Feeley gives the example of a defendant with no prior record: "While a prosecutor might respond with lenience in one case, in another he might decide to follow a harsher strategy, believing that 'a firm hand' at an early point might be the most effective deterrent against future misconduct" (1979, p. 163). This raises the possibility that prior record, in some instances, is used, like offender-related factors, in a selective and contextual way rather than as a mere starting point for further negotiation.

[13] Chiricos and Waldo (1975, p. 769), however, observe that specifying the contingencies surrounding the relationship of a given factor to sentencing may be a relatively boundless task. (Their specific concern is with socioeconomic status.)

may be utilized in decision making. Whether any are used, which ones, and how, cannot be known beforehand.[14]

GESTALT APPROACH TO DEFENDANT ATTRIBUTES

Research on the relationship between defendant attributes and sentencing has insufficiently recognized the ways those attributes are selectively and contextually employed in negotiations that produce disposition decisions. The relative influence of offender-related as opposed to offense-related characteristics on outcomes has not been determined, to the extent that prior research has neglected these methodical features of the bargaining process and has utilized misspecified models. We might now ask, how can the relation between defendant attributes and case outcomes be profitably studied? First, the model of decision making should have a gestalt perspective (see Nettler, 1979, p. 40). Second, with this approach, the structure of commonsense discourse, which is the medium of decision making, can be investigated. Finally, there must be a confrontation of the issue of what concept of justice is relevant to the sociological understanding of the criminal justice process.

In the examples viewed so far, it would be possible to itemize the offender-related factors used in negotiations. From Example 1, we would obtain this list:

1. The defendant had her house burned.
2. She was a mother of three children.
3. She had traveled back and forth to court several times.

From Example 2:

1. The defendant was a young guy.
2. He was a student at the college where the theft occurred.
3. He did not consider himself a thief.

However, these listings fail to capture how the descriptions were selected to do the work of soliciting a lesser penalty (Example 1) or lesser charge (Example 2), as well as the way each description was defined by its

---

[14] The same point is raised by Feeley, who found that organizational and attitudinal factors crucial to the handling of cases were "most visible *during* rather than before the research process" (1979, p. 123). In Blumer's terms, the discourse through which decisions were made is not just an intervening event, but "a formative or creative process in its own right" (1956, p. 135).

relationship to other descriptions and the specific arguments for disposition. In Example 1, the consequences of the defendant's house having burned are exacerbated by her having three children. Taking care of the children under these circumstances and having to travel back and forth to court were related to themes of responsibility and her having already "gone through enough hell," which could justify the argument that 24 hours in jail would be unnecessary punishment. In Example 2, the defendant's youth complements his status as a student. Being a student at the college where the theft occurred makes his act appear as one that is incidental to his campus activities rather than as one that reflects a primary orientation to thievery. And clearly, this depiction fits with his not considering himself a thief. Together, the items help claim the relevance of a noncriminal charge for the defendant.

Consider then, that "who" a person is, in talk, is something constructed in the way that a gestalt phenomenon is put together. Each of the separate descriptions has a meaningful function only in relation to the other elements featured in the talk, including the other person-descriptions and the activity (in these examples, justifying proposals for disposition) being accomplished (see also Gurwitsch, 1964; Maynard & Wilson, 1980; Wieder, 1974). Zimmerman and Pollner's (1970) discussion of the "occasioned corpus" is relevant:

> The work of assembling an occasioned corpus consists in the ongoing "corpusing" and "decorpusing" of elements rather than the situated retrieval or removal of a subset of elements from a larger set transcending any particular setting in which that work is done. . . . the elements organized by the occasioned corpus are unique to the particular setting in which it is assembled, hence ungeneralizable to the other settings. (Zimmerman & Pollner, 1970, pp. 95–96)

The use of defendant descriptions in actual negotiations is like assembling and disassembling a set of elements in a corpus rather than selecting a subset of stable elements and using them in checklist fashion in each and every decision.

That the relationship between offender-related factors and sentences is something produced in each negotiation regarding a particular case need not imply that the process is unsystematic, but only that it is not systematic in the way research methodologies presuppose it to be. A basic and generalizable methodicalness is displayed in the ways negotiators put together an occasioned corpus or gestalt of defendant characteristics within an argument for or against some sentence. Recognizing this, researchers can focus on the structure of legal practitioners commonsense knowledge, as this displays aspects of social and cultural organization intrinsic to criminal justice decision making.

The Structure of Commonsense Knowledge

Investigating commonsense knowledge does not imply an inquiry into members' psychologies but into the social organization of subjectivity. It is in practitioners' mutual discourse that orderly reasoning practices are displayed and made available for sociological description (Coulter, 1979). The next two examples display such practices and provide the opportunity for addressing the justice issue, since both concern "minority" defendants.

Example 3

The case involves a woman defendant who allegedly stole some clothes from a local department store.

```
(20) (1.014)
  1   PD1:   On the face of it, it looks pretty bad. But investigating
  2          the case comes up with some beautiful defenses that I'm
  3          anxious to go to trial on if the D.A. is. Situation is this,
  4          she's a sixty-five-year-old lady, speaks uh Castillian Span-
  5          ish, she's from Spain. Uh she goes into Davidson's—Oh,
  6          incidentally, by way of background, for twenty years she's
  7          worked in the Catholic Church of San Ramon as the
  8          housekeeper for the nuns and the father 'n all this stuff,
  9          and uh very religious, well known. I've interviewed half
 10          of San Ramon concerning her background. Wonderful
 11          lady, no problems, sixty-five years old. But on this par-
 12          ticular occasion, she goes into Davidson's, goes into a
 13          fitting room, pins them up underneath her dress, and leaves.
```

Douglas (1967, p. 281–283) has argued that a distinction is made, in everyday life, between "situated" and "substantial" selves, where a substantial self is the reality lying behind situated behaviors. Similarly, Goffman (1974, p. 293) has remarked that a person's activities and roles are regarded as an expression of a real and perduring self. In this segment, the person-descriptions (lines 4–11) are assembled in a selective and contextual manner to audibly document a good moral character lying behind the defendant's various situated activities and everyday role behaviors.

After giving the sequence of actions leading to her arrest (lines 11–13), the PD goes on to assert that she had been taking two different kinds of pain-killing drugs.

```
(21) (1.055)
  1   PD1:   Now I've checked with the county pathologist and he
```

9 The Analysis of Plea Bargaining Discourse

```
        2           researched the thing out. He says that if those drugs are
        3           mixed it will cause a state of confusion, delirium, and put
        4           the person in a situation where they're just in a dream
        5           world, don't know what in the world they're doing
```

Subsequently, the PD, responding to a question of the judge, tells how much medication was taken and when. After the judge remarks on what the drugs might do (pain-killing drugs could produce "some odd effects"), the PD provides additional expert opinion on the matter, quoting a doctor who said that with "elderly people" the drugs sometimes have "strange or adverse effects that it would not have normally." Then the following occurs:

(22) (1.096)
```
 1  PD1:   So we feel like that she certainly wasn't acting with her
 2         normal characteristics
 3  J1:    Has she ever had any violations for anything
 4  PD1:   That's it, she's had nothing, for twenty years she worked
 5         up there in the Church of San Ramon with all these
 6         people. She's a very religious lady. All these uh, these
 7         uh Mexican Catholics up there who just think the world
 8         of her say my god I couldn't believe it. I spent uh was
 9         it Monday this week? . . . up there talking with 'em and
10         uh they just you know I've got uh some sisters who're
11         willing to come in and state they've known her for all
12         this period of time and she's just had a tremendous
13         reputation for honesty and very religious
14  J1:    What do you want?
15  PD1:   Want it dismissed
```

Here, PD1 states his position that the defendant was not acting normally (lines 1–2), and in response to the judge's question regarding prior violations (line 3), he goes on to repeat and reformulate the earlier person-descriptions (lines 5–13). Finally, he asserts the defense want that the case be dismissed (line 15).

Clearly, PD1's person-descriptions are involved in building an argument for this particular outcome. The judge, at various points, indicated his alignment with the defense attorney's view of the case. The district attorney, on the other hand, at first resisted the defense argument but eventually dismissed the case. The focal point, however, is that the defendant's attributes were integral to a procedure, or commonsense reasoning pattern, developed over the course of the negotiations; it consists of three parts. First, person-descriptions are produced to establish the nature of the defendant's real self or character. Second, drawing on cultural assumptions to the effect that facts of a persons' biography cannot be contradictory (Goffman, 1961), or that they should be consistent with one another and with the real self of the defendant, the shoplifting act is reported as not normal. Third, this anomalous behavior is explained by reference to the extraordinary circumstances (drug effects) that could produce it.[15]

Example 4

The defendant is this case was charged with disorderly conduct and resisting arrest. In the first segment, here, the public defender relates a version of the incident that caused the defendant's arrest.

(21) (24.208)
```
 1   J1:    And now that brings us to Frank Bryan. Is he the poor
 2          chap sitting out there all by himself?
 3   PD2:   Yeah, he's the sweet man with the nice smile . . . See
 4          he's drunk and he comes home to his own house where
 5          he had a fight with his family, and he's out in his own
 6          front yard apparently having such a fight or at least—
 7   DA3:   His mother having called the police
 8   PD2:   Mother have ca(h)ll(h)ed the (h) co(h)ps. It's a family
 9          thing, he's screaming and saying "fuck" and all that kind
10          of stuff. And this is, I mean, the same very happy go
11          lucky good natured guy, as you can tell, he's sitting out
12          in the courtroom and when the police come into his own
13          home, his castle, he decides he ain't going without making
14          some trouble
```

Although there are a number of matters relevant to the overall negotiations concerning Bryan's case (see Maynard, 1983), of specific interest here is the construction of the defendant's character. The PD draws a clear distinction between the public and private activity of his client. Although the defendant is acknowledged to be drunk, fighting, and cursing (lines 3–10), these activities occur at his home as part of a "family thing" (line 8). While the DA reminds the PD that the mother called the police (line 7), PD2 treats the matter lightly by inserting laughter tokens (the *h*'s in parentheses) in the utterance that acknowledges the DA's reminder (line

---

[15] The contradiction set up between the character of the defendant and the behavior she engaged in is a phenomenon related to the occurrence of "reality disjunctures" in members' discussions of "facts." One way of explaining such disjunctures is the use of "extraordinary circumstances," including the faulted subjectivity of a party to the disjuncture. See Pollner (1974, 1975).

8; see Jefferson, 1979). PD2 subsequently depicts the police as coming into the defendant's home and castle (line 13), and the defendant's resistive behavior as being precipitated by their intrusiveness (lines 12–13). But if the defendant was combative at home, in the courtroom he can be described as a "sweet man with a nice smile" (line 3) who has been sitting happily during the pretrial conference (lines 1–2, 10–12).

The contrast exhibited here draws on cultural conceptions of a natural separation between public and private life, a distinction that is recognized in the law (Stinchcombe, 1963). As Flacks (1975, p. 265) has stated, one's private sphere, in U.S. society, is regarded as "immune from the intrusions and controls of unwanted others," including police. What one does in public, on the other hand, is and should be subject to social convention; that is where interference by authorities, if needed, is properly done. According to this conception, the defendant can be depicted as acting according to his rights at home and his obligations in public. PD2's use of this argument was to diminish the defendant's culpability and solicit a dismissal of the resisting arrest charges. The DA eventually acceded to this proposal.

However, when the negotiators went on to discuss what penalty would be appropriate for the disorderly conduct charge, they engaged in further discussion of the defendant's background.

(22) (24.126)

1	DA3:	He has uh one prior conviction in this jurisdiction with
2		the um sheriff's office of, interestingly enough, uh striking
3		a public officer and uh disturbing the peace
4	PD2:	Will you knock it off, you wanna make a federal case
5		out of this
6	DA3:	No, I- I just think that its not uh this uh happy go lucky
7		chap's uh first encounter with uh (the law)
8	PD2:	Statistically if you got black skin you are highly likely to
9		contact the police, uh substantially more likely than if
10		you're white, now c'mon, what do you want from him.
11		He's got a prior

Here, DA3 brings up the defendant's prior conviction (line 1), which is acknowledged by PD2 (*He's got a prior,* line 11). Between these two utterances, there is a dispute over the meaning of the prior record. DA3 notes the similarity of the prior to the present charge (lines 1–3), while PD2 devaluates that topic (*Will you knock it off,* etc., lines 4–5). Next, DA3 undercuts PD2's earlier description of the defendant (*happy go lucky chap*) by juxtaposing it with the fact that the present charge is not the defendant's first encounter (line 7). But PD2 produces an utterance minimizing the importance of the prior offense by invoking the defendant's race and its effect of contacts with the police (lines 8–10).[16]

In summary, several commonsense reasoning patterns were exhibited in the negotiations regarding Bryan. One pattern concerned the distinction between public obligations and private rights. PD2 drew the distinction while arguing over the appropriateness of dismissing the resisting arrest charge by describing the defendant as a person who might behave violently at home but who displays a nice public demeanor. When the issue of sentencing was discussed, DA3 pointed to the defendant's prior conviction for offenses similar to those presently charged, thereby suggesting a continuity to his behavior that might demand a more severe sanction. PD2 downplayed the importance of the record by using the defendant's race to account for a high likelihood of contacting the police.

Reasoning patterns such as those in Examples 3 and 4 clearly reveal lay and professional theories about the kinds of persons who commit crimes, why they commit them, and how such persons should be treated (Cicourel, 1968). Research into such reasoning patterns, of necessity, proceeds with a relatively small number of cases and does not provide an easy remedy for the large-scale assessment of the equal-treatment issue. But it does provide the advantage of revealing how discrimination might be manifested in concrete forms of discourse. Given that there are differences in history and across regions in sentencing practices (Kleck, 1981; Thomson & Zingraff, 1981), bias in the criminal justice process may occur in particular times and places by the way that the discourse is organized, and this may not be evident in aggregate-level data.

In the data here, gender, race, and class characteristics of defendants were generally used as mitigating factors in negotiations: In Example 3, the characteristics of the defendant were used to suggest her good character; in Example 4, the race of the defendant was explicitly invoked, but only to argue that blacks are victims of police harassment, and as a way of explaining the defendant's prior record. In other jurisdictions, however, the examination of reasoning patterns might reveal the use of race or other attributes in deprecatory and defamatory ways.

The general point is that if assessments of the equal-treatment issue are to break new ground, they must be predicated on a knowledge of the social organization of interaction as it proceeds and as it is constructed by participants. This means increased attention must be paid to the

---

[16] PD2 employs a categorical "you" to speak about the consequences of having black skin. The defendant is clearly an incumbent of the category "persons with black skin."

structure of language in institutional settings, such as the court, for discourse is the medium by which decisions are made and through which organized discriminatory or nondiscriminatory reasoning practices are sustained.

The Concept of Justice

The question of whether defendants receive equal treatment before the law is a complicated one because the concept of 'justice' itself has varying definitions. As Nettler (1979) has argued, the standard of justice employed in sentencing research is that defendants be considered without regard for various background factors, including age, gender, race, class, and so on. The absence of systematic effects from these variables indexes no bias, while their presence indicates discrimination. A different view of justice emphasizes that equality lies in the treating of people as individuals, which means making decisions fit with known features of a person's biography (Nettler, 1979). The two principles are usually referred to as "formal" and "substantive" rationality, respectively (Weber, 1946, p. 220).

In all the cases considered, the second standard is clearly employed. In Example 3, although the defendant was "old" (65 years), a woman, and a member of a minority (Spanish-speaking) group, such attributes were a functional aspect of argument for dismissal. Thus, they were not universally relevant in the way that discrimination would be measured by the first standard of justice. Rather, they were specifically (selectively and contextually) used to construct the suggestion that the woman was good person, one who would not have taken clothing from a store without being under the adverse influence of drugs. It was precisely on the basis of background factors, in other words, that a claim for the fairness of a disposition was made. The same can be said of Examples 1, 2, and 4. To the extent that prosecutors, defense attorneys, and judges make and accept claims like these, we can speak of a courtroom subculture with a systemic orientation to individualized dispositions.

Here again, a tension exists between methods (including conceptions of justice) imposed upon a social process by a research model and the actual practices that make up that process (Needleman, 1981). Sentencing studies largely employ a principle of formal rationality to calculate fairness in a process where, at least in part, substantive justice is the mode of operation (Horwitz & Wasserman, 1980; see Feeley, 1979; Rosett & Cressey, 1976).

CONCLUSION

So far researchers have taken the contradictory and inconclusive findings of their studies as having ambiguous or negative import for theory. With respect to the labeling perspective, Bernstein, Kelley, and Doyle have argued, "the emphasis that interactionists place on the role of the deviant's social attributes in explaining variation in societal reaction seems very much over-stated" (1977, p. 754). On the conflict and legal consensus theories, Chiricos and Waldo have remarked that the former "does no better" than the latter in explaining "the class and racial characteristics of convicted and sentenced criminals" (1975, p. 769). An organization perspective, in opening awareness of different decision-making points and the number of variables relevant to courtroom decisions, has yielded useful insights regarding the complexities of the process.

But if the empirical arguments in this paper are correct, the lack of explanatory power in all these theoretical views points toward the following needs. First, it is necessary to model defendants' attributes as elements selectively and contextually assembled in a specific corpus for each case. Second, more investigation of practitioners' commonsense reasoning is required to fully clarify the ways in which defendant attributes affect outcomes. Finally, while it is easy to assess whether defendants receive equal treatment using a standard of formal rationality, different criteria must be established for evaluating the process on its own substantive terms. In all, determinations about the egalitarian or oppressive nature of sentencing, plea bargaining, and other discretionary activities depend upon further knowledge of the organization of discourse as an ongoing accomplishment within the criminal justice process.

REFERENCES

Abel, R. L. (1980). Redirecting social studies of law. *Law and Society Review, 14*, 805–829.

Atkinson, J. M., & Drew, P. (1979). *Order in court*. London: MacMillan.

Bernstein, I. N., Kelley, W. R., & Doyle, P. (1977). Societal reaction to deviants: The case of criminal defendants. *American Sociological Review* (October), 743–755.

Bernstein, I. N., Kick, E., Leung, J. T., & Schulz, B. B. (1977). Charge reduction: An intermediary stage in the process of labelling criminal defendants. *Social Forces, 56*(2), 362–384.

Blumer, H. (1956). Sociological analysis and the variable. *American Sociological Review 21:* 683–690.

Buckle, S. R. T., & Buckle, L. G. (1977). *Bargaining for justice: Case disposition and reform in the criminal courts*. New York: Praeger.

Chiricos, T. G., & Waldo, G. P. (1975). Socioeconomic status and criminal sentencing: An empirical assessment of a conflict proposition. *American Sociological Review, 40*, 753–772.

Chiricos, T. G., Jackson, P. D., & Waldo, G. P. (1972). Inequality in the imposition of a criminal label. *Social Problems, 19*(4), 53–72.
Cicourcel, A. (1968). *The social organization of juvenile justice.* New York: Wiley.
Clarke, S. H., & Koch, G. G. (1976). The influence of income and other factors on whether criminal defendants go to prison. *Law and Society Review, 11*(1), 57–92.
Coulter, J. (1979). *The social construction of mind: Studies in ethnomethodology and linguistic philosophy.* Totowa, NJ: Rowman and Littlefield.
Douglas, J. D. (1967). *The social meaning of suicide.* Princeton: Princeton University Press.
Eisenstein, J., & Jacob, H. (1977). *Felony justice.* Boston: Little, Brown.
Farrell, R. A., & Swigert, V. L. (1978). Prior offense record as a self-fulfilling prophecy. *Law and Society Review, 12,* 437–458.
Feeley, M. (1979). *The process is the punishment: Handling cases in a lower criminal court.* New York: Russell Sage.
Flacks, R. (1975). Making history vs making life: Dilemmas of an American left. *Sociological Inquiry, 46*(3–4), 263–280.
Garfinkel, H. (1967). *Studies in ethnomethodology.* Englewood Cliffs, NJ: Prentice Hall.
Garfinkel, H., & Sacks, H. (1970). The formal properties of practical actions. In J. C. McKinney & E. Tiryakian (Eds.), *Theoretical sociology: Perspectives and development* (pp. 338–365). New York: Appleton-Century Crofts.
Gibson, J. L. (1978). Race as a determinant of criminal sentences: A methodological critique and a case study. *Law and Society Review, 12,* 455–477.
Giddens, A. (1979). *Central problems in social theory: Action, structure and contradiction in social analysis.* Berkeley, CA: University of California Press.
Goffman, E. (1961). *Encounters.* Indianapolis: Bobbs-Merrill.
Goffman, E. (1974). *Frame analysis.* New York: Harper Colophon.
Greenberg, D. F. (1977). Socioeconomic status and criminal sentences: Is there an association? *American Sociological Review, 42,* 174–176.
Gurwitsch, A. (1964). *The field of consciousness.* Pittsburgh: Duquesne University Press.
Hagan, J. (1974). Extra-legal attributes and sentencing: An assessment of a sociological viewpoint. *Law and Society Review, 8*(3), 357–384.
Hagan, J. (1975a). Parameters of criminal prosecution: An application of path analysis to a problem of criminal justice. *Journal of Criminal Law and Criminology, 64*(4), 536–544.
Hagan, J. (1975b). The social and legal construction of criminal justice: A study of the pre-sentence process. *Social Problems, 22*(5), 620–637.
Hagan, J. (1977). Criminal justice in rural and urban communities: A study of the bureaucratization of justice. *Social Forces* (March), 567–612.
Hagan, J., Hewitt, J. D., & Alwin, D. F. (1979). Ceremonial justice: Crime and punishment in a loosely coupled system. *Social Forces, 58*(2), 506–527.
Hagan, J., Nagel (Bernstein), I. H., & Albonetti, C. (1980). The differential sentencing of white-collar offenders in ten federal district courts. *American Sociological Review, 45,* 802–820.
Hanushek, E. A., & Jackson, J. E. (1977). *Statistical methods for social scientists.* New York: Academic Press.
Heumann, M. (1977). *Plea bargaining: The experiences of prosecutors, judges, and defense lawyers.* Chicago: University of Chicago Press.
Hogarth, J. (1971). *Sentencing as a human process.* Toronto: University of Toronto Press.
Hopkins, A. (1977). Is there a class bias in criminal sanctioning? *American Sociological Review, 42,* 176–177.

Horwitz, A., & Wasserman, M. (1980). Formal rationality, substantive justice, and discrimination: A study of a juvenile court. *Law and Human Behavior*, 4(1–2), 103–115.
Jefferson, G. (1979). A technique for inviting laughter and its subsequent acceptance/declination. In G. Psathas (Ed.), *Everyday language: Studies in ethnomethodology* (pp. 79–96). New York: Irvington.
Kleck, G. (1981). Racial discrimination in criminal sentencing: A critical evaluation of the evidence with additional evidence on the death penalty. *American Sociological Review*, 46(6), 783–805.
Lizotte, A. J. (1978). Extra-legal factors in Chicago's criminal courts: Testing the conflict model of criminal justice. *Social Problems*, 25, 564–580.
Mather, L. M. (1974). Some determinants of the method of case disposition: Decision-making by public defenders in Los Angeles. *Law and Society Review*, 8, 187–217.
Maynard, D. W. (1982). Person-descriptions in plea bargaining. *Semiotica*, 42: 195–213.
Maynard, D. W. (1983). Social order and plea bargaining in the court. *Sociological Quarterly*, 24: 233–251.
Maynard, D. W., & Wilson, T. P. (1980). On the reification of social structure. In S. G. McNall and G. N. Howe (Eds.), *Current perspectives in social theory: A research annual* (pp. 287–322). Greenwich, CT: JAI Press.
Myers, M. A. (1979). Offended parties and official reactions: Victims and the sentencing of criminal defendants. *Sociological Quarterly*, 20, 529–540.
Myers, M. A., & Hagan, J. (1979). Private and public trouble: Prosecutors and the allocation of court resources. *Social Problems*, 26, 439–451.
Needleman, C. (1981). Discrepant assumptions in empirical research: The case of juvenile court screening. *Social Problems*, 28(3), 246–262.
Nettler, G. (1979). Criminal justice. In A. Inkeles, J. Coleman, & R. H. Turner (Eds.), *Annual Review of Sociology* (pp. 27–52). Palo Alto, CA: Annual Reviews.
Neubauer, D. W. (1974). *Criminal justice in middle America*. Morristown, NJ: General Learning Corporation.
Nimmer, R. T. (1974). Judicial reform: Informal processes and competing effects. In H. Jacob (Ed.), *The potential for reform of criminal justice* (pp. 207–234). Beverly Hills, CA: Sage.
Pollner, M. (1974). Mundane reasoning. *Philosophy of the Social Sciences*, 4, 35–54.
Pollner, M. (1975). 'The very coinage of your brain': The anatomy of reality disjunctures. *Philosophy of the Social Sciences*, 5, 411–430.
Reasons, C. E. (1977). On methodology, theory, and ideology. *American Sociological Review*, 42, 177–180.
Rosett, A., & Cressey, D. R. (1976). *Justice by consent: Plea bargaining in the American courthouse*. Philadelphia: Lippincott.
Sacks, H. (1972). Notes on police assessment of moral character. In D. Sudnow (Ed.), *Studies of social interaction* (pp. 280–293). New York: The Free Press.
Schegloff, E. A., & Sacks, H. (1974). Opening up closings. In R. Turner (Ed.), *Ethnomethodology* (pp. 233–264). London: Penguin.
Stinchcombe, A. (1963). Institutions of privacy in the determination of police administrative practices. *American Journal of Sociology*, 69: 150–160.
Sudnow, D. (1965). Normal crimes: Sociological features of the penal code in a public defender's office. *Social Problems*, 12, 255–283.
Swigert, V. L., & Farrell, R. A. (1977). Normal homicides and the law. *American Sociological Review*, 42, 16–32.
Thomson, R. J., & Zingraff, M. T. (1981). Detecting sentencing disparity. *American Journal of Sociology*, 86(4), 869–880.

Weber, M. (1946). Bureaucracy. In H. Gerth & C. Wright Mills (Eds.), *From Max Weber: Essays in sociology* (pp. 146–221). New York: Oxford University Press.

Wieder, D. L. (1974). *Language and social reality: The case of telling the convict code.* The Hague: Mouton.

Wilson, T. P. (1970). Normative and interpretive paradigms in sociology. In J. D. Douglas (Ed.), *Understanding everyday life* (pp. 57–70). Chicago: Aldine.

Zimmerman, D. H. (1974). Fact as practical accomplishment. In R. Turner (Ed.), *Ethnomethodology* (pp. 28–43). London: Penguin.

Zimmerman, D. H., & Pollner, M. (1970). The everyday world as phenomenon. In J. D. Douglas (Ed.), *Understanding everyday life* (pp. 80–103). Chicago: Aldine.

CHAPTER **10**

The Interaction between Judge and Defendant

Ruth Wodak

INTRODUCTION: THE AIMS AND GOALS OF SOCIOLINGUISTICS

The study of institutional discourse, such as interaction at court, can be motivated by different intentions and can have several goals:

1. Every restricted and explicitly defined speech situation (Labov & Fanshel, 1977; Leodolter, 1975a, 1975b; Wodak, 1981a, 1981b, 1981c) allows the linguist to arrive at constitutive rules of interaction, of language behavior and discourse, that are never found so clearly in everyday conversation (turn taking is defined, the roles of the participants are laid out from the beginning, norms are explicitly stated). The goal of the interaction in court is known—to find the truth or a "truth" that can be believed in and defined in legal terms (e.g., Garfinkel, 1967; Lautmann, 1972).

2. Socio- and psycholinguists have intentions that go beyond the linguistic and ethnographic description of the court procedure. The main interest is to find typical (language) behavior correlated to certain sociological (class, age, sex) or psychological (concentration, affectivity) variables, using an interdisciplinary framework (like role theory; Dressler & Wodak, 1981; Leodolter, 1975b). What are the consequences of different types of behavior in terms of the sentence, who succeeds in establishing a good image of himself or herself (Wodak, 1981b, 1981c)? What kind of language barriers exist, not only between legal and everyday language, but also between different styles and strategies in everyday speech?

3. This kind of research leads us to a third group of interests: on a

theoretical level, to be able to explain certain types of behavior in terms of different cultural and class- or sex-specific socialization processes (Leodolter, 1975a); on a practical level, to draw conclusions for the education of lawyers, for the change of court procedures, and for the adaptation of legal language to modern society.

Several linguists and scholars of discourse analysis have become interested in the court situation, motivated by all three goals (Leodolter, 1975a; O'Barr, 1981; Wodak, 1981b, 1981c), and applying very different methods of analysis (speech act theory, conversational analysis, storytelling models, and sociophonological techniques).

REVIEW OF THE LITERATURE: THE IMPACT OF INSTITUTIONAL AND CULTURAL NORMS ON LANGUAGE BEHAVIOR

Many sociological, especially ethnomethodological, studies have pointed to the importance of language behavior in the courtroom. Yet, until the 1980s, legal discourse and interaction was not studied in explicit terms. (Lautmann, 1972; Garfinkel, 1967).

Studies of "natural institutionalized speech situations" have shown that the rules and norms of discourse are dependent on the setting and the explicit rules of the culture and society. Thus, for example, therapeutic discourse functions in a completely different way than does communication in court. Most of the everyday rules and norms of institutionalized situations (like school, court, doctor–patient interactions) are not valid in the therapeutic situation: This allows patients to present their "real self," to break down their image (which they have to carry and play on the "outside"), to discover their underlying and often unconscious (subconscious) traumatic experiences, and to reconstruct their biographies. Due to the different setting in therapy, the conversation and discourse follows other rules than in everyday life (e.g., Wodak, 1981a). But even cultural norms may influence the same institutionalized situation and will have tremendous impact on the discourse strategies allowable and possible. This is the case in the courtroom. U.S. justice functions in a completely different way from that in Western Germany, and again different from the procedures in Austria: In U.S. trials, the lawyers have many more functions than in Europe; they are trained to put their questions very subtly and often enough to discover contradictions. In West Germany, the lawyer also plays a greater role than in Austria. In analyzing and comparing different sociolinguistic studies of the interaction between judge and defendant, we have to bear these differences in mind.

In O'Barr's (1981) study of the function of silence in court, three types of this certainly verbal strategy were distinguished: Silence can be ambiguous or can have only one interpretation. It can also be inherent in the discourse. The defendant can be silent due to misunderstandings, due to the planning of his or her response, or due to interruptions. Some of these phenomena have to do with the specific language used at court, with "legal language." On the one hand, the explicitness of the language of law is necessary. On the other hand, speech and language barriers are the consequences: The defendant cannot or does not understand the question posed (certainly one of the reasons for class-specific justice). This is followed by the larger function of lawyers, who are schooled in this specific language and can interpret it for the defendants. This is certainly a condition that sociolinguistics should examine: the functions of legal language and the resulting language barriers. Again, this can only be done for a specific culture and legal system (e.g., Wodak et al., 1983).

Hoffmann (1980) analyzed courtroom interactions in West Germany, a completely different legal system from those in the United States or Austria (see below). He distinguished two different narrative forms that can be offered in response to a judicial demand for a report of an event. In the Austrian system, the question posed by the judge is merely, "Tell me what happened?" or just "Well, what happened?" Such questions trigger several different discourse strategies, for example, stories (narrations), scenic representations, or reports. The choice of one of these text types depends on the class and sex of the speakers, as well as on their preparation by the lawyer (e.g., Leodolter, 1975a, Wodak, 1981a). Defendants answer with reports or descriptions, and occasionally with narrations. This is a very good example of the impact of the institution on discourse or conversation.

Hoffman was able to categorize the answers of the defendants more precisely: Reports can be "eyewitnesses reports" or reports of the course of events (impersonal speakers' perspective with no narrative tense); descriptions can be dominated by comments (*Kommentierung*) or strategic formulas (stereotypes used at court and learned by heart); some narrative elements may appear.

The two studies mentioned here (O'Barr, 1981; Hoffman, 1980) are descriptive: A first attempt was made, from a linguistic and ethnographic point of view, to categorize the language behavior or some of the aspects of the communication at court explicitly. The samples are too small to allow generalizations. Sociolinguistic interests did not have any impact on the interests of these two researchers and no conclusions of a socially relevant nature were drawn. In the study that I present below, the aims of the explicit investigation of the interaction between judge and defendant were different, of a sociolinguistic nature.

THE LANGUAGE OF DEFENDANTS IN AUSTRIAN COURTS

Due to space limitations, it is impossible to contrast different research strategies, methods, and results; I therefore summarize some of my own results from a large empirical study of language behavior and interaction in a Viennese courtroom, dealing with trials on severe car accidents (15 entire trials were tape-recorded and analyzed; for details see Leodolter, 1975a; Wodak, 1981b, 1981c). I concentrate on analyses of two accounts: a middle-class defendant and a female working-class defendant, telling their "story" of the car accident. The goal of the investigation is to arrive at an explicit definition of courtroom interaction (the dialogue between court and defendant) and to discover the significance of socially derived linguistic barriers (especially their contribution to communicative difficulties) in an interaction that has serious consequences for the participants. The central hypothesis claims that, due to different modes of class- and sex-specific socialization, some defendants will be more able to cope with the authority situation at court than others (e.g., middle-class defendants know the role expectations better than working-class defendants). Are those who are unfamiliar with the system therefore discriminated against? Does the defendants' linguistic behavior contribute to the outcome of the hearing?

Rules and Norms at Court: How to Present a Positive Image

Based on psychological and sociological parameters, the interaction between judge and defendant is divided into subsituations (sociopsychological speech situations) (Table 10.1). The language behavior along these parameters is then analyzed on the discourse and phonological levels. Three levels are distinguished: psychological factors, sociological factors, and interaction sequences. These parameters have a great influence on the interaction and discourse between judge and defendant. Certain linguistic manifestations (SPS) correlate with these factors. The text analysis therefore allows interpretations of why certain discourse types are used or not used. These factors depend on the interaction, social class, and sex of judge and defendant.

The defendant's own version of an accident (SPS 3) is one of the most important phases of the interrogation. Some text-linguistic studies of speech behavior correlate styles of speech with the construction of a socially acceptable image (Holly, 1977; Wodak-Leodolter, 1980). They show that it is important not only to behave in an adequate manner, but

10 The Interaction between Judge and Defendant

Table 10.1
Courtroom Interaction

Sociopsychological Speech Situations (SPS)	Psychological Factors	Sociological Factors	Interaction with Judge
1. judge's dialect	fear; emotional topic	low tolerance for ambiguity	judge threatens punishment
2. parenthetic remarks	trivial questions; lower attention	lack of flexibility	judge poses rapid or incomprehensible questions
3. extended narratives	neutral topic; little emotion	well-known role	defendant's account not interrupted
4. stereotyping	practice; familiarity with material	no detachment from one's own role	question of guilt and remorse
5. emphasis	insisting; being convinced of one's own opinion	no empathy	judge insists upon or repeats a question

also to answer all the questions by the judge "correctly" to get a fair hearing. The strategies used in "storytelling" create a good or a bad image for the defendants. Does the story fit the facts? Is it obviously memorized, or does the defendant succeed in convincing the court that he or she is telling the truth? Does the defendant use technical vocabulary? Is the story consistent and coherent? How does the defendant evaluate the situation? By using categories provided by an interactionist theory of role relationships, I first observed how the defendants built their images (Krappmann, 1972; Leodolter, 1975a). Second, I compared the implicit rules of the court (gained by observation of the hearings) with the explicitly stated rules voiced by the judge and the defendant. It was obvious that occupation played an important role in the evaluation of the defendant. In addition to this, some defendants were able to succeed in showing their own identities by using the strategies of maintaining 'role-distance', or 'role ambiguity'. It was important, finally, for the defendant to combine the role of a guilty person and, simultaneously, the role of a socially acceptable, humble person. A further difficulty arose because most working-class defendants pleaded "not guilty," although everybody knew they were guilty. Yet another factor was the adaptation of the defendant in role taking. If the defendant demonstrated flexible verbal behavior—was able to adapt quickly to all of the questions and expectations of the judge—he or she was likely to fare much better than a defendant who memorized a version of what had happened. With flexible responses, interrogations developed variously; therefore, the defendant had an impact on the question strategies of the judge. Such a defendant presents a first version of their story in a standard but unfamiliar German norm. When the judge questioned him or her, the defendant found himself or herself in the position of having to replay and rephrase in their own, less acceptable dialects (Leodolter, 1975b).

"Storytelling"

(1)

J: G.F.?
D: Yes. Good morning.
J: You are a Doctor of Philosophy?
D: Yes.
J: In which field?
D: Philosophy, pure philosophy.
J: Pure philosophy? How does that relate to your sporting activities?
D: For many years, I have been a member of the Austrian Alpine Club. I have led expeditions and have undertaken arduous ascents.
J: You are single, you live at _____?
D: Yes.
J: You are a university instructor?
D: Yes.
J: Average income?
D: 6000 shillings.
nJ: 6000 shillings. No capital, no financial obligations?
D: No.
J: No previous convictions. Do you plead guilty or not guilty?
D: I plead guilty to having overlooked the woman, despite paying full attention . . .
J: Flötzersteig, near the Wilhelminenspital. Now what happened?
D: Yes, I was in the center lane, because there were cars parked on the right side and about at the place where the accident later occurred, the row of parked cars ended on the right side, and therefore I wanted to change lanes because the right lane was then clear and also I looked into the mirror and suddenly I see in front of me, or rather, left of me, a figure, and my first thought was that it's completely impossible

10 The Interaction between Judge and Defendant

and I was really shocked that this could be possible at all, that now in front of me something to my left, a human being appears, and before I could start braking, the collision happened and somehow I had also realized that the vehicle behind me skidded. With this I had realized that woman was thrown towards the curb and there this was my first thought: no further accident, if behind me cars crash into me and therefore—eh—I went to the left. After this, upon later consideration, this had to be explained that due to the deformation of the fenders on the right side, braking occurred. I already wanted to steer the car to the right in order to stop it in this way against the curb, therefore I had the impression that the car was going to the left. I then could orient myself and braked and stopped right at the curb.

...

[after sentence has been passed]

D: Yes, I wish to thank you for the conduct of the trial and especially for the mild sentence, and I accept the sentence.
J: Hopefully, it will go all right in June. Then you will become a professor?
D: This can be applied for, after a certain time, the professorship, after the habilitation, after 3 years it can be applied for—it is difficult.
J: Will you earn more then?
D: Professorship? Yes, one can live on that quite well.
J: More than now?
D: I think the starting salary is about 10,000 shillings, the starting salary.
J: O.K. Thank you.

(2)

J: Religion?
D: Catholic.
J: Married?
D: Yes.
J: Have a household?
D: Yes.
J: And you live?
D: In the 22 [district—a remote, inelegant area of Vienna (RdB)].
J: Vienna 22, _____ Road. So, and then we need your education.
D: Primary and secondary school.
J: Each for 4 years.

D: Yes . . .
J: Yes, and what else?
D: Yes, I was near the crossing, suddenly the car came from the right, I saw it, but I couldn't manage to brake anymore. So—
J: You couldn't brake, couldn't you try to swerve somehow?
D: No.
J: Do you know what that is?
D: No.
J: No again. You can't answer this question either?
D: Yes—to steer somewhere else did you mean? Or?
J: Yes—every vehicle has a steering wheel. If one turns it around, the direction changes, doesn't it? If it's not broken. If one turns this thing, it is called swerving—to put it briefly. Understood? Yes?

The strategies used in (1) and (2) to answer the question "What happened?" are completely and significantly different, constituting two text types (Wodak, 1981a), derived from the same underlying frame, with the same function in discourse. In the first account, the defendant tells a consistent story (narrative text-type) embedded in a metacommunicative framework. He expresses the shock, his feelings of guilt and fear, and delivers a complete evaluation of the accident to the judge. The technical vocabulary is so well applied that no questions need to be asked to fill in the details. Very precisely woven into the story are all the details that might be important in judging an accident. Although the story is obviously prepared beforehand, it does not constitute a completely different speech style from the defendant's own usual one. The defendant switches very little and seems perfectly secure. By presenting a valid explanation for the accident, he makes work easier for the judge. Linguistically, the text is characterized by personal perspective, by the completeness of the story structure (Labov & Waletzky, 1967; Werlich, 1975; Wodak, 1981a), by the explicitness of evaluative speech acts, and by very coherent phrasing (almost like written discourse). The second story is almost no story at all. A scene is described, but no metacommunicative frame, no orientation, no evaluation, and no explanation are given. The event itself is pointed to, the minute of the crash and the panic felt, but no other parts of the story are told. Wodak (1981a, §3.9) puts forward a theory on text types in which 'scene' is derived from the same underlying text-thematic macrostructure as 'story'. Statistical results show that this text type is very common for the working class and for women. The switch to a different speech style during the narrative discourse is obvious. It

10 The Interaction between Judge and Defendant

seems that the defendant has learned her version by heart. Under the situational stress, it is impossible for her to rephrase ("I couldn't brake" is repeated 20 times during the trial). She is blocked and the judge makes it worse with his cynical questioning. This may be a consequence of her doubly negative status role: She is a woman and from the working class. He uses her momentary uncertainty about the verb *swerve* as a basis for lecturing her on the purposes of the steering wheel. The outcome of these two trials is not surprising: The first defendant had to pay a nominal fine, although he was guilty of manslaughter. The second defendant received a 3-month jail sentence, although she was less guilty.

The qualitative presentation of "storytelling," of discourse strategies used in Austrian courtrooms, was complemented by a quantitative sociophonological analysis. The interactions between judge and defendants were analyzed in terms of sociophonological parameters (Table 10.1; Figure 10.1). Phonological indicators with a sociolinguistic function were chosen to distinguish the code switching between the Viennese dialect (used by the working class) and Austrian Standard German (used by the middle class and upper class). (For details of the sociophonological theory and Austrian language situation, see Leodolter 1975a, 1975b).

Code switching turned out to be an adequate indicator of security or anxiety in this situation. Defendants who were secure, who were able to build and present a positive image, switched very little, significantly less than defendants who did not know how to cope with the rules and norms of the court (or in other authority situations). This does not mean that the use of the Austrian Standard German was the only register accepted: Defendants who knew the court situation from experience (who had at least 10 sentences and were of the working class) kept their dialect and did not switch like middle-class defendants who also felt secure.

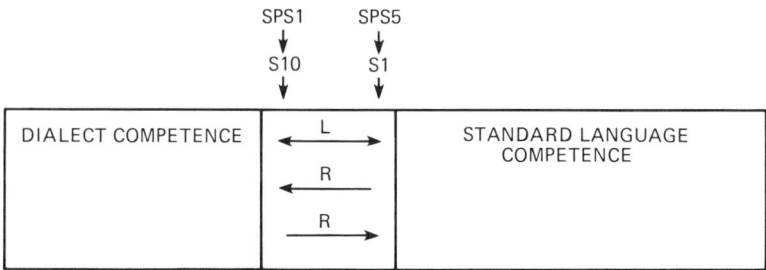

Figure 10.1 Competence model of Viennese colloquial language. The two competences (almost a diglossic situation) allow many variations due to phonological rules (R) and lexical input shifts (L). These styles depend on parameters of a sociological and psychological nature (SPS) in every speech situation. (S), fast speech styles.

This conversation in the dialect with the previously convicted defendants gives evidence for the fact that the use of dialect by itself is not stigmatized; the "wrong" (language) behavior is sanctioned by the judge and this language behavior can manifest itself in the dialect or the standard norm; code switching therefore is the central indicator on the phonological level, discourse strategies (types of "storytelling") on the text level.

CLASS-SPECIFIC JUSTICE: THE GOALS OF INTERDISCIPLINARY RESEARCH

This short text-linguistic analysis of an important subinteraction during the interrogation suggests the following conclusions:

1. Middle-class individuals are able to build a positive image; they know the strategies and values dominating courtroom interaction. They plead guilty. Their stories are consistent and coherent, the facts plausible: An accident happened because of some "objective misfortune" (Sykes & Matza, 1968).
2. Working-class defendants do not succeed in the courtroom. They do not know what to expect and their language behavior reinforces a variety of prejudices and stereotypes held by the judge.

Thus, discourse analysis, the discrimination of typical text types used by defendants of different social class and sex, not only allows us to build theories on socialization processes and language acquisition (in a broad sense) on discourse rules in conversation and interaction rituals; it is also of practical relevance: Judges should be trained to consider language behaviors differentially. They should be taught the results of socio- and text-linguistic studies on text production and text variation, and they should alter their behavior according to these findings. Decision making should be more explicit and transparent, understandable for the defendants. Only then is there a chance that justice can function objectively rather than on the basis of everyday intuitions and prejudices.

REFERENCES

Cicourel, A. (1968). *The social organization of juvenile justice*. New York: Wiley.
Dressler, W., & Wodak, R. (1982). Sociophonological methods in colloquial Viennese. *Language in Society 11:* 339–370.
Garfinkel, H. (1967). Some rules of correct decisions that jurors respect. In H. Garfinkel (Ed.), *Studies in ethnomethodology*. Englewood Cliffs: Prentice Hall.

Hoffman, L. (1980). Zur Pragmatik von Erzählformen vor Gericht. In K. Ehlich (Ed.), *Erzählen im Alltag* (pp. 28–64). Frankfurt/Main: Suhrkamp.
Holly, W. (1977). Gesprächssteuerung und Imagearbeit. Unpublished Ph.D. Dissertation, University of Heidelberg.
Krappmann, L. (1972). *Soziale Dimensionen von Identität*. Stuttgart: Klett.
Lautmann, R. (1972). *Justiz—die stille Gewalt*. Frankfurt: Rowohlt.
Labov, W., & Fanshel, D. (1977). *Therapeutic discourse*. New York: Academic Press.
Labov, W., & Waletzky, J. (1967). Narrative analysis: Oral versions of personal experience. In J. Helm (Ed.), *Essays on the verbal and visual art* (pp. 12–44). Seattle: University of Washington Press.
Leodolter, R. (Wodak) (1975a). *Die Sprache von Angeklagten bei Gericht*. Kronberg/Taunus: Scriptor.
Leodolter, R. (Wodak) (1975b). Interaktion und Stilvariation. In W. Viereck (Ed.), *Sprachliches Handeln—Soziales Verhalten* (pp. 139–170). München: Fink.
O'Barr, M. (1982). *Linguistic evidence: Language, power and strategy in the courtroom*. New York: Academic Press.
Skolnick, J. (1966). *Justice without crime*. New York: Wiley.
Sykes, G., & Matza, D. (1968). Techniken der Neutralisierung: Eine Theorie der Delinquenz. In F. Sack & R. König (Eds.), *Kriminalsoziologie* (pp. 360–371). Frankfurt: Rowohlt.
Werlich, E. (1975). *Typologie der Texte*. Heidelberg: Quelle und Meyer.
Wodak-Leodolter, R. (1980). Problemdarstellungen in gruppentherapeutischen Situationen. In K. Ehlich (Ed.), *Erzählen im Alltag* (pp. 179–208). Frankfurt/Main: Suhrkamp.
Wodak, R. (1981a). *Das Wort in der Gruppe*. Linguistische Studien zur therapeutischen Kommunikation. Wien: Verlag der Akademie der Wissenschaften.
Wodak, R. (1981b). Discourse analysis and courtroom interaction. *Discourse Processes, 3*, 369–380.
Wodak, R. (1981c). The language of defendants at court. In C. Kramerae & M. Schulz, *Language and power*. Los Angeles: Sage.
Wodak, R. (1984). *Hilflose Näge?—Mätter und Töchter erzählen*. Wien: Deuticke.
Wodak, R. et al. (1983). *Verstandlichkeit von Gesetzestesttexten*. Wien: Niederösterr Landesregierung.

CHAPTER **11**

Doctor–Patient Discourse

Aaron V. Cicourel

Communication between a physician and patient in western societies is a relentless form of discourse. The social context of the discourse provides us with a microcosm of broader organizational and institutional constraints and resources that reflects status and power differences in a society. The language used by the physician not only reveals status differences inherent in the social stratification system of the society in question, but the language used also reveals codes or registers that mark differences in the participants' knowledge base, beliefs about illness and its causes, and attempts by doctor and patient to control and direct the discourse.

In the brief discussion that follows, I review some of the central ideas on doctor–patient communication (Cicourel, 1981) and provide an example of differences in knowledge base and beliefs between a doctor and his patient.

ASPECTS OF DOCTOR–PATIENT COMMUNICATION

One view of doctor–patient communication (Francis, Korsch, & Morris, 1969; Korsch, Gozzi, & Francis, 1968; Korsch & Negrete, 1972) states that the physician contributes to poor communication because of a use of technical and turgid language that confuses patients. Doctors are said to lack appropriate personal rapport or empathy in a setting where the patient or the parent of an infant patient needs emotional reassurance about the condition of the child. The research by Korsch and her associates suggests that physicians do not show enough interest in the patient, may fail to greet the parents, and do not explain what is wrong with the child. One consequence of the doctor's perfunctory attention to the parents is that they may not follow the physician's instructions and thereby seek another remedy because they do not understand the reasons for the remedies prescribed. The parents may not return for a follow-up visit and the doctor may view this as negligence.

Research directed by Waitzkin (Waitzkin & Stoeckle, 1972, 1976; Waitzkin & Waterman, 1974) was concerned with the control of information in doctor–patient communication as a way of examining the exercise of power while sustaining a stratified relationship. One focus of the Waitzkin-directed studies is how much information should be given the patient by the physician. The authors report that this decision depends on the life circumstances of the patient at the time, the family's wishes, perhaps the family's religious background or beliefs, and the kind of illness involved.

Additional research on doctor–patient communication is consistent with the results reported by Korsch and her associates and Waitzkin and his associates and includes the point that patients seem to be more likely to follow the doctor's advice when they receive more information from the physician about their illness (Davis, 1968, 1971; Haggerty & Roghmann, 1972). Research by Shuy and his associates (Shuy, 1976) provides us with information about the way patients come to feel that they must simulate the doctor's vocabulary during the medical interview and the extent to which patients feel that physicians do not understand the patient's problems; and also that patients feel it is difficult to tell the physician their problems (45% of 100 interviewed), and that doctors withhold information the patient should be told (70%).

A study in West Germany by Siegrist (1977) of interviews in three hospitals found that doctors often disregarded the patients' demands for information, and this was particularly true when the patient was identified as coming from low social-status settings such as prisons and state mental hospitals. The physicians would ignore the patients' requests or simply keep talking while emitting paralinguistic cues that suggested the patients' questions were trivial or irrelevant. The doctors resorted to sudden shifts in topic to avoid difficult or sensitive issues or situations, and thus avoided having to provide the patient with delicate information. The patients were often left with uncertainty when no clinical results were available.

A general theme that emerges from studies of doctor–patient communication is that culture and language strongly influence the understanding of each participant. For many patients the physician's life-style, ways of thinking, and dialect are perceived as different and troublesome. Specific problems of miscommunication occur in the medical interview when the patient's cultural background is ignored or not taken into account (Kimball, 1971).

Doctors, however, report that patients may arbitrarily stop taking a particular prescription, miss important appointments, ignore important medical advice, and not reveal what is bothering them the most about their illness. The patient's feelings and inferences about the doctor's sensitivity and explanations or lack of them can lead to doubts about the physician's competence and thereby further weaken the trust necessary to follow medical advice and remedies. The patient often feels that the physician is insensitive to the patient's point of view and leaves the patient in the dark about the nature of the illness and its prognosis. The doctor, however, feels that patients are often confused about what is bothering them, or unwilling to be explicit about their problems, and that patients do not pay adequate attention to the explanations given by the physician.

Social class and ethnic differences can lead to problems of trust and the withholding of information, and a general reluctance to ask direct questions and provide direct answers. Physicians may not always be aware of ethnic differences in reports of pain, the choice of symptoms, and the extent to which the same problems can be minimized, overstated, or generalized.

The use of specific vocabularies by the patient might result in the physician suspecting that the patient is hypochondriacal. But many patients often use a vocabulary that is different from the "middle-income" oriented language commonly used by the doctor. Thus there may be class-oriented or cultural norms that constrain the way distress will be voiced.

The patient often sees the physician as using a vocabulary that is intended for someone familiar with medical communication and may feel constrained to adopt a similar use of language in order to be understood by the doctor. Physicians are increasingly being made aware of the necessity of using a vocabulary that the patient can understand. But breakdowns in communication occur, because many patients feel obligated to use "doctor language" but are often unable to sustain this type of communication.

Doctor–patient discourse may reveal status and power differences as reflected in the way intonation and stress are employed, the way questions are asked by the physician, or the way doctors ignore questions by the patient. The office or hospital seems to make many patients feel uncomfortable or vulnerable, especially during the physical examination, when they may be asked to remain undressed while the doctor, nurse, or technician enters and leaves.

In conducting a medical interview, the physician is often constrained by the bureaucratic environment in which he or she works. The language employed not only reflects the doctor's training and the desire to be accurate and concise, but also reflects his or her professional image and status vis-à-vis patients and others working in the same office or hospital. The use of a specific linguistic code or register reflects general principles associated with the practice of medicine and can also reveal the doctor's medical speciality. The medical specialty and level of income desired can affect organizational conditions of work, such as the costs associated with maintaining a particular type of office, clinic, or laboratory. Financial and daily work conditions can infuence the number of patients scheduled for interviews, examinations, or tests. The physician may thus be required to adjust to different forms of communication while he or she moves from one office to another, from a preliminary interview to a physical examination, or from an emergency or routine telephone conversation to a postphysical examination discussion with the patient. The work conditions can impose a set of communication routines that can prove difficult for physician, staff, and patient. There is very little research that addresses the way the bureaucratic and financial conditions of the work setting can influence doctor–patient discourse.

In a medical setting where medical students, interns, or residents or fellows are in training, the bureaucratic conditions can be further complicated. Tannen and Wallat (1983) note the way that a pediatrician can address three audiences with different linguistic registers. The pediatrician uses three codes, each having its particular intonation, voice quality, content, and lexical and syntactic structures. The three audiences consist of a training audience in pediatrics, a parent, and the parent's child.

The use of different registers presumes that each listener may be capable of comprehending one or more specific domains of knowledge, while simultaneously revealing the pediatrician's professional competence. The use of a particular register can imply several goals on the part of the speaker. One goal may be a clear and carefully worded delivery that is intended to inform the parent about the child's illness but at the same time to assure her that there is no cause for alarm. A professional register may be designed to convey the doctor's competence and range of experience with an illness or procedure. The register used with the child may be intended to distract the child in order to perform a specific procedure, or to comfort a child when it appears that the child is becoming apprehensive.

The setting itself, therefore, makes specific demands on the physician's information-processing capabilities and also constrains the kinds of responses that can be expressed. A medical interview can touch on many topics and several of them can be associated with emotionally charged conditions. The doctor must, therefore, be sensitive to a social context that can change momentarily, depending on the way the physician seeks to control the interview and reactions to the kinds of topics introduced by both participants.

The sharpness or directness of the doctor's words, or their indirectness or ambiguity, can be intended or not, but their impact on the patient may or may not be discerned by the physician. Some lexical and syntactic choices by the doctor can be designed to mitigate the gravity of a situation, but we do not always have access to subsequent information from the patient that would clarify the success of the physician's intentions. Many doctors are quite sensitive to the power of language during a medical interview and physical examination, and they seem to employ specific intonation, stress, lexical items, and syntactic structures with considerable deliberateness, while others seem to have less control over their use of language and its effects on the patient. But even when the physician is sensitive to the importance of language use during a medical interview and physical examination, the patient's comprehension of what is said by the doctor is not always clear from the patient's remarks during the interview. There are, of course, cases in which doctor and patient misunderstand each other for a good part if not most of the interview.

CONTRADICTORY BELIEFS ABOUT ILLNESS: AN EXAMPLE OF MISCOMMUNICATION

In the remainder of the paper I illustrate the problem of miscommunication in medical interviews by focusing on a specific case in which a patient harbors contradictory beliefs and also misunderstands her physician. The case involves a 62-year-old woman who consulted a gynecologist because of vulva irritation. A more detailed discussion of the case can be found in Cicourel (1982). Here I only summarize some of the highlights of the case and then present excerpts from an interview I conducted with the patient some 16 months after she had originally consulted her physician about the vulva irritation. The case is not a typical one, by any means, but it helps to illustrate a few problems of doctor–patient discourse.

The doctor's progress notes describe the patient as widowed for 9 months and depressed. She had seen an internal medicine specialist 4 months earlier because of vulva irritation and was started on estrogen, which she stopped because of breast soreness. The interview began with a typical question by the doctor, a request for information ("What can I do for you?"). The patient was invited to provide the physician with information that could clarify the patient's condition. The interview that followed is fairly routine and terminated with the physician telling the patient that she seemed to be in good condition but that some routine tests would be necessary. The tests proved to be abnormal and the doctor called the patient to tell her she would have to come in again and have biopsies taken. The biopsies were done during the second visit and proved abnormal. The physician called a second time to state that an operation was necessary to remove the patient's uterus. The operation was discussed during a third visit.

When I interviewed the patient 16 months after her initial visit to the doctor, she expressed beliefs about her illness that were at variance with the physician's views. The patient had been told repeatedly that she required an operation to remove a cancerous uterus, and the matter was discussed with her family present. My interview with the patient provided the occasion for her to construct a set of beliefs about her illness. I suspect but cannot confirm that her beliefs existed at the time of her original interview with the doctor. According to the physician, the patient resisted his explanations of her illness at the outset and throughout the many months that she was under his care. Two types of contradictions seemed to emerge from this case, which, while not typical in the content reported here, nevertheless reveal problems common to doctor–patient discourse.

Some background for the first contradiction revolved around the patient's doubts about the adequacy of the explanations she received about her illness and the necessity of the operation, but she also expressed a desire to have the same gynecologist remain her physician and perform the operation. She perceived a contradiction between the doctor's initial statements about her condition made during the first interview (and the first telephone call after the first interview), where she felt that she was being told that things looked pretty good and that perhaps nothing serious existed, and the subsequent claim that she had a cancerous uterus. This perceived contradiction was subsequently strengthened by a notice from the hospital that was waiting for her when she arrived home after the operation that stated that her recent pap smear test had been normal. This was perceived by the patient to be completely at odds with the physician's views.

The second, but related contradiction refers to the patient's belief that she did not have cancer and that the operation may have been performed on the wrong person. But she also expressed the belief that she and her children had contracted cancer from a "contagious" husband and father who had died of pancreatic cancer 9 months prior to her initial visit to the gynecologist.

The reader can perhaps grasp some idea of the basis for the patient's beliefs about the contradictions in the following passage taken from my interview with her 16 months after the initial visit to the doctor.

> P: I had two thoughts, was this somebody else's letter stuck in my envelope, or uh . . . or was that normal and somebody in, along the line somewhere said it wasn't normal, and I, as I say, then I, I just didn't know what to think, when you get, open up a letter like that. . . . see . . . it's a shock particularly I think I hadn't gotten over the shock of my husband's death yet and all this kep, came upon me.
> I: Okay . . . okay, and you did speak to the doctor . . .
> P: Apparently he said something to them, so I'm getting a date on it now but still as you see I don't have a name on it.
> I: Yeah.
> P: What's so hard about typing in a name? I think this is an important procedure that we do these Pap tests and I think (I: yes) they should be (I: I agree) covered well instead of just haphazardly. (Each dot = 1 second pause)

The above remarks by the patient indicate that she assumed that perhaps someone had made a mistake. Her remarks are not clear. First she stated that someone's letter had gotten into her envelope. We could also infer that the patient was thinking that perhaps her pap test was normal and that someone then said it was not normal. The patient's view that perhaps a bureaucratic mistake had been made seems to have triggered thoughts that questioned the original diagnosis and the need for a subsequent operation. The interview continued with additional remarks about how she came to choose her physician and how she decided to remain with him rather than going to a military hospital where her husband had died.

The patient then described the pap smear test that was done during her first visit to the gynecologist and the subsequent telephone call from the doctor saying she had cancer. But the patient's remarks are not always clear:

> P: . . . But, uh, Dr. B. gave me the examination, and took this Pap test and then I don't remember, it wasn't very long after he called me and he, on the phone, and he said that . . . uhm . . . uhm, we found cancer cells, or cancer, cancer cells, I don't remember just how he said it, and of course I was, as I say, still in shock from my husband's death.

The patient does not clarify the sequence of events clearly. She confused the first interview and the first telephone conversation with a second and third interview and a second telephone conversation.

During her first interview the physician's remarks ("Well . . . from uh

... the .. uh standpoint of uh, a gynecologist, I think everything is, is really pretty good.'') were interpreted as indications that nothing serious was found. The pap smear test, however, proved abnormal and led to the first telephone call telling the patient that a D and C (dilation and curettage of the uterine cervix) might still be in order, while also stating that biopsies should be performed. Despite the abnormal biopsies after the second visit, and the second telephone call, the patient was not convinced that the diagnosis of cancer was the result of appropriate medical practice. During her description of the visits and telephone calls, 16 months later, she noted: "But, uhm, then reading that letter I thought well, something got mixed up there, maybe somebody is walking around with cancer and I didn't have it. I, all this was going through my mind, you know . . ."

The gist of the confusion seems to be an apparent discrepancy between the physician's remarks of what the patient took to be a routine condition and the progressively serious consequences that led to the operation for the removal of her uterus. The patient did not realize nor did she accept the physician's explanations that a D and C is not necessarily a routine procedure—that it can also be the basis for discovering a more serious condition. But the biopsies made the D and C irrelevant because they confirmed an adenocarcinoma.

The second contradiction is revealed by lengthy remarks by the patient. Space permits us to only briefly indicate the patient's belief that her husband's type of cancer must be contagious:

> P: . . . maybe, the cancer is contagious and nobody warned us, and my, me dear son, he always kissed his dad on the forehead and, uh my uh daughter did too, and you know that last three weeks or so, they really perspire and I wonder if the germs don't come out with the perspiration . . .

The patient suggested that her son's current urological illness might be linked to her husband's cancer, and that the daughter's recent lump on her neck was due to the same contact with the father. The family conditions seem to have provided coherence to the patient's belief about cancer.

The hospital records and our contacts with the physician indicate the way the patient was given explanations at variance with her belief. But the patient felt the doctor had not pursued the matter adequately despite many discussions about her misunderstanding. The patient seems to have linked what she thought was a benign diagnosis by a prior visit to an internal medicine specialist and the first visit to the gynecologist to her claim that the gynecologist had mentioned the option of a D and C. The central contradiction revolves around the belief that cancer is contagious, and that the patient and her children probably contracted the disease from her husband. But this belief contrasts with the patient's claim of an option of a D and C by the gynecologist, who she said had told her she was in good condition when he examined her during the first office visit, and with the receipt of a normal pap smear report from the hospital upon returning home from surgery. The patient concluded that perhaps she did not have cancer and that the wrong person had received the operation and treatment.

CONCLUDING REMARKS

In this brief essay I have illustrated some aspects of doctor–patient discourse by focusing on the way patients can sustain beliefs about their illnesses despite repeated attempts by the physician to change the patients' misconceptions. The present case is not typical in terms of the kinds of details that the patient used to provide coherence for her beliefs, but this more dramatic case underscores common aspects of misunderstanding in doctor–patient discourse. Patients often doubt the doctor's assessment of their condition despite following a course of treatment. Yet physicians also report patients taking themselves off of medication despite being told that the treatment is essential for good health.

The patient's memory and language limitations and the doctor's technical descriptions are often unavoidable aspects of doctor–patient discourse. The patient's knowledge base or beliefs can be a significant limitation for answering the physician's questions, just as the doctor's limited knowledge of sociocultural and cognitive–linguistic issues can lead to a failure to recognize how the patient's mental or folk models can affect the patient's conceptions of illness and technical information about illness and treatment. The medical setting affords an environment in which we can examine the way a medical history captures the prior discourse of an interview. Interviewing the patient and the physician after doctor–patient discourse can illuminate the intentions, goals, and understanding of the participants of prior discourse.

REFERENCES

Cicourel, A. V. (1981). Language and medicine. In C. A. Ferguson & S. B. Heath (Eds.), *Language in the USA* (pp. 407–429). Cambridge: Cambridge University Press.

Cicourel, A. V. (1982). Language and belief in a medical setting. In H. Byrnes (Ed.), *Contemporary perceptions of language: Interdisciplinary dimensions*. 33rd Round Table on Language and Linguistics. Georgetown University, Washington, DC: Georgetown University Press.

Davis, M. S. (1968). Variations in patients' compliance with doctors' advice: An empirical analysis of patterns of communication. *American Journal of Public Health, 58,* 274–288.

Davis, M. S. (1971). Variation in patients' compliance with doctors' orders: Medical practice and doctor–patient interaction. *Psychiatric Medicine, 2,* 31–54.

Francis, V., Korsch, B. M., & Morris, M. J. (1969). Gaps in doctor–patient communication: Patient response to medical advice. *New England Journal of Medicine, 280,* 535–540.

Haggerty, R., & Roghmann, K. (1972). No compliance and self-medication. *Pediatric Clinics of North America, 19,* 101–115.

Kimball, C. P. (1971). Medicine and dialects. *Annals of Internal Medicine, 74,* 137–139.

Korsch, B. M., & Negrete, V. F. (1972). Doctor–patient communication. *Scientific American, 227,* 66–74.

Korsch, B. M., Gozzi, E. K., & Francis, V. (1968). Gaps in doctor–patient communication: Doctor–patient interaction and patient satisfaction. *Pediatrics, 42,* 855–871.

Shuy, R. W. (1976). The medical interview: Problems in communication. *Primary Care, 3,* 365–386.

Siegrist, J. (1977). Empirische Untersuchungen zu Kommunikationsprozessen bei Visiten. *Osterreichische Zeitschrift für Soziologie, 3,* 4.

Tannen, D., & Wallat, C. (1983). Doctor/mother/child communication: Linguistic analysis of a pediatric interaction. In S. Fisher & A. D. Todd (Eds.), *The social organization of doctor–patient communication.* Washington, DC: The Center for Applied Linguistics.

Waitzkin, H., & Stoeckle, J. D. (1972). The communication of information about illness: Clinical, sociological, and methodological considerations. *Advances in Psychosomatic Medicine, 8,* 180–215.

Waitzkin, H., & Stoeckle, J. D. (1976). Information control and the micropolitics of health care: Summary of an ongoing research project. *Social Science and Medicine, 10,* 263–276.

Waitzkin, H., & Waterman, B. (1974). *The exploitation of illness in capitalist society.* Indianapolis, IN: Bobbs-Merrill.

CHAPTER **12**

Cross-Cultural Communication

Deborah Tannen

INTRODUCTION: THE IMPORTANCE OF CROSS-CULTURAL COMMUNICATION

The study of cross-cultural communication is central to both theoretical and applied linguistics. Examining the causes of misunderstandings in cross-cultural communication sets in relief the processes that underlie all communication but often go unnoticed when it proceeds successfully. Thus discourse analysts find cross-cultural communication a useful research site, apart from any real-world interest in cross-cultural relations.

In fact, however, most discourse analysts have a genuine concern with real-world issues, and cross-cultural communication is crucial to nearly all public and private human encounters. At the most global level, the fate of all people, indeed the fate of the earth, depends upon negotiations among representatives of governments with different cultural assumptions and ways of communicating. Moreover, in order to accomplish any public or private goals, people have to talk to each other, and in more and more cases, the people communicating come from more or less different cultural backgrounds. Furthermore, as my research demonstrates and as I illustrate with brief examples from that research, the notion of "cross-cultural" encompasses more than just speakers of different languages or from different countries; it includes speakers from the same country of different class, region, age, and even gender.

PARALINGUISTIC SIGNALS IN COMMUNICATION

As the work of Gumperz (1982a) and his coworkers (Gumperz & Tannen, 1979; papers collected in Gumperz, 1982b) makes clear, speakers use paralinguistic and prosodic features—for example, tone of voice, pitch, loudness, pacing, pauses—to establish cohesion, that is, to show the relationship between ideas (what is foreground, what is background? What is cause, what effect? What is given, what new?) and to show their attitude toward what they say (Are they earnest, joking, or sarcastic? Being friendly or rude? Implying "come closer" or "stay back"?)

These signals about how one means what one says, which Gumperz calls "contextualization cues," are automatically processed. A speaker does not stop and think, "Now I am angry, should I raise my voice or lower it?" A listener doesn't stop and think, "Now if he is raising his voice, does that mean he is angry?" Rather, people encode and decode automatically—"I'm angry," or "He likes me"—without thinking about what tone of voice, loudness, pacing or pitch gives that impression. In the terms of Bateson (1972), these signals indicate a metamessage about how the message, or propositional content of the words spoken, is intended. In other words, how an utterance is said communicates metamessages about the relationship between interactants.

In intracultural communication, expectations about how paralinguistic features signal how an utterance is meant—that is, the interpretation of metamessages—is likely to be shared by speakers and hearers, so they are not noticed; they seem self-evident and "logical," just as the word for a chair in one's own language seems like the real word for chair, when in fact it is arbitrary and no more logical than the words *asiento, karekla,* or the word for chair in any other language.

In cross-cultural communication, however, expectations about how paralinguistic signals are used to indicate what is meant by what is said are not shared. Therefore, in asking what led to misunderstandings, one is forced to notice that a certain tone of voice or use of pitch or other paralinguistic or prosodic feature was intended to mean one thing and taken to mean another. For example, Gumperz (1982a) shows that when speakers of Indian English use increased volume to perform the conversational business-as-usual of getting the floor, it seems to speakers of British English that they are angry. A speaker of British English typically gets the floor by repeating an initial phrase until she or he has audience attention. When the speaker of British English responds in kind to what she or he has perceived as a flareup of temper on the part of the Indian, both interlocutors feel that the other unaccountably introduced the tone of anger into the interaction.

Research on communicative style (Lakoff, 1973, 1976), politeness phenomena (Brown & Levinson, 1978), what Goffman (1967) calls deference and demeanor, as well as indirect speech acts (Searle, 1975) have all contributed to the realization that most communication is characterized by indirectness. While it may seem at first glance that people use words to say what they mean, a little thought and even less observation indicate that they usually do not come right out and say what they mean. Rather, they negotiate, hint at what they mean, try to get an idea of what the other person might think of what they might mean, and be ready to adjust or take back what they might have meant.

As the work of Lakoff demonstrates and explains, social requirements are too pressing for people to barrel ahead with their thoughts and ideas. Rather, there are two main benefits to indirectness. The first is rapport: It is better to be understood, to get what one wants, without saying what one means. Then the very fact of mutual understanding is proof of rapport, of sharing background and style. The second is defensive: In case one's intentions are not received well, one can avoid outright disagreement by not having gone "on record" (Brown & Levinson, 1978). Cultures differ with regard to whether speakers would rather risk threatening rapport, and therefore appear distant, or risk threatening independence, and therefore appear imposing.

There are cultural differences with respect to how much and what type of indirectness is expected in particular settings. For example, as my own research (Tannen, 1981a) and that of others (for example, Goody, 1978) shows, there are cultural differences with respect to how likely a person is to interpret questions as requests for information, as opposed to interpreting them as indirect ways of communicating something else. Of course all people are capable of interpreting questions both ways. They rely on information about the context, the habits of the other person, and how something is said to decide whether a question or any other utterance is meant literally or not. But the inclination to look for hidden meaning can be more or less strong depending on whether one has come to expect people in this setting to hint or not, and how. My research (Tannen, 1981a) shows that misunderstandings commonly arise when one person asks a question intended as a request for information, for example, "John's having a party. Do you want to go?" while the other interprets this as a hint, for example, "I want to go."

In presenting a sample conversation beginning with this question, I found that Greeks in my study were more likely to interpret such a question as an indirect way of hinting one's own preference than were Americans in my study. Furthermore, for Americans but not for Greeks, women were more likely than men to interpret the question as a hint. These findings may give some indication of the sources for the stereotype of Greeks and of women as being untrustworthy (you can't believe what they say), as well as the stereotype among Greeks of Americans as childlike (they haven't yet learned the subtle ways of hinting but, like children, blurt things out).

Indirectness (or the possibility of it) makes misunderstandings a danger in any conversation, but they are even more likely when people come from different cultural backgrounds. The automatic and seemingly self-evident elements of conversational style are arbitrarily agreed on by speakers from a given culture; speakers from different cultures have different conventions for use of these elements to accomplish conversational goals. Most speakers simply assume that their system is self-evidently appropriate. Rather than question our basic ways of doing things, most of us are ready to draw conclusions (possibly negative) about people who are different.

EXAMPLES OF CROSS-CULTURAL DIFFERENCES

Research in which I taped 2½ hours of Thanksgiving dinner table conversation among six friends (Tannen, 1984b) showed that although all participants spoke the same language and seemed to understand each other, nonetheless there were subcultural differences that resulted in repeated misunderstandings of each other's intentions. For example, three of the dinner conversation participants, who were from one part of the United States, New York City, seemed to dominate. However, this was the result not of their intention to dominate but of the differences in their turn-taking habits and ways of showing friendliness. When any two or more people talk, each one waits until the other has finished talking before taking a turn to talk. However, this seemingly simple criterion is really complex, because there are cultural and subcultural differences in how much pause one expects speakers to allow within turns and between turns. Whichever party expects less pause will repeatedly and predictably be the first to interpret a turn-taking pause as an uncomfortable silence, an indication that the other has nothing to say. As a result, if that person has friendly intentions and wants the interaction to go smoothly, she or he will fill the silence with talk. In other words, what is intended as a friendly act of keeping conversation going is interpreted as an unfriendly act of not giving the other person a chance to talk. This is what happened in the conversation I recorded and analyzed. Because three of the speakers expected shorter turn-taking pauses, they continually took the floor before the others felt there had been enough pause for them to start talking. The slower speakers felt the faster ones were not giving them a chance to talk, but the faster ones thought the others had nothing to say and were not holding up their end of the conversation.

Another device used by the three faster speakers involved overlap. These speakers, like those of many other cultural groups that have been reported in the literature (for example, Erickson, 1982; Riesman, 1974), expected a lively casual conversation at dinner to include overlap. That is, they expected that more than one person would talk at a time. One function of overlap is for a listener to show understanding by talking at the same time as the speaker: by loud exclamations of understanding, by finishing sentences with or instead of the speaker to show that the listener knows where the sentence is going (hence has been a good listener), by asking questions the answers to which obviously were about to come anyway. This can be seen in the following example segment, in which the listener (B) is talking at the same time as the storyteller (A) for much of the time. (See Appendix for transcription conventions.)

(1)
    A: In fact one of my students told me for the first time, I taught her for over a year. [.5] That she was adopted. And then I thought—uh—[.5] THAT explains SO many things.
    B: What. [That she was →
    A: 'Cause she's so:: different [from her mother
    B: smarter than she should have been? Or stupider [than she should've been.
    A: It wasn't smart or stupid, actually, it was just she was so different. [2.] Just different.
    B: lhmJ

For much of the time that A is telling his story, B is talking, asking questions that A obviously would have answered anyway. It can be seen from the transcript that B's overlapping does not stop A from continuing his story, and during playback (a session in which the segment is played for the participants and they have a chance to comment) A stated that he did not mind B talking along with him; he took it as a sign of interest in his story. This tactic worked fine among those three speakers. Often they were all speaking at once. However, the other speakers did not expect overlap. Their idea of a conversation was that only one speaker could speak at a time. As a result, when an overlap-favoring speaker began to speak to show listenership, an overlap-avoiding speaker interpreted this as an interruption and stopped talking. The irony is that from the point of view of the culturally different speakers, each one thought the other created the interruption: The overlap-avoiding speaker thought the overlapper intended to interrupt, but the cooperative overlapper cannot understand why the speaker interrupted himself by stopping.

A special instance of this phenomenon occurred when a fast, overlapping speaker uttered a particularly loud or paralinguistically exaggerated show of appreciation of the talk of a slow, overlap-avoiding speaker. This expressive use of paralinguistic features often had the effect of stopping the speaker in his or her linguistic tracks, wondering what caused the outburst. This can be seen in the following example, in which the main speaker (C) is telling about a meeting at which a speech pathologist suggested that "gay" (homosexual) speakers' identifiable voice quality might be the result of hormonal differences. This is an idea that all those present found preposterous. However, the way that two listeners, (A) and (B), (the same speakers quoted in the earlier segment) show their agreement with the speaker (C) is so unexpected to him that rather than being encouraged to continue, he is thrown off balance:

(2)
        C: Yeah. Whether the gay voice was hormonal.
        B: ⌊YOU'RE KIDDING!⌋
             [2 sec.]
        B: Wo::w.
             [1.5 sec.]
        A: Oh God! [softly]
             [1 sec.]
        C: Or whether it was learned behavior, or w whether it was [.5] uh learned behavior, o:r genetic, or hormonal or what.
             / ? as they were gonna /

The paralinguistically gross reactions of A and B, who are fast, overlapping, expressive speakers, were meant to encourage the main speaker (C), but because he is a slower, overlap-avoiding speaker, he was shocked by the first overlapping and extreme reaction, *YOU'RE KIDDING!* and stopped talking. This led both A and B to remedy the situation by giving more expressive encouragement, but these only exacerbated C's confusion. Therefore when he resumed his story, it was with much hesitation, repetition, and vagueness.

A similar phenomenon occurred with a way of asking questions that I have dubbed "machine-gun questions" (Tannen, 1981b, 1984b). The fast, overlapping, expressive speakers often showed interest by asking a series of questions that, typically, were personal in focus and were characterized by reduced syntactic form, high or low pitch, and an appearance of abruptness. An extreme but not atypical example of the negative effect of such questions with others who do not expect them can be seen below. Again, the speakers are the same as the ones seen in the previous examples:

(3)

        [4 sec. pause]
- B: You live in LA?
- C: Yeah.
- B: Y'visiting here?
- C: Yeah.
- B: What do you do there?
- C: [1.5] uh: I work at General Stu— [.5] General Studios [1.]
- B: ₋a:nd
     [You an artist?
- C: No: no.
- B: Writer?
- C: Yeah:. I write [.5] advertising copy.

B's questions were intended to draw C out, to show interest in him, to encourage him to talk. However, they had the opposite effect. Because they seemed so unexpectedly pointed, personal, and abrupt, they caught C off guard. B tried to remedy the situation by showing more interest, asking more such questions. This, of course, because of their style differences, only made things worse.

When such questions were asked of others who used this style, however, a variety of possibilities existed. They were answered sometimes immediately, sometimes very quickly, and sometimes at length. Sometimes they were suspended and answered later; and sometimes they were not answered at all. In any case, the quick questions had the effect of keeping conversation snappy and smooth. Machine-gun questioners knew that such questions were intended as a show of friendliness and did not have to be answered. Non–machine gunners, however, felt that questions have to be answered, so they felt compelled to stop whatever they were saying and answer the question, though often minimally, as a way of passive resistance, and because they resented the imposition. The machine gunner could not understand why the other was so resistant to making conversation, and the machine gunned could not understand why the asker was so pushy.

EFFECTS OF CROSS-CULTURAL DIFFERENCES

In all these examples, no participant realized that the other's way of talking was a reaction to his or her own, but simply attributed it to the unaccountable and possibly negative personality or intentions of the other. In all these examples, too, it is clear that the devices that make up conversation—the way people use pacing, tone of voice, pitch, loudness, and so on to show how they mean what they say and to show how ideas are related to each other (what's important and what's by the way)—are conventional. When conversationalists share expectations about how these conventions are used, then communication is smooth. One can pretty much assume that what the other means is what one would have meant if one had said the same thing in the same way. But if conversationalists have different habits about use of these conventions, then interpretation becomes very tricky. Others may not mean what their utterances seem to mean. When the conversational habits of the person from the other culture have no meaning in one's own repertoire, then the utterance is likely to be dismissed as unprocessable. But, as is more often the case, since the basic features of tone, pitch, pausing, and loudness are the universal ways of showing how one means what one says, and in fact are the substance of which talk is made, when the utterance of a person from another background has meaning in one's own repertoire, a listener simply assumes that he or she intended the perceived effect. If he seems angry, one assumes he intended to show anger. If he seems pushy, or resistant, one assumes that he is a pushy or unfriendly person. This is the tragedy of cross-cultural communication.

It should be noted, however, that cross-cultural differences do not always have negative effects. The possibility of misinterpretation can lead to positive as well as negative misattributions. As a simple example, the turns of phrase and common expressions of another language, when translated into one's own, can seem especially charming, novel, or creative, and one can therefore attribute special creative verbal ability to speakers of other languages who are simply translating common expressions from their native language.

Furthermore, features that have one meaning to one person and another meaning to the other may nonetheless have a positive meaning to the listener and a positive effect on the interaction. For example, Suprapto (1983) shows that in interaction between an Indonesian gynecologist and American patients, the doctor uses laughter in a conventional Indonesian way, for example when potentially embarrassing subjects are broached. The patients are not familiar with this conventional use of laughter, but they interpret it as a sign that this doctor has an easy-going, informal, and good-humored personality, and they therefore like to deal with him.

Another example of positive effects of style differences is demonstrated by Adger (1984) based on analysis of children's interactions in a multicultural classroom. One child comes from a cultural background in which the style of argumentation requires the winner to get the last word. Another child comes from a cultural background in which value is placed on avoiding confrontation and winning over the long haul. Thus, in arguments between these two children, it is possible for the first child to get the last word and the second child to back down to achieve harmony, with the result that both feel they have won what they set out to achieve.

It might seem, logically, that increased exposure should lead to increased understanding. When people of different groups communicate with each other frequently, they should come to understand each other better. Sometimes this is the case, or, if the differences have positive rather than negative effects, the mutual misinterpretation does not lead to friction. But just as often, and tragically, increased exposure and contact can lead to increased mutual negative stereotyping, as Vassiliou, Triandis, Vassiliou, and McGuire (1972) have found. When people have not had much contact with others from a certain other group, they have no reason to develop negative stereotypes. But when they have had dealings with people of the other group, have tried sincerely to be fair and have ended up frustrated, each blames the other. People are not likely to assume that both are genuinely trying but are misunderstanding each other.

Stereotypes of ethnic groups develop partly, at least, from impressions made on people from one culture by habits that have a different meaning for people in the other. For example, the stereotype of the pushy New Yorker is the non–New York view of such Mediterranean habits as standing close, talking loud, and talking at the same time. In contrast, New Yorkers expecting these expressions of rapport find many non–New Yorkers cold and dull.

There are many such pairs of mutual stereotypes. The image of the American Indian as silent and stony probably grows out of the cultural convention of many American Indians to remain silent in situations in which non-Indian Americans engage in chitchat, for example, when meeting new acquaintances. The corresponding stereotype among Indians is that white people are ridiculously talkative, insincere, and superficial, trying to act like your friend when they are not. (Basso, 1979; Scollon & Scollon, 1981).

The inscrutable Chinese is a speaker merely fulfilling the Chinese expectation that one start somewhere off the point and work in to the point by indirection. Getting right to the point seems hopelessly rude or foolishly childlike, or is taken to be an indirect way of implying something else (Young, 1982).

Cross-cultural communication is like trying to follow a route on which someone has turned the signposts around. The familiar signposts are there, but when you follow them, they take you in the wrong direction. As Becker (1982) eloquently demonstrates, interpreting discourse across cultures exaggerates the dilemma that is inherent in all communication: One's interpretation is "deficient" because it misses intended subtlety and is also "exuberant" because it reads in unintended meaning. When one is unfamiliar with the constraints of another's system, one cannot distinguish business-as-usual cohesion from individual variation by deviation from convention.

Similarly, cross-cultural communication exaggerates the paradox, inherent in all communication, that grows out of the fact that humans are simultaneously individuals and yet need others for survival. As Scollon (1982) points out, all communication is a double bind, simultaneously showing interpersonal involvement and respect for individuality. Thus, in cross-cultural communication, showing respect for cultural differences is a violation of rapport, denying ways that all people are alike. (That is why some people object to any research documenting cross-cultural differences, which they see as buttressing stereotypes and hence exacerbating discrimination). At the same time, ignoring cultural differences leads to misinterpretation and hence discrimination of another sort.

When the setting of cross-cultural communication is a Thanksgiving dinner, and the participants are friends or friends of friends, people are disposed to ignore or pass over negative impressions. If they do not succeed, the repercussions are not serious; perhaps they will invite different friends to dinner next time. But when the setting is crucial to one's personal life (e.g., a job interview), or when the misunderstandings are repeated (e.g., if one has moved to a new country or region, or married someone of different cultural background), the misunderstandings can mount to cumulative and serious frustration. When the arena is international affairs, the results of cross-cultural misinterpretation can be tragic indeed.

APPENDIX: TRANSCRIPTION CONVENTIONS

Length of pause is indicated in brackets.
Brackets across lines indicate overlap: both lines spoken simultaneously.
— indicates glottal stop: sudden cutting off of voicing
: indicates lengthening of vowel sound.
/?/ indicates words not transcribed because incomprehensible.
/words/ in slashes indicate uncertain transcription.
CAPS indicate stress through pitch and loudness.
? indicates rising intonation, not syntactic question.
. indicates falling intonation, not syntactic sentence.
→ indicates that utterance continues without pause.

BIBLIOGRAPHY

Adger, C. (1984). Communicative competence in the culturally diverse classroom: Negotiating norms for linguistic interaction. Unpublished Ph.D. dissertation, Department of Linguistics, Georgetown University.

Basso, K. (1979). *Portraits of "The Whiteman."* Cambridge: Cambridge University Press.

Bateson, G. (1972). *Steps to an ecology of mind.* New York: Ballantine.

Becker, A. L. (1979). Text-building, epistemology, and aesthetics in Javanese shadow theatre. In A. L. Becker & A. Yengoyan (Eds.), *The imagination of reality* (pp. 211–243). Norwood, NJ: Ablex.

Becker, A. L. (1982). Beyond translation: Esthetics and language description. In H. Byrnes (Ed.), *Contemporary perceptions of language: Interdisciplinary dimensions* (pp. 124–138). Georgetown University Round Table on Languages and Linguistics 1982. Washington, DC: Georgetown University Press.

Brown, P., & Levinson, S. (1978). Universals in language usage: Politeness phenomena. In E. Goody (Ed.), *Questions and politeness* (pp. 56–289). Cambridge: Cambridge University Press.

Erickson, F. (1975). Gatekeeping and the melting pot: Interaction in counseling encounters. *Harvard Educational Review, 45*(1), 44–70.

Erickson, F. (1979). Talking down: Some cultural sources of miscommunication in interracial interviews. In A. Wolfgang (Ed.), *Nonverbal behavior* (pp. 99–126). New York: Academic Press.

Erickson, F. (1982). Money tree, lasagna bush, salt and pepper: Social construction of topical cohesion in a conversation among Italian–Americans. In D. Tannen (Ed.), *Analyzing discourse: Text and talk* (pp. 43–70). Georgetown University Round Table on Languages and Linguistics 1981. Washington, DC: Georgetown University Press.

Erickson, F., & Shultz, J. (1982). *The counselor as gatekeeper: Social interaction in counseling interviews.* New York: Academic Press.

Forster, E. M. (1924). *A passage to India.* New York: Harcourt.

Freedman, D. (1979). Ethnic differences in babies. *Human Nature,* January 1979, pp. 37–43.

Goffman, E. (1967). *Interaction ritual.* Garden City, NY: Doubleday.

Goody, E. (1978). Towards a theory of questions. In E. Goody (Ed.), *Questions and politeness* (pp. 17–43). Cambridge: Cambridge University Press.

Guilmet, G. M. (1979). Maternal perceptions of urban Navajo and Caucasian children's classroom behavior. *Human Organization, 38*(1), 87–91.

Gumperz, J. J. (1978). The conversational analysis of interethnic communication. In E. Lamar Ross (Ed.), *Interethnic communication* (pp. 13–31). Southern Anthropological Society Proceedings, No. 12. Athens, GA: University of Georgia Press.

Gumperz, J. J. (1982a). *Discourse strategies.* Cambridge: Cambridge University Press.

Gumperz, J. J. (Ed.). (1982b). *Language and social identity.* Cambridge: Cambridge University Press.

Gumperz, J. J., & Tannen, D. (1979). Individual and social differences in language use. In C. Fillmore, D. Kempler, & W. S.-Y. Wang (Eds.), *Individual differences in language ability and language behavior* (pp. 305–324). New York: Academic Press.

Hall, E. (1959). *The silent language.* New York: Doubleday.

Kempton, W. (1980). The rhythmic basis of interactional microsynchrony. In M. R. Key (Ed.), *Verbal and nonverbal communication* (pp. 67–75). The Hague: Mouton.

Kochman, T. (1981). *Black and white styles in conflict.* Chicago: University of Chicago Press.

Lakoff, R. (1973). The logic of politeness, or minding your *p*'s and *q*'s. Papers from the Ninth Regional Meeting of the Chicago Linguistics Society, 292–305.
Lakoff, R. (1975). *Language and woman's place*. New York: Harper and Row.
Lakoff, R. (1976). Why you can't say what you mean. Review of Edwin Newman, *Strictly speaking*. *Centrum, 4*(2), 151–170.
Michaels, S. & Cook-Gumperz, J. (1979). A study of sharing time with first grade children. *Proceedings of Fifth Annual Meeting of the Berkeley Linguistics Society* (pp. 647–659). Department of Linguistics, University of California, Berkeley.
Philips, S. U. (1972). Participant structures and communicative competence: Warm Springs children in community and classroom. In C. Cazden, V. John, & D. Hymes (Eds.), *Functions of language in the classroom* (pp. 370–394). New York: Teachers College Press.
Reisman, K. (1974). Contrapuntal conversations in an Antiguan village. In R. Bauman & J. Sherzer (Eds.), *Explorations in the ethnography of speaking* (pp. 110–124). Cambridge: Cambridge University Press.
Saville-Troike, M. (1980). Cross-cultural communication in the classroom. In J. E. Alatis (Ed.), *Current issues in bilingual education* (pp. 348–355). Georgetown University Round Table on Languages and Linguistics 1980. Washington, DC: Georgetown University Press.
Scollon, R. (1982). The rythmic integration of ordinary talk. In D. Tannen (Ed.), *Analyzing discourse: Text and talk* (pp. 335–349). Georgetown University Round Table on Languages and Linguistics 1981. Washington, DC: Georgetown University Press.
Scollon, R., & Scollon, S. B.-K. (1981). *Narrative, literacy and face in interethnic communication*. Norwood, NJ: Ablex.
Searle, J. (1975). Indirect speech acts. In P. Cole & J. Morgan (Eds.), *Syntax and semantics* (Vol. 3) *Speech acts*. (pp. 59–82). New York: Academic Press.
Suprapto, S. A. (1983). Negotiation of meaning in cross-cultural communication: A study of doctor/patient interaction. Unpublished Ph.D. dissertation, Department of Linguistics, Georgetown University.
Tannen, D. (1980). Implications of the oral/literate continuum for cross-cultural communication. In J. Alatis (Ed.), *Current issues in bilingual education* (pp. 326–347). Georgetown University Round Table on Languages and Linguistics, 1980. Washington, DC: Georgetown University Press.
Tannen, D. (1981a). Indirectness in discourse: Ethnicity as conversational style. *Discourse Processes, 4*(3), 221–238.
Tannen, D. (1981b). The machine-gun question: An example of conversational style. *Journal of Pragmatics, 5*(5), 383–397.
Tannen, D. (1981c). New York Jewish conversational style. *International Journal of the Sociology of Language, 30,* 133–149.
Tannen, D. (Ed.). (1982a). *Analyzing discourse: Text and talk*. Georgetown University Round Table on Languages and Linguistics 1981. Washington, DC: Georgetown University Press.
Tannen, D. (Ed.). (1982b). *Spoken and written language: Exploring orality and literacy*. Norwood, NJ: Ablex.
Tannen, D. (Ed.). (1984a). *Coherence in spoken and written discourse*. Norwood, NJ: Ablex.
Tannen, D. (1984b). *Conversational style: Analyzing talk among friends*. Norwood, NJ: Ablex.
Tannen, D., & Saville-Troike, M. (Eds.). (1985). *Perspectives on silence*. Norwood, NJ: Ablex.

Young, L. Wai Ling. (1982). Inscrutability revisited. In J. Gumperz (Ed.), *Language and social identity* (pp. 72–84). Cambridge: Cambridge University Press.

Vassiliou, V., Triandis, H., Vassiliou, G., & McGuire, H. (1972). Interpersonal contact and stereotyping. In H. Triandis (Ed.), *The analysis of subjective culture* (pp. 89–115). New York: Wiley.

Biographical Notes

JANET BEAVIN BAVELAS holds a B.A. and Ph.D. (1970) in psychology from Stanford University and an M.A. (1968) in communication research, also from Stanford. Since 1961 she worked with the Palo Alto Group at the Mental Research Institute in California, where (as Janet Beavin) she coauthored works on interpersonal discourse, including *Pragmatics of Human Communication,* with Paul Watzlawick and Don D. Jackson. In 1970 she joined the Department of Psychology at the University of Victoria, Victoria, B.C., where she is currently an associate professor. Her research interests center on methods for studying interpersonal communication, verbal and nonverbal.

AARON V. CICOUREL is a professor of sociology in the Department of Sociology and the School of Medicine at the University of California, San Diego, where he has been a member of the faculty since 1970. He has held visiting appointments at several universities, including Northwestern, California at Berkeley, London, Buenos Aires, Mexico City, Madrid, Konstanz, Vienna, and the Max Planck Institute (Starnberg). He has conducted field research in Argentina, Mexico, England, Spain, and the United States. His current research activities include reading comprehension in children, diagnostic reasoning and doctor–patient communication, general discourse processes, socioeconomic development in rural Spain, and language and community life among Sephardic Jewish groups.

NORBERT DITTMAR is a professor of linguistics in the Department of German at the Free University of Berlin and has held visiting professorships at the Ontario Institute for Studies in Education (Toronto), Université de Paris VIII, and the University of Victoria (Canada). His research domains are sociolinguistics, bilingualism, second-language learning, semantics, pragmatics, and conversational analysis. He is author of *Sociolinguistics: A Critical Survey of Theory and Application,* coauthor of *Sprache und Kommunikation ausländischer Arbeiter*, and, with Wolfgang Klein, coauthor of *Developing Grammars: The Acquisition of German by Foreign Workers*. He is a member of the editorial board of the journals *Linguistics* and *Linguistische Berichte*. Currently, he is supervising projects on the urban vernacular of Berlin, semantics and pragmatics of elementary second-language learner registers, and verbal interaction of therapist and patient in therapies after attempted suicide.

ROGER FOWLER is a graduate of London University and is now a professor of English and linguistics at the University of East Anglia, Norwich, England. He has held visiting professorships at the University of California at Berkeley and at Brown University. Much of his work has been in the linguistic criticism of literary texts and linguistic contributions to the theory of literature: *Essays on Style and Language, The Languages of Literature,* and *Style and Structure in Literature*. His research in sociolinguistics and discourse analysis is best represented by Fowler, Hodge, Kress, and Trew, *Language and Control*, in which the authors argue for a critical, socially committed, application of linguistics to the articulation of ideology in discourse. Recently Fowler has begun to combine sociolinguistic and stylistic approaches to literature, as in his *Literature as Social Discourse*.

GUNTHER KRESS is presently Dean of the Faculty of Humanities and Social Sciences at The New South Wales Institute of Technology in Sydney. His theoretical interests in the study of language are broadly Hallidayan; in his publications he has investigated the interrelations of social structure and language, as for instance in *Language as Ideology*, cowritten with Bob Hodge, and *Language and Control*. A recent interest is the investigation of the distinction of speech and writing, which he has explored in relation to a specific problem, namely, how children learn to write, in *Learning to Write*.

DOUG MAYNARD is an assistant professor in the Department of Sociology, University of Wisconsin, Madison, Wisconsin. His primary teaching and research interests are in ethnomethodology and conversational analysis. He has published *Inside Plea Bargaining*, which pursues some of the ideas in his contribution to this volume. His current research interests center on children's disputes and the delivery and reception of diagnostic news.

FRANK E. MILLAR received a Ph.D. from Michigan State University in 1973 and is an associate professor in the Department of Communication at Cleveland State University. His main research interests are the description of interpersonal communication patterns and the dynamic interplay between communication behaviors and consciousness. He has published in *Communication Monographs, Human Communication Research, Communication Yearbooks, Communication,* and *the Communicator* and has contributed chapters to other edited books. He is coauthor of the book *Messages and Myths*.

L. EDNA ROGERS received a Ph.D. from Michigan State University in 1972 and is an associate professor in the Department of Communication at Cleveland State University. She has held national offices in the International Communication Association and the Speech Communication Association and has served on the editorial boards of several communication journals. Her research on family communication patterns is published in *Family Process, Communication Monographs, Human Communication Research, Communication Yearbooks* and in related edited volumes.

GILL SEIDEL has been a lecturer in French studies and sociolinguistics at Bradford University, England, since 1973. Her work is concerned with the political dimension of language: the representation of the political in texts and the politics of communication. She has shifted her focus from the discourses of the left—sociolinguistic investigation into French political tracts of May 1968—to an analysis of the language and ideology of the right and the far right. Her recent book *The Holocaust Denial* reflects these concerns. She has also published articles on the discourse of the National Front and the French New Right in *Langage et Société* and in *Mots*. Seidel coordinates an international research team based in Paris, l'Equipe "droites," part of the Laboratoire de Lexicologie et Textes Politiques (INALF and CNRS), Ecole Normale Supérieure de Saint-Cloud, directed by Maurice Tournier, which is investigating the vocabulary and discourses of the contemporary right. She is currently editing a collection of papers on sexist and racist discourse.

MARY SYKES received a B.A. (1970) and M.A. (1974) in economics from the University of Manchester. Since 1971 she has been a lecturer in sociology at the University of East Anglia. Her research interests are in the sociology of welfare and state race-relation bodies and in discourse analysis.

DEBORAH TANNEN is an associate professor of linguistics at Georgetown University. She received her Ph.D. in linguistics at the University of California, Berkeley in 1979. She was a Danforth Fellow and has held a Rockefeller Humanities Fellowship. Her publications have been in the area of conversational analysis, spoken and written discourse, frames theory, doctor–patient communication, cross-cultural communication, and modern Greek discourse. Her most recent research compares ordinary conversation and literary discourse. She is the author of *Conversational Style: Analyzing Talk among Friends,* and *Lilika Nakos,* on the work of the modern Greek writer. She edited *Analyzing Discourse: Text and Talk* (Georgetown University Round Table on Languages and Linguistics 1981); *Spoken and Written Language: Exploring Orality and Literacy; Coherence in Spoken and Written Discourse;* and, with Muriel-Saville Troike, *Perspectives on Silence.* She is on the editorial board of *Discourse Processes* and is an associate editor of *TEXT.*

TEUN A. VAN DIJK is professor of discourse studies at the University of Amsterdam, from which he received a doctorate in linguistics. After earlier work on linguistic poetics, text grammar, and discourse pragmatics, he did research (with Walter Kintsch) on the psychology of discourse processing. This work is currently extended toward the field of social cognition, with applications in the analysis of ethnic prejudice in discourse (media, textbooks, conversations) and of news in the press. His books in English include *Some Aspects of Text Grammars; Text and Context; Macrostructures; Studies in the Pragmatics of Discourse; Strategies of Discourse Comprehension,* with Walter Kintsch; *Prejudice in Discourse;* and *News as Discourse* (in preparation). He has edited several books and special journal issues and founded and edited *Poetics* and *Text.*

CHRISTIANE VON STUTTERHEIM completed her Ph.D. with a dissertation on the expression of temporality in a second language in 1984 at the Free University of Berlin. She is author of the articles "When Language Barriers Become Mind Blocs" and "Temporality in Learner Varieties." Currently, she teaches linguistics and German as a second and foreign language as an assistant at the Institut für Deutsch als Fremdsprachenphilologie in Heidelberg. She is associated with the European Science Foundation project on second-language learning, analyzing data on the learning process of reference in German as a second language.

RUTH WODAK is a professor and head of the Department of Applied Linguistics at the University of Vienna and has carried out research in various domains of sociolinguistics, including language behavior in court and therapeutic communication. Her publications include *Das Sprachverhalten von Angeklagten bei Gericht* (*Language Behavior of Defendants in Court*), *Das Wort in der Gruppe* (The Word in the Group), and, with Muriel Schulz, *The Language of Love and Guilt.* She edited *Therapeutische Kommunikation,* with D. Flader, and, under the names Leodolter, Wodak-Leodolter, and Wodak, has published many articles in the fields of socio- and psycholinguistics.

DON H. ZIMMERMAN is a professor of sociology in the Department of Sociology, University of California, Santa Barbara. His current research topics include the conversational organization of citizen calls to a police department, with particular emphasis on the reflexive relation between talk and work activities. His recent publications include several journal articles and contributions to studies of institutional language and language in institutional settings.

Index

A

Accent, 74
Accommodation, 125–126, 135
  principles of, 132
Address
  forms of, 64, 67
  terms of, for women and men, 105
Advertisement, 39–41
Afro-Asian, discriminatory usage of term, 96
Agency, 28
Agent deletion
  dehumanizing effect, 98–99
  mystificatory effect, 90–93
American Indian, 211
Appeal to authority, 129
Approximation, 129
Argument, *see* Conflict, interpersonal
Argument sequence, 11
  escalation in, 11
  inversion in, 11
  repetition in, 11
Argumentation, 43, 211
Austrian Standard German, 189
Authority, 33
Avoidance of conflict, 19–22

B

Baby-talk register, 67–68, 72–74
Beliefs, patient, 193, 201
Black English, and working-class speech, 106, 119
Blaming the victim, 89, 92

C

Car accident, 184
Case grammar, 44
Categories, natural, 65–66
Causality of events, 34
Child discourse, 115
Children, quarrels among, 10–11, 12–13

Chinese, 211
Class, 55, 174, 155–156
Classroom, 211
Code switching, 131–132, 189
Cohesion, 204
Comment, 183
Commonsense knowledge, 170–174
Communication
  code, 136
  cross-cultural, 203–212
  doctor–patient, 193
    and organizational constraints, 196
    and social class, 194
  intracultural, 204
  mode, restricted, 137–142
  strategy of immigrant, 128–133
Communicative style, 204
Competence, 137–138
Competitive sequence, 14
Complexity, syntactic, 72
Conflict, interpersonal, 9–26
  avoidance of, 19–23
  methods for studying, 9–26
  obtaining data, 22–23
  as organized, 12, 14, 15
  as a speech event, 9, 12, 15, 19
Conflict theory, 154
Contextualization cue, 136, 204
Convergence, 126, 135
Conversation
  between children, 113
  competition and cooperation in, 113–115
  and dominance in cross-sex discourse, 115–119
  topics and gender, 111–113
  work in interaction, 111
Conversational dominance, in cross-sex discourse, 115
Conversational skills
  clinical assessment
    topic maintenance, 85
    repairs, 87–88
    reference specification, 89–90

development, 83
language impaired, 83, 84
linguistic knowledge, 84, 88–90
research assumptions, 84
Couples Interaction Scoring System
 (CISS), 16–17, 20–21
Couple's verbal conflict, 15–16, 18,
 moves in, 18
Courtroom
 interaction, 6, 153–176, 181–190
 language, 182
 silence, 183
Critical discourse analysis, 6–8
Cross-cultural
 communication, 203–212
  and discourse analysis, 203
  misunderstandings in, 203
 differences, 206–212
 effects of, 209–212
Cultural variation
 ethnography of speaking, 68
 language acquisition, 68

D

Defendant
 attributes, 166–174, *see also* Person
  description
 –judge discourse, 181–190
 language of, 184–190
 working class, 185
Deference and demeanor, 204
Dehumanization, through lexicalization
 and syntax, 95–100
Deletion, 71
Description, person, in plea bargaining,
 159–164
Deviance, 154
Directives
 aggravated vs. mitigated forms, 114–115
 use by girls and boys, 114–115
Discourse
 and class, 55
 and discrimination, 83–101
 doctor–patient, 193–202, *see also* Communication, doctor–patient
 and gender, 108–120
 genres, 108
 and ideology, 30
 of immigrant workers, 125–149

institutional, 181
native–immigrant, 125–149
 in the classroom, 127
 in medical institutions, 127
 at work, 127,
official, 68, 75–81
and pidgin speech, 137–142
plea bargaining, 153–176
and power, 61–82
between sexes, 110–113
sexist, 28, 39
therapeutic, 182
vs. text, 27–28, 31
about women and men, 54
Discourse analysis
 applications of, 2
 ideological, 27–41
 political, 43–55
 relevance of, 3–6
 in society, 1–8
Discourse disorder
 causal factors 81, 83, 84, 88, 90–91
 developmental disorder, 79
 existence, 90–91
 functionalism, 79, 90–91
Discrimination, *see also* Racial
  discrimination
 definition of, 83–84
 in discourse, 83–101
Discursive process, 47
Disorder, developmental
 autism, 79, 81
 dysphasia, 79, 83, 88
 mental retardation, 79
Disqualification, 21
Divergence, 126, 135
Doctor–patient discourse, 193–202
Dyads, kinds of, 22

E

Ellipsis, 71
Encounter, native–immigrant, 127
Enunciation, 43
Equal treatment, 174–175
Escalation, 11–12, 15
 symmetrical, 18–19
Ethnic
 attitudes, 5
 boundary, 136

Index

minorities, 5
prejudice, 6
Ethnicity, 4
Ethnocentrism, 3, 5, 8

F

Facial expression, 12
Feminist research, 45-46
Fictional argument, 15
Fillers, use by women and men, 106
Foreigner talk, 133-135
Formulas, in court, 183
Functionalism, linguistic, 66

G

Gastarbeiterdeutsch, 138
Gender, 28, 174
 and discourse, 108-120
 and language, 103-120
Genderlect, 106
Generic masculine, 105
Genre, 28-29
Grammar, generative-transformational, 70
Greeks, 205-206

H

Headline, 51-52
Historical materialism, 46

I

Ideological
 formation, 47
 structures, 27-41
 superstructure, 46
 variation, 87-88
Ideology, 2-3, 29-32, 44, 52-53, 64-68
 and discourse, 30
 and lexical choice, 34-35
 meaning of, 29
 and sex roles, 39-41
 and syntax, 31
 and transitivity, 34-35, 37-38
Illocutionary force
 autism, 81
 affective disturbance, 81, 83
 clinical assessment, 81-83
 development, 81

Immediacy, 20
Immigrant worker, 125-149
Immigration, unfavorable representation
 of, 94-99
Implicature, 73-74
Indirect speech act, 204
Indirectness, 20, 205-206
Institution, social, 28
Institutional discourse, 181
Insult, 9-14
 personal, 14
 ritual, 13-14
Intensifiers, use of by men and women,
 106
Interaction, in court, 181-190
Interethnic communication, 125-149
 sociopsychological perspectives on,
 135-137
Intergroup relations, 135-136
Interlanguage, 137
Interpersonal conflict, 9-23
 of couple, 15-16, 18-19
 dyads in, 22
 as discourse, 9
 and facial expression, 12
 methods of study of, 9-10
 moves in, 18-19
 organized nature of, 12, 14
 research methods of, 23
 as speech event, 9
 studies of, 10-22
Interruptions
 definitions of, 115-118
 between women and men, 115-116,
  118-119
Intracultural communication, 204
"Inventory of Marital Conflict," 23
Inversion, 11

J

Judge, 181-190
 –defendant discourse, 181-190
Justice, 153-154, 175-176
 class-specific, 183

K

Knowledge base, 193

L

Lag sequential analysis, 16
Language
  and gender, 103–120
  and ideology, 29–32
  and power, 61–82
  barriers, 181
  legal, 181
  structure,
    and sexism, 105
    separation from language use, 119
    vs. language use, 104–105
Laughter, 210
Learner narrative, 142–148
Legal
  consensus, 154
  language, 181
Lexical studies, 43
Lexicalization, 69, 77–78
  and the presentation of causality, 90
  and racial discrimination, 94–99
Linguistic registers
  and interview control, 197
  in medical interviews, 196
Locatives, mystificatory effect of, 91

M

Marital interaction, 15–16, 18, 23
Marxist tradition, 44–46
Media, 23
Medical interview, 196, *see also* Doctor–patient communication
Men and women, discourse about, 54
Metamessage, 204
Miscommunication, doctor–patient, 194, 197–198,
  data of, 199–200
  and social class, 195,
Misunderstandings, in cross-cultural communication, 203
Modality, 72–73, 77
Modes of talking, 27–28
Move, 18
Multicode text, 39
Mystification
  through agent deletion, 90–93
  through use of locatives, 91

N

Name, 64, 67
Narrative
  function, 44
  temporality in, 142–148
Negotiation, in plea bargaining, 157–158
News, 7, 32–39
Nominalization, 37–38, 71
  dehumanizing effect of, 98–99
Non-immediacy, 21–22
Nonverbal behavior, 12–13, 16
Norm, 181

O

Offender-related
  factors, in plea bargaining, 159–164
  variables, 155
Offense-related factors, in plea bargaining, 157–158
Official discourse, 68, 75–81
Overcorrection, 67
Overlap, 207–208
Overlexicalization, 69

P

Paralinguistic
  feature, 208–209
  signal, 203–204
Paraphrase, 43, 46–48, 129
Participant, 69–70, 77–80
Passive, 71
Person description, 157, 159–164
  contextuality of, 166–167
  Gestalt approach to, 168–175
  selectivity in, 165
Pidgin speech, 139
  and context dependence, 139
  and discourse organization, 140–141
  and implicit reference, 139–140
  and temporal reference, 142–148
Pitch and intonation, gender differences in, 107
Plea bargaining
  discourse, 153–176
  negotiation in, 157–158
Politeness phenomena, 204

Political discourse
  and enunciation, 53–55
  forms of, 45
  and paraphrase, 46–48
  and synonymy, 46–48
  and syntax, 48–53
Political discourse analysis, 43–55
  approaches to, 43–46
Power, 4–5, 7, 28, 61–82
Practice
  constitutive, 64–65, 67–68
  directive, 64
Pragmatic mode, 139
Predicate, 69–70, 79–80
Prejudice, 126, *see also* Race; Racism
Pronouns, of power and solidarity, 63–64
Pronunciation by women and men, 107

Q

Quarrel, 9, 11
Question, 70, 205–206, 208–209
  tag, 109–110

R

Race, 51, 170, 174
Racial discrimination
  definition of, 83
  in discourse, definition of, 85–86
  problems in identification of, 83–85
Racism, 3, 7–8, 55, *see also* Racial discrimination
Reasoning, commonsense, 170–174
Register, 66
Relational control coding system, 16–21
Relevance of discourse analysis, 3–6
Repair, 132
Repetition, 11
Reporting on race, 51–53
Rhetorical studies, 44
Ritual insult, 13–15
Role, 4–5, 62
  ambiguity, 185
  distance, 185
  -playing, 10–12
  -taking, 185
  participant, 181
Rule, constitutive, 181

S

Second-language acquisition, 137–138
Self-correction, 129–130
Semiotic, social, 65–68
Semiotics, 44
Sentencing decision, 154, 156–164
  theory and research on, 154–156
Sequencing, 71
Sex role, 39–40
Sex-exclusive forms vs. sex-preferential forms, 103, 108
Sexism, 7, 55
Social context, 4–5
  and discourse, 109
  and identity, 116
Social practice, language as, 61
Socialization, 70–71, 182
Society, the role of discourse analysis in, 1–8
Sociolinguistics, correlational, 62
Sociology of discourse, 5
Sociophonological analysis, 189
Solidarity, pronouns of, 63–64, 67
Sounding, 13–14
Speech act, 73
Speech situation, sociopsychological, 184
State apparatus, ideological, 67–68
  repressive, 67
Status, 4, 62
  role, 189
Stereotype, 205–206, 211
  linguistic, 130
  racial, 126
Story, 183
Storytelling, 185, 188
Strategy, 188
Synonymy, 43, 46–48
Syntax, 43, 48–53, 70–72
  and ideology, 31

T

Tag questions
  in women's speech, 109–110
  varieties of, 110
Temporal reference, 142–148
Temporality in narrative, 142–148
Terms of address for women and men, 105

Terms of endearment, use by women and men, 106
Text
 vs. discourse, 27
 political, 43
 type, 188
Thematic structure, 35, 37
Therapeutic discourse, 182
Thought units, 16
Titles
 occupational and organizational, for women and men, 105
 and terms of address for women and men, 105
Topic abandonment, 128
Topic-comment, 140
Transact, 18–21
Transactive clause, 34–35, 37–38
 and the representation of causality, 86, 90–93
Transfer, 131
Transitivity, 69–70, 77–80
 and the representation of causality, 89–90
Turn taking, 74, 206–207

U

Underlexicalization, 69

V

Variables
 psychological, 181
 sociological, 181
Variety, sociolinguistic, 65–68
Verbal conflict, *see* Conflict
Viennese dialect, 189
Visual code, 39
Visual text, 33, 35, 39

W

Welfarization
 definition of, 93
 and race, 93–94
Women
 discourse about, 39–41
 and men, discourse about, 54
Women's speech
 characteristics of, 104
 and genderlects, 106
 pitch and intonation in, 107
 and pronunciation, 107
 research on, 103
 use of intensifiers in, 106
 use of fillers in, 106
 use of tag-questions, 109–110
 use of terms of endearment in, 106,